POLITIMETRICS

POLITIMETRICS

An Introduction
to Quantitative
Macropolitics

Ted Robert Gurr
Northwestern University

PRENTICE-HALL, INC., Englewood Cliffs, N.J.

Grateful acknowledgment is made to Sage
Publications, Inc., for permission to reprint
quotations from the following: J. Zvi Namenwirth
and Harold Lasswell, *The Changing Language
of American Values: A Computer Study of
Selected Party Platforms,* Sage Professional Papers
in Comparative Politics No. 01-001 (1970).

Library of Congress Catalog Card Number: 72–1130

ISBN: 0–13–685586–5

Printed in the United States of America

10   9   8   7   6   5   4   3   2   1

Prentice-Hall International, Inc., *London*
Prentice-Hall of Australia, Pty. Ltd., *Sydney*
Prentice-Hall of Canada, Ltd., *Toronto*
Prentice-Hall of India Private Limited, *New Delhi*
Prentice-Hall of Japan, Inc., *Tokyo*

Contents

Preface

This book was originally planned as an introduction to the comparison of nations using what are called "aggregate data." Such data are widely used in student papers as well as in professional articles, but there seemed to be no textbook in political science that surveyed the particular problems and procedures of this kind of research. The first draft was written far away from computers and classrooms, in a Thames-side village in England. From that perspective I came firmly to the conclusion that I was not dealing just with the technical problems of one kind of data or one kind of political comparison. There were instead many interrelated problems of how we do systematic research on political entities, as distinct from political individuals. So I have attempted to answer the particular questions about aggregate comparisons by posing and answering the more general methodological questions about how we can and should do quantitative research in macro-politics. And I became convinced that the subject was sufficiently distinct from other methodologies to deserve a new name: *politimetrics*. These decisions have since been subject to much scrutiny and criticism by my colleagues, and the manuscript has been thoroughly revised several times. It remains an introduction, one which should be straightforward enough for most undergraduates in political science. I hope also that it increases awareness of politimetrics as a distinct subfield of political science and stimulates my colleagues to write the better and more advanced texts that will make this one obsolete.

A number of scholars provided helpful advice on this book in manuscript form. I am especially indebted to Professor J. Zvi Namenwirth, who read it with a degree of care and attention to detail far beyond what an author can ordinarily expect. I would also like to thank Professors J. Merrill Shanks and J. David Singer for their critical advice and encouragement, and my colleague at Northwestern, James A. Caporaso, for sharpening my awareness of many issues in the philosophy of science. Of course any errors or inadequate interpretations that may exist in the book are my own responsibility. I also am grateful to my editor at Prentice-Hall, Roger Emblen, for encouraging me to go ahead with this project. Mrs. Terri Beard of London prepared the original manuscript. Raymond Duvall of Northwestern gave the galley proofs a final, critical reading. A note of appreciation also is due the Ford Foundation, whose Faculty Fellowship program made time available for me to think through and organize many of the arguments presented here.

POLITIMETRICS

Introduction
to
Politimetrics

"Politimetrics" is the quantitative study of political groups, institutions, nations, and international systems. It is a way of doing research on politics, or, more precisely, a number of related ways of doing research whose common object is to identify, measure, and explain regularities in the properties and dynamics of political entities. Politimetrics is an approach to systematic knowledge, not a substantive field or a set of findings. Some of its practitioners are concerned with questions of international relations, others with comparative government and politics, still others with the American political process. Its findings are part of the corpus of knowledge of these subjects, and part of the empirical basis for their theories. Politimetrics is not the only quantitative approach to political questions. There is a parallel and longer-established tradition loosely called political behaviorism, which is concerned with micropolitics: how *individuals* think and act politically. What I call politimetrics is distinguished by its empirical focus on macropolitics: it deals with political *collectivities* rather than the individuals who make up those collectivities.

This book is a text, though not a conventional one. Politimetrics does not have a unique set of methods for collecting and analyzing data. It consists of many techniques borrowed from other fields of social research which are applied to the particular problems of macropolitical comparisons. What is distinctive about politimetrics is the ways these techniques are adapted and applied to these problems. Throughout the book my procedure will be, first, to present general principles of political research design, and second, to illustrate them by showing how practicing researchers applied or ignored these principles. Three contrasting studies which use macropolitical data will provide most of the illustrations. We will dissect their conceptual origins,

1

methods, and results in the process. The presentation thus will be sometimes abstract, but never far removed from actual usage.

Many of the more specialized and technical methods used in politimetrics are not discussed in this book. Some kinds of macropolitical phenomena can be studied in laboratory simulations, for example, by having people play the parts of decision-makers in nations at war (for an introduction see Coplin 1968, and Guetzkow 1962). Formal mathematical methods also are used to study some macropolitical questions. Basic axioms, or assumptions, about some political subject are stated in mathematical form, and logical methods are used to derive propositions from these assumptions. These propositions identify conditions that should be found in the "real political world." They can then be tested, for example in simulation studies. They also can be tested using the kinds of political measurement and statistical comparison described in this book. These latter methods are now the most widely used in politimetrics, and probably will continue to be our most common procedures for testing generalizations about macropolitics for some time to come.

There also are numerous research techniques developed in other fields of social research that are potentially applicable to macropolitics, but are not yet widely understood or employed by politimetricians. The two leading "metrics" in social science are psychometrics and econometrics. Many of the psychometricians' techniques for measuring and analyzing psychological phenomena have been used by political scientists, especially for the study of micropolitics. Many have also been adapted to macropolitical analysis, and are reflected in this book. The techniques of econometrics are more appropriate to macropolitical questions but less fully used. Econometricians have long dealt with the relations of micro to macro economic phenomena, and with diverse problems of data error, time-series analysis, reciprocal causation, and forecasting, all of which are increasingly important to politimetricians. Econometric approaches to these and other problems will be more and more used in politimetrics in the future. They are not much discussed in this book because its principal objective is to present the basics of contemporary politimetrics.[1]

The first chapter provides a general introduction to quantitative, macropolitical research. The second chapter introduces the three studies. One of them, by J. Zvi Namenwirth and Harold Lasswell, shows how the value concerns of American political parties have changed from the mid-nineteenth to the mid-twentieth century. Another, by J. David Singer and Melvin Small, asks whether the formation of alliances among nations has

---

[1] Two of the basic works in psychometrics are J. P. Guilford, *Psychometric Methods*, 2nd ed. (New York: McGraw-Hill, 1954) and Edwin E. Ghiselli, *Theory of Psychological Measurement* (New York: McGraw-Hill, 1964). Two highly regarded surveys of econometrics are J. Johnston, *Econometric Methods* (New York: McGraw-Hill, 1963) and Carl F. Christ, *Econometric Models and Methods* (New York: John Wiley, 1966).

increased or decreased the extent of war, across an even longer span of time. The third study, my own and not previously published, examines the causes of civil strife in contemporary democracies. These studies are used in Chapter 2 to show how theoretical arguments are formulated, what variables might be chosen for analysis, and what kinds of worlds in time and space can be chosen in which to study them.

Once a research question is formulated, we must develop measures of its variables and collect the data necessary to test it. Politimetrics has some distinctive problems of measurement, and has developed some distinctive ways of dealing with them. These are the topics of the third through fifth chapters. In Chapter 3 I survey some basic principles about measuring macropolitical phenomena and suggest how researchers engaged in such measuring can satisfy competing demands of theoretical relevance, technical accuracy, and practicality. The sources of available data and some procedures for "making" data are reviewed in Chapter 4, which concludes by discussing some effects of "missing data" and solutions for them. Chapter 5 shows how data were collected in the three studies and how measures were constructed from them.

Chapters 6 and 7 survey the methods we commonly use to analyze macropolitical data. Graphic and statistical methods for comparing two measures are described in Chapter 6. The next chapter deals with some of the more challenging problems of analyzing changes over time, comparing three and more variables, and testing causal explanations. The beginning student is not expected to understand the details of these techniques, but is provided a survey of the kinds of research problems for which they are designed. The three studies provide examples of all these techniques. Chapter 8 reports some basic results and interpretations of each of the three studies, relying largely on the conclusions of the researchers who carried them out.

In preparing this book I have tried not only to provide a guide to the research process in politimetrics, but to equip the reader for doing his or her own quantitative political comparisons. The book assumes some prior knowledge of the substantive interests of political science, but not a great deal. It should be comprehensible to anyone who can read and understand the substance of a quantitative journal article. The treatment is necessarily technical at some points, but the reader who boggles at a technical discussion can expect to find a clarifying explanation or application further on. Chapters 6 and 7, on statistical methods, should be generally understandable by people without a formal background in statistics. Nevertheless, students who have had a basic statistics course will understand them more easily and in more detail.

The reader who is accustomed to the traditional footnotes of political science, with book titles, ibid.'s, and op. cit.'s cluttering the bottom of the printed page, will not find them here. The referencing system used in the natural sciences is increasingly used in politimetrics, and is followed in this book. A reference to a published work or a quotation is followed by a reference in this form: (Zinnes 1967, pp. 271–72). The Bibliography at the end of the book lists all such references in full detail.

No one should think that this book is definitive. My colleagues doing quantitative political research certainly will not. What I call politimetrics is a relatively new field. Its methods and assumptions are changing rapidly and are being applied with increasing imagination to more and more subjects. Many practices and interpretations—and restrictions—that were accepted without question a few years ago are now subject to debate and revision. So it is much too soon to attempt to codify the principles and procedures of politimetrics. John Tukey's remark about statistics can be applied equally well to politimetrics: "As we face more complex problems, just those things we once thought immoral must become our salvation" (1961, p. 91). This book, in brief, is an introductory survey of and commentary on present principles and practices, not all of which are necessarily ideal and many of which we are likely to change.

1

Purposes and Processes of Quantitative Political Research

Almost all systematic political research, whether engaged in by students or professional scholars, is inspired by unanswered questions. The questions may be descriptive ones, such as: How under-represented are the cities in my state legislature? What kinds of countries have coups d'état? Or the questions may be about connections and causes: Are political leaders of middle-class background more conservative than those of blue-collar background? Do nations with large military establishments get more involved in wars than nations with small ones?

The answers to questions like these require comparisons. We must compare legislative districts, countries, ideologies, and military establishments to answer them. Verbal comparisons are useful but limited. The advantage of *quantitative* methods is that they help us make rather precise comparisons among large numbers of legislatures, or coups, or countries. No sensible scholar would claim that the use of numbers automatically ensures that answers to political questions will be accurate and free from deliberate or unconscious bias. Many people, professional researchers among them, "lie with statistics"; many also commit homicide with their autos, which is an argument not against the use of autos but against their *mis*use. The fact is that the collection and comparison of data on politics makes available to the researcher powerful tools which, if properly used, can greatly increase the accuracy and validity of answers to political questions.

The objective of this book is to show how political and other social scientists do and can collect and use macropolitical data to answer political questions. There is no one, "correct" way in which this is done. At every step, from precise formulation of the question to final report, there are many options. Depending on the question, there may be many nations and eras in which to study it, a multitude of information sources, many different ways of collecting and processing that information, and a vast stock of statistical techniques for analyzing the data. This book describes some of these options, how they are used, and how to choose among them. Throughout I have tried to convey something of the spirit of the scientific enterprise in quantitative political science, for it is a fascinating one. The important questions we want to ask far outnumber the answers at hand. The technical tools for attempts at answering political questions extend well beyond their present applications. Thus the innovative student who is armed with the basic techniques and approaches described here can make explorations and discoveries at almost every turn. He or she also can profitably duplicate and reanalyze published studies, for, unlike the basic experiments of physics, biology, or psychology, few of those in political science have been subject to the verification that is required if we are to accept their findings as definitive. Even if the student does not plan to do his own quantitative research, this book should help him to understand better the merits and limitations of the data, results, and policy implications of contemporary political research.

This initial chapter has two objectives. The first is to identify the basic, theoretical purposes of quantitative political research and to show how the methods of politimetrics contribute to them. The second is to describe the basic steps in the quantitative research process.

1.1 Objectives of Political Research

The ultimate goal of almost all empirical political research is the development of better theory. We are not talking about ethical or normative "theory" that tells us what we should do in politics, but about *empirical theory*. Empirical political theory is, ideally, a set of general and thoroughly tested statements that describe and explain the patterns of political reality. In other words, empirical theory deals with the "is" of political life: it is intended to explain the origins and consequences of different kinds of political conditions and actions. (Empirical political theory is highly relevant to our political preferences, in at least two ways. Our preferences help us decide which political questions to try to answer. The more accurate and precise our empirical political theory is, the more likely it is that we will be able to work toward realizing our political preferences.)

Quantitative, macropolitical research contributes to theoretical development in one or both of two ways. One is to discover political regularities, called "descriptive generalizations." One apparent regularity in American party politics is that, in non-Presidential national elections, the party out of power almost always gains congressional seats. Such "facts" or regularities are eventually to be incorporated in theories, to be explained by showing how they are connected with other regularities. The other common objective of macropolitical research is to test theoretical statements. These statements, called theorems or hypotheses, are theoretical predictions about regularities that ought to hold in the real political world. In brief, the two theoretical purposes of empirical research are to contribute the building blocks of theory by adding to our knowledge of political regularities, and to test theoretical statements already at hand.

So political scientists mostly agree that the goal of their work is "theory." But there is much disagreement about what we should theorize on, how we should arrive at theory, what forms we should express it in, and how we should go about testing it. What we lack, in other words, is agreement on a *scientific paradigm,* which is a set of guiding ideas that gives organization and direction to an area of scientific investigation. Most scientific fields agree on a paradigm. Physicists and biologists have their dominant paradigms, and so do economists and experimental psychologists. As a result they seldom debate about the principal "puzzles" or problems to be solved. They have partially or fully developed theories, using agreed-upon concepts, which they are cooperatively testing and extending. As this implies, they have an agreed-upon set of methods for testing theories, and concur about what kinds of evidence support or contradict a theoretical statement.

I have three points to make to the reader about the lack of a dominant paradigm in political science. One is simply that the analysis of this problem is beyond the scope of this book. The reader interested in the paradigmatic issues of political science might begin by reading Kuhn (1964) and especially Holt and Richardson (1970). The second point, which is especially important for students to appreciate, is that much of the confusion in contemporary political science does not result from stupidity or willful antagonism. It is because we lack a shared scientific "language" that it is difficult, if not impossible, for us to agree about the correctness of competing claims to knowledge. The third is that the methods and techniques described in this book are consistent with many different paradigmatic points of view. Three topics of dispute that affect politimetrics are discussed below.

INDUCTIVE VERSUS DEDUCTIVE SCIENCE.   The methods and techniques of politimetrics are usually associated with the "inductive" search for descriptive generalizations about politics, which is often distinguished from the testing of theorems deduced formally from theoretical assumptions. This distinction between inductive and deductive science is artificial. All processes for gaining knowledge require us to make some initial assumptions (axioms) and hypotheses (theorems) about the nature of social and political reality. The effective difference is that in one research style the hypotheses are largely implicit until after the analysis of data, while in the other they are offered boldly at the outset. Thus there is no completely "inductive" political science, only varying degrees of explicitness in initial theorizing. The procedures of politimetrics are suited to testing all kinds of conjectures, however they are derived. The future of political science will be brightest, though, if politimetrics becomes as widely used for evaluating formal theories as it has been for testing ad hoc hypotheses.

MACRO VERSUS MICRO PHENOMENA   Politimetrics is defined here as the quantitative study of political groups, institutions, nations and international systems. It is thus distinct from the study of individuals' political orientations, voting choices, and modes of political participation. This distinction does not rest on a paradigmatic assumption that micropolitical phenomena are irrelevant. Quite the contrary: many important political questions must be studied at both the individual and collective levels. Some, like the connection between personality types and political orientations, can be studied only in individuals. Nor does the distinction assume that different scientific logics are used when studying groups rather than individuals: the logic of assessment is generally the same. One of the two reasons for the distinction is the practical one that the methods of measuring and comparing collectivities are substantially different from the interview, questionnaire, and small-group observation methods that are used when we study individuals. Many of the principles and strategies of politimetrics that are discussed in subsequent chapters apply to research on individuals as well as collectivities. But the student who is concerned with the specific problems of micropolitical research should consult some of the many good introductions to the subject.[1]

The second reason for dealing here with macro phenomena is that most of the important questions of political science are about collectivities. How are power and authority allocated among groups and institutions? How well do institutions perform their tasks? How do movements for political reform arise and what effects do they have? How does conflict among groups, and nations, arise and play itself out? These are macropolitical questions, and politimetrics offers direct and powerful methods for dealing with them.

INDIVIDUAL VERSUS AGGREGATE DATA   A basic distinction is often made in political research between individual and aggregate data. The distinction parallels that between micro- and macropolitical phenomena, and is just as clear-cut—or is it? Literally, "aggregate" data means data that are a sum or composite, and some aggregate statistics are summed up from information on individuals. For example, we might ask each individual in a community about his political party preference, thus obtaining a set of individual data. But when we express this information in percentage terms for the community —say, 40% Republican, 36% Democratic, 3% other, 21% independent— they are aggregate statistics and can be compared with similar aggregate estimates for other communities. Aggregate measures based on summed or averaged data are called *summation* variables, and are distinguished from *syntality* variables. The latter are characteristics or products of a collectivity

1 E.g., see Claire Selltiz et al., *Research Methods in Social Relations,* rev. ed. (New York: Holt, Rinehart & Winston, 1963) and Frederick F. Stephan and Philip J. McCarthy, *Sampling Opinions: An Analysis of Survey Procedures* (New York: John Wiley, 1958).

as a whole, rather than the sum or average of its parts. They are sometimes called "emergent" properties. Examples are the extent of political inequalities between social classes, the durability of a political regime, or the extent of hostility expressed in a diplomatic exchange between nations (see Merritt 1970, Chap. 2). Politimetric methods are applicable to both summation and syntality variables, and many studies make use of both.

1.2 The Research Process

One image of scientific research, for which the thirteenth-century English scholar Friar Roger Bacon is sometimes blamed, is that the researcher collects as much information on a specific subject as possible, thinks about it, and then marvelously arrives at new generalizations. The tradition lives on in many a student term paper. According to another image, "science" is repeated physical experiment, preferably using complex apparatuses, whose results are expressed in mathematical notations. In a third approach, doctors of medicine and psychology have been observed to get practical, quite possibly "scientific," information by administering a drug to a group of patients or an educational film to a group of students and then determining its effects, by comparing this "experimental" group with an otherwise-similar "control" group that did not get the drug, or the message.

The fact is that all these procedures, and many others, have been used to increase our systematic knowledge of men and nature. Each kind of subject requires its own kinds of research procedures, and political scientists have been just as adept as others in borrowing, adapting, and creating their procedures for analyzing political questions. Mulling over masses of raw information, for example, has developed into complicated statistical searches for patterns in quantitative data. Similarly, the political scientist usually cannot perform physical experiments on political groups or governments, any more than geologists can experiment with mountain formation or astronomers can manipulate supernovas; he *can*, however, question men and observe governments at different points in time to determine what happens to them under the impact of external events. Nor can the political scientist set up and manipulate "experimental" and "control" groups to answer most of his questions. But what he can and does do is to look at political events, groups, and nations as if they were a set of natural political experiments, then measure and compare the conditions which seemed to cause some of them to turn out one way, and others another way.

What follows is an outline of the procedures used in making quantitative comparisons of political phenomena. It does not describe *how* to do it; that is the subject of subsequent chapters. It is instead an outline map of the research process, one which shows how its specific steps relate to the whole.

Formulating the Questions

Logically the first step in the quantitative political research process is to formulate one's questions precisely, a step called "problemation." Such questions might be concerned with *description, correlation*, or *explanation*— or all of them. If one is interested in violent conflict, for example, these are some of the *descriptive* questions one might have in mind:

> How much violent conflict occurs in various cities, or regions, or countries?
> What are the most and least common kinds of violent conflict?
> What kinds of groups are typically involved in different kinds of violent conflict?
> What tactics most often lead a group to success in violent conflict?

The question of equality in legislative representation offers other examples of descriptive questions:

> Which regional or political groups have proportionally the least representation in a legislature, and which have the most?
> Which groups have changed in their relative representation over time, and how much?
> When a number of states or nations are compared, which have the most equitable and which the most disproportionate representation?

Descriptive questions about one condition or variable usually lead quickly to *correlational* questions. We are seldom satisfied with knowing how groups or events or nations differ on one variable, but usually are curious about how one condition relates to others. These are a few of the relational questions that might be suggested by the two examples above:

> Do the most democratic or most developed nations have less violent conflict than others?
> What kinds of social and political changes are likely to occur in the decades after a major episode of violent conflict?
> Is legislative representation most unequal in the most urbanized, or the most industrialized states?
> Is there a connection between the amount of political party competition in a state, or nation, and the equality of legislative representation?

Explanatory questions can be thought of as attempts to show what general law or cause-and-effect relationships are manifest in a correlation. Say that we observe, or have a hunch, or are told that the most developed countries have less violent conflict than underdeveloped ones. Very probably we will want to know what the dynamics are. Stinchcombe suggests one strategy for dealing with such a question: "invent at least three theories, not now known to be false, which might explain these relations; choosing appropriate indicators, derive at least three different empirical consequences from each theory, such that the factual consequences distinguish among the theories" (1968, p. 13). It is not at all difficult to suggest three alternative explanations, or theories, for the correlation between violence and development:

> Economic development may *lead to, or cause,* a decline in violent conflict.
>
> Economic development may *depend upon,* or *require,* a decline in violent conflict.
>
> The correlation may be *coincidental,* or *spurious,* the result of some fundamental cultural or structural differences that make some countries both developed and peaceful, and others both underdeveloped and violent.

Stinchcombe goes on to suggest that "Any student who has difficulty thinking of at least three sensible explanations for any correlation that he is really interested in should probably choose another profession" (1968, p. 13). Alternative explanations are usually easy to propose. The more complex task is how the student may then *test* his alternative explanations, or any single explanation. That is the principal subject of this book.

Three more general points can be made about the process of problemation. First, and most obvious, the researcher usually does not have just one question in mind. He may have a related set of descriptive and relational questions, or one central hypothesis that is broken down into a series of more specific ones.

Second, to answer any of the three kinds of questions we usually have to find, or assume, answers to the other questions. There is no such thing as a "pure descriptive study" of violent conflict, for example. Before we can count or measure "violent conflict" we have to have some initial theoretical ideas about what is violent and what is not, what is conflict and what is not. And if we want to study *correlations* we need answers to descriptive questions about the "things" we are correlating. To test *explanations* about how conditions or events affect one another, we need information about how they are related. All this does not mean, as some critics charge, that the science process is a circular one in which we end up seeing only what we want to see, or confirming the implicit theories with which we began. The scientific process should be a spiral: each improvement in theory makes for better description the next time round, which increases the precision of correlations, which may need different theoretical explanations, which suggest that the "object" described be redefined, and so on.

Finally, there is no hard and fast rule about how much attention is given to specifying a research question before going on to the next stages of the research process. Some empirical studies begin only after an exhaustive search of the literature for ideas and evidence, and the formulation of careful theoretical systems, comprised of interrelated sets of assumptions, definitions, and hypotheses. Other studies begin with one or two simple questions, which may or may not be restated and elaborated after some evidence is gotten. But there is no doubt that a *clearly stated* set of questions, whether simple or elaborate, will lead to more efficient and informative research than a

TABLE 1.1 *The Data Matrix*

	Variable 1	Variable 2	Variable 3	...	Variable j
Case 1	datum 1.1	datum 1.2	datum 1.3	...	datum 1.j
Case 2	datum 2.1	datum 2.2	datum 2.3	...	datum 2.j
Case 3	datum 3.1	datum 3.2	datum 3.3	...	datum 3.j
.	.	.	.		.
.	.	.	.		.
.	.	.	.		.
Case i	datum i.1	datum i.2	datum i.3	...	datum i.j

vague desire, however well-intentioned, to collect a lot of data that have something to do with coups, or kings, or Kenya.

Specification and Operationalization

At least three other tasks have to be dealt with before any significant amount of data is collected. The researcher carries out these tasks by deciding what kind of *data matrix* he or she will need to answer questions, and then deciding how to go about filling it. An empty data matrix is shown in Table 1.1. (1) One of the three preliminary tasks in filling the data matrix is to decide on the *universe of analysis*: the kinds of events, or institutions, or political entities about which the data are to be collected. Each "thing" studied is a *case* and is listed one per row in the matrix. (2) The second task is to specify precisely the *variables* for which data are to be collected. A variable is a quality or characteristic that varies among the things being studied. The number of political parties in a country is a variable, ranging from zero to as many as 15 or 20. The power of political parties is also a variable, ranging from very low to very high. In a data matrix variables are almost always represented as columns, one column per variable. (3) The third task is to develop operational *measures* or *indicators* for the variables, or, in other words, to spell out the rules by which the *data* (scores, numbers) for each case on each variable are gotten.

Solutions to each of the three tasks are strongly influenced by the scientific paradigm of the researcher. He has many different cases to choose among, an almost infinite variety of variables, and many alternative approaches to measurement. Practical considerations will help him decide on some of these issues. His special interests also influence his decisions. But he almost always has some basic scientific assumptions, acquired in his training and reading, about what kinds of units and variables are most worth studying, and what kinds of operational methods are best to use.

To help illustrate how these tasks can be solved, let us assume that we want to answer a question about how conflict and political democracy are related. We have in mind a correlational hypothesis: the greater the degree of political democracy in a collectivity, we speculate, the lower the intensity (but not the frequency) of conflict. In other words, democratic bodies are likely to have as many occasions for conflict as nondemocratic ones, but conflict in democratic ones will usually be less disruptive or bitter.

UNIVERSE OF ANALYSIS   Two kinds of decisions must be made about the universe of analysis. If we plan to gather data on conflict and democracy, we must first choose among various *kinds* of cases in which the relationship could be studied. In practice, most studies using the methods of politimetrics compare a number of nations at one point in time, but depending on the question, there are many other alternatives. The connections between conflict and democracy could be studied quantitatively among the 50 American states. They could be examined among private organizations like labor unions or universities. They also could be studied in one country over time, or on a situation-by-situation basis.

The related question is the *range* of cases to be included. If nations or states are to be studied, for example, we could choose all of them, or all those for which information is easily available. We might instead select a subset—all Latin American countries, or all Southern states—or a representative sample. Similar sets of alternatives can be identified for other kinds of cases. The various kinds and ranges of cases, and how to choose among them, are discussed in more detail in Section 2.3.

VARIABLE SPECIFICATION   Our formulation of the initial question about the connection between conflict and democracy identifies the basic variables on which data will be collected. They are *conflict intensity, conflict frequency,* and *political democracy.* The contingent questions are, What is *meant* by the concepts "conflict" and "democracy?" In practice, politimetrics has two ways of dealing with the problem of variable specification. One is to begin with verbal definitions of the concepts. The researcher considers how others have used and defined each of the variables mentioned in his research question, and spells out in some detail what he means by each of them. Then detailed procedures are proposed for observing and measuring each concept; these are the concept's "operational definition." The second procedure is to ignore the conceptual problem and rely solely on operational definitions; verbal terms like "conflict" and "democracy" are used only as labels for whatever is operationally identified.

OPERATIONALIZATION   The way the researcher has formulated his initial research questions often provides the answers to the problems of which variables are to be studied, and for what cases. The hard question is, What procedures can be used to obtain reliable and valid data for each case on each variable? For demographic variables like urban population, and economic ones like national productivity, there are readily available, internationally standardized measures. Standard measures also are sometimes available for variables like proportion of registered voters who turn out for an election, and budgeted military expenditures. But measures are seldom available for many of the most interesting and important political variables, like "intensity of conflict" and "degree of democracy." To operationalize such variables the researcher must adapt existing measures or devise new ones. Measures of hard-to-measure variables often are referred to as *indicators,* a term which usually signifies that the measures are not as direct and complete as the researcher would like.

Politimetricians have a Pandora's box of techniques for collecting data and constructing indicators. Much ingenuity, foresight, and a degree of luck are needed for the researcher to reach a satisfactory compromise among the often-contradictory demands of his research questions, the techniques available to him, and the kinds of information he can get. These are only some examples of the kinds of indicators of conflict:

> Counts of the number of conflict events like strikes, riots, and coups d'état in each case (frequency).
>
> Judgment of the severity of conflict in each case, on a standardized scale ranging from low to high (intensity).
>
> Tabulations of the number of casualties from, or participants in, or duration of conflict in each case (intensity).

No set of indicators will satisfy all the critics. Most conflict researchers, for example, would say that the indicators listed above represent only part of what is meant by conflict frequency and intensity. The intensity of conflict in a country may be reflected as much or more in political emigration, suicides, and executions as it is in overt clashes like riots and coups. The politimetrician must accept as a fact of professional life that there is disagreement about what constitutes adequate measures of concepts in almost all subfields of political science.

Operationalization is in many ways the most crucial step in the whole research process, for how the researcher decides to index his variables will largely determine whether and how well his initial questions are answered.

Some of the many problems of operational measurement, and approaches to their solution, are reviewed in Chapter 3.

Data Collection and Processing

For the researcher working with macropolitical data, filling in the data matrix is a long and routine process of recording, comparing, and judging information from case studies, archives, newspaper files, statistical year-books, and data cards. Though it may be routine, it seldom is uninstructive. The kinds of sources available to him are reviewed in Chapter 4. During the process the investigator who does his or her own data collection can acquire much substantive information about the events being analyzed. This information helps provide him with an invaluable sense of both the inadequacies and implications of the data, a kind of sixth sense that is of great value when he later interprets the results.

After the data are recorded they must be processed. Many different kinds of processing may be required. Sometimes a number of partial indicators of a variable must be combined into a summary index. If narrative information was recorded, it will have to be evaluated and converted into numerical scores. Often the data must be transformed. Some procedures used in collecting and processing data are described in Chapter 5.

Analysis and Interpretation

To analyze data is to subject them to some explicit tests, the results of which hopefully will provide answers to the researcher's initial questions. A descriptive question about the number of demonstrations in different cities can be answered simply by summarizing the data in a table. If the question is whether one group of cities has more or different kinds of demonstrations than another group, analysis requires some statistical tests of differences among them. If the question is whether two or more variables are related to one another and how, analysis can become complex indeed. It can be as complicated as a series of correlation, regression, and factor analyses requiring hours of computer time and expressed in a stack of computer printout that stands as high as the researcher. The kinds of analysis vary according to the kinds of question asked at the outset and the kinds of data collected. They also depend on the skills of the researcher, for many collections of political data have been only incompletely and sometimes improperly analyzed.

The final substantive step in the research process is the interpretation of the results. Interpretation proceeds as much by insight as by established procedure. The researcher almost always has some kind of initial expectations about what his descriptive and correlational results will look like. These expectations are sometimes intuitive, sometimes based on case studies, and sometimes formally theoretical, as when he is testing a hypothesis. Thus, one of the tests of the adequacy of the study is how well his expectations are confirmed. But some "striking" results are serendipitous ones: important, unexpected patterns in the data. There often will be many small surprises in the ways particular expectations are confirmed, and sometimes big surprises in the form of new patterns and relationships that require us to revise our understanding of the phenomena being studied.

If testing explanations was the initial purpose of the empirical study, the researcher will ordinarily have some rather precise standards against which to measure his results. The kind of question he is most likely to ask is, Are the relationships of the sort predicted by one of my hypothetical explanations? and, Are the results as strong as expected? Needless to say, the results are seldom exactly as expected. Usually they lead the researcher toward modifying his explanations and doing further empirical work. In the course of the typical empirical study, the researcher goes through a whole series of analyses, interpretations, reanalyses, and reinterpretations. Only the final and most satisfying results are likely to be reported fully in his research papers.

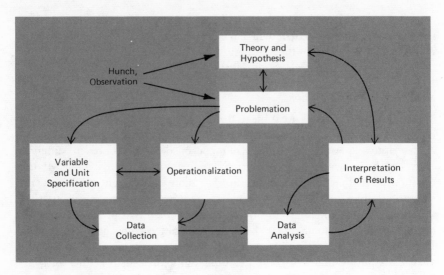

FIGURE 1.1. Map of the research process in politimetrics.

There are a great many statistical procedures and tests used in analyzing political data, and various approaches to interpreting their results. These are the subject of Chapters 6, 7, and 8.

The foregoing outline of the political research process is summarized in Figure 1.1. You should note that the relation of theory to the process varies considerably. Researchers who prefer the inductive method, for example, begin with no more than a vaguely formed question that they formulate into a hypothesis only after collecting some data. Others follow the widely recommended procedure of forming one or more hypotheses carefully in advance. Some, as noted above, test theorems derived from formal, axiom-based theories. Once a question is formulated, some researchers may short-cut "specification" and "operationalization" stages by going from questions directly to an existing collection of data. This is especially convenient for students who are doing research exercises, and for investigators who want a "quick look" before doing a more ambitious project. Sometimes, too, a quantitative research project begins with a critique of someone else's data analysis or reinterpretation of their results. But essentially the cycle in Figure 1.1 characterizes all quantitative research in political science, and indeed all systematic social research. It has a number of payoffs. Generalized descriptions of the properties of political conditions and events are one of them. A better, more precise understanding of the correlations among political and other phenomena is another. Most important of all, the process contributes to the development of general, explanatory theory about the causes and effects of what men, groups, and nations do in politics.

2

Setting Up the Problem: Three political studies

As one way of illustrating the process of political research, we follow three recent studies from their conceptual origins to their analytic conclusions. These studies are used in this chapter to illustrate how political questions can be posed for quantitative research. Capsule descriptions of the studies lead to a comparison of their conceptual origins. The kinds of variables included in them are examined next. Finally we consider the investigators' choices of temporal and spatial worlds from which to gather evidence. For a sociologist's view of such questions see Abell 1971.

2.1 The Three Studies: Problems and Concepts

A word of explanation is needed about the studies chosen. They are not paragons of social scientific excellence, but by prevailing standards they are competent, and also innovative and substantively interesting. They are not simple exercises of a sort that students might hope to accomplish for a research paper, but on the other hand almost every part of them could have been accomplished by an imaginative and well-trained graduate student. The central rationale for their selection is that, jointly, they represent a wide range of substantive problems and approaches.

The first study, by J. Zvi Namenwirth and Harold D. Lasswell, is concerned with how Democratic and Republican political party platforms reflect, in their language, changes in American values between the mid-nineteenth and mid-twentieth centuries. The study is American and primarily descriptive; the data are collected by verbal content analysis and are compared within and across time periods, using both simple and complex statistical techniques. A major finding is that there has been a substantial decline across time in American political concern about questions of morality and authority, and a great increase in concern about material welfare. Differences between the parties are almost but not entirely inconsequential by comparison. The study was carried out at Yale University in 1966–67. A partial account by Namenwirth appeared in 1968: "Some Long and Short Term Trends in One American Political Value: A Computer Analysis of Concern with Wealth in Sixty-Two Party Platforms," *Computer Studies in the Humanities and Verbal Behavior*, Vol. I (October 1968). A fuller report was published in 1970, titled *The Changing Language of American Values: A Computer Study of Selected Party Platforms* (Beverly Hills, Calif.: Sage Professional Papers in Comparative Politics, Vol. I, No. 01–001, 1970). It is referred to below as the "American Values" study.

The second study is a previously unpublished set of analyses from my research on the social causes of group protest and violence. It is a cross-national study of pluralistic democracies during the early 1960s, and is designed to test a general theory about the effects of different kinds of social conditions on the types and extent of strife. The data are collected by a variety of methods from many sources. They are analyzed using techniques of correlation, multiple regression, and causal modeling. The theory is generally supported, with some surprises, and a large proportion of the variation of strife among nations is statistically explained. The study is referred to as the "Causes of Strife" study, and represents part of a long-term research project begun at Princeton University in 1965. The theoretical argument is presented in my *Why Men Rebel* (Princeton University Press, 1970). Three empirical articles reporting other aspects of the analysis are listed in the bibliography: Gurr 1968, 1969, and 1970b.

The last study, dealing with "Alliances and War," was conducted by J. David Singer and Melvin Small as part of Professor Singer's long-term study of the correlates of war, at the University of Michigan. The research deals with a major issue of international relations: the effects of alliance formation among nations on the onset and extent of war. Data are collected on all the alliances and wars that occurred in the "international system" of nations between 1815 and 1945, and compared with one another using correlational techniques. The information on alliances and war is intrinsically interesting. The most striking finding is one not predicted by any current theory. In the nineteenth century, when alliances increased, the severity and frequency of war tended to decline. Between 1900 and 1945 the relationship is strongly reversed: as alliances increased, so did wars. The primary published report on the study is "Alliance Aggregation and the Onset of War, 1815–1945," in J. David Singer, ed., *Quantitative International Poltics: Insights and Evidence* (New York: Free Press, 1968). A number of related articles and monographs by Singer and Small are listed in the bibliography of this book.

The three studies thus represent all three kinds of questions that can be asked of political phenomena: "American Values" is primarily *descrip-*

tive; "Alliances and War" deals principally with a *correlational* question; and "Causes of Strife" is concerned with testing a *theoretical* explanation. They also represent the range of phenomena that can profitably be examined using quantitative techniques. These include human values and ideologies, sociopolitical dislocations such as war and civil disorder, and also more commonly studied subjects like economic growth and political structure. The cases studied include subnational groups (parties), nations, events (wars), and relationships (alliances). We shall see in later chapters that the studies are equally diverse in their use of sources, methods of data collection, and analytic techniques. Here we shall look closely at the theoretical and conceptual questions that inspired them.

American Values

"For years the study of value change has been a central topic in intellectual, political and social history," write Namenwirth and Lasswell. "Unfortunately, speculating about causes and consequences of value change is far easier than determining accurately the magnitude and direction of such change" (1970, p. 5). This is the general question to which the study is addressed: what have been the long-range changes in values, especially in Western societies, and what questions do the observed changes raise about the causes and consequences of value change? The authors brought a number of concepts and categories to the question. Lasswell has long been concerned with classifying peoples' values, defined here as their "preferred goal states" (p. 6), and with working out the logic and practice of men's attempts to attain their various, often competing goals. He assumes that individuals, and collectivities, have hierarchies of values: they want some conditions more than others, and are likely to give more attention to (and talk more about) those that are most important to them.

The basic conceptual tool of the study, therefore, was the eightfold classification of values proposed by Lasswell and Kaplan (1950). These values are of two general types, listed and briefly defined as follows:

> *Welfare values* are "those whose possession to a certain degree is a necessary condition for the maintenance of the physical activity of the person." They include:
>
> > *well-being,* "the health and safety of the organism";
> >
> > *wealth,* including goods and services as well as monetary income;
> >
> > *skill,* "proficiency in any practice whatever," on the argument that people have an intrinsic need to acquire and use physical and mental skill; and
> >
> > *enlightenment,* "knowledge, insight, and information...."
>
> *Deference values* are "those that consist in being taken into consideration (in the acts of others and of the self)." They include:

power;

respect, "the value of status, of honor, recognition, prestige. . .";

rectitude, the moral values such as virtue, goodness, and righteous-
ness; and

affection, "the values of love and friendship." (From Lasswell and
Kaplan 1950, pp. 55–56, quoted in Namenwirth and Lasswell 1970,
p. 9.)

Two important conceptual distinctions are also made. These eight
values can be regarded either as means or as ends in themselves—in Lasswell's terminology, *scope* and *base* values. For example, some people seek
power for its own sake, others because it is a means to respect or well-being.
The second distinction is between types of verbal references to each value.
Such references can be to *substantive values* per se, or to *value transformations.* Words such as "administration," "constitution," and "presidency"
refer to the substantive aspects of power. "Protect," "civil rights," "recommendation," and "punish" are references to value transformations—the
ways in which power values are created and shared. These distinctions are
used in constructing indicators and collecting data.

The objective of the "American Values" study, then, is to determine
the relative frequency with which these different values, and aspects of
them, have been referred to in American party platforms. Such changes are
intrinsically interesting if we want to know something of American political
history, or if we want to know how the apparent social concerns of American
political parties differ, and how they have changed from the nineteenth
to twentieth centuries. The more important question, in the authors' view
and probably for most political scientists, is how value change and social
change affect one another. The research design suggests only a fragmentary
answer for the United States, but this reflects the limited scope of the study,
not the impossibility of dealing with the question by these means. (See
Namenwirth 1968, pp. 126–27; Namenwirth and Lasswell 1970, pp. 7–8).

Causes of Strife

The theoretical basis for this study is an attempt to tie together different levels of explanation for group protest and violence. The argument is
that our predilections for doing violence to one another can be fully understood only if three levels of explanation are taken into consideration. The
first is the purely psychological kind of explanation, about the sources and
consequences of frustration. The second is the social psychological explanation of peoples' attitudes about violence and about society and politics. The
third, social level of explanation deals with the institutional conditions that
determine how free or circumscribed people are in their actions. These
motivational, attitudinal, and social aspects of explanation interact with one
another. A theory of group action needs to specify what kinds of social pro-

cesses and conditions cause particular kinds of frustrations and patterns of attitudes, as well as how collective grievances and hostile attitudes can disrupt social institutions. The basic hypotheses of the study are sketched below.

Collective discontent is the necessary precondition for civil strife, a statement that is all but truistic. What is not truistic is the hypothesis derived from it: *the greater the intensity and scope of discontent in a population, the greater the likely magnitude of strife.* "Discontent" is a psychological variable, but there are objective social conditions from which we can infer and predict it. Its social origins are attributed to "relative deprivation," that is, widespread perception of discrepancies between the goals of human action and the prospects of attaining those goals. "Strife" is collective, overt attacks on people or property in which private citizens participate, including both violent attacks and nonviolent protests. The strife events included in the study range from demonstrations and interracial clashes to coups d'état, terrorism, and guerrilla wars. The violence used by regimes in attempts to maintain social control is included only when it occurs as part of these events. It is assumed to have somewhat different origins than popular attacks and protests, which implies that a somewhat different theory be used to explain it.

Discontent and strife are causally connected both rationally and nonrationally. Rationally, angry men may resort to public protest and to violence on the basis of their calculations that it will help improve conditions. Nonrationally, much psychological evidence suggests that aggression against something that frustrates us is satisfying, even if the frustrating conditions remain unchanged. Thus, intensely angry men often rebel even when rebellion is hopeless. These two motivations sometimes reinforce one another. At other times the nonrational impulse to aggression is inhibited because people calculate or believe that it is undesirable. This suggests the second basic hypothesis of the theoretical argument: *the greater the normative and utilitarian justifications for strife in a discontented group, the greater the likely magnitude of strife.* "Normative justifications" are the basic attitudes men have about the desirability of violence. These range from cultural dispositions learned in childhood about how to deal with anger, to traditions and ideologies that variously praise order or celebrate violence. "Utilitarian justifications" are beliefs about the success of strife. People are as likely to develop such beliefs from other groups' successes as from their own careful calculations.

Various social causes of justifications for violence are specified in the theory. One is the historical extent of strife in a community. Groups and societies with high levels of past strife are likely to develop and hold attitudes and beliefs which offer greater justifications for future strife than societies with more peaceful histories. Similarly, the more successful strife has been in the past for a group or for an entire society, the greater its future justifications. Irrespective of other attitudes about violence, people will be relatively unlikely to oppose a political system and its representatives violently if they think those agencies are legitimate.

The outcome of motivations and attitudes toward strife is finally and most immediately determined by two aspects of social organization: the balance of social control, and the balance of institutional support, between contending groups. In contemporary societies the contending groups usually are the regime and those who support it, on the one side, and those who oppose or ask reforms from it on the other. The "institutional balance" between regimes and dissidents refers to their relative capacity to organize and command men. If regimes are supported by a pervasive network of organizations, as they are in Communist countries, dissidents have little space in which to organize. The "coercive balance" refers to the capacities of the contenders to fight. If dissidents can arm substantial cadres, or win over some of the military, they can carry on a protracted internal war. The general hypothesis is that *the greater the institutional and coercive capacities of the dissidents relative to the regime capacities, the greater the magnitudes of strife.* The relation holds only up to the point of equality. Beyond the point at which dissidents gain the upper hand, regimes will collapse more quickly and the violence contingent on their collapse is likely to be less. (See Gurr, 1970a, for a fuller presentation and documentation of the above argument.)

Two cross-cutting distinctions among types of strife are particularly important. One is between violent and nonviolent strife, the latter including such events as demonstrations and political strikes. The second is between two general forms of strife:

> *Turmoil* is relatively spontaneous, short-lived strife whose initiators usually have limited, "reformist" objectives. Its principal forms are political demonstrations and strikes, riots, political and ethnic clashes, and local rebellions.

> *Rebellion* is highly organized, often long-lasting strife with intensive, usually "revolutionary" objectives. Its main forms are terrorism, coups d'état, guerrilla and civil wars, and "private wars" among communal groups.

The general purpose of the "Causes of Strife" study is to determine whether indicators of discontent, justifications, and social balance are related to strife in the directions predicted by the hypotheses, and how strongly. The better they jointly explain variation in strife in the democratic nations, the greater our confidence in the accuracy of the theory.

Alliances and War

One of the classic questions of international relations is how the "balance of power" affects the stability of the international system. A traditional and contemporary argument is that international peace can indeed be maintained without strong supranational institutions (such as a powerful United Nations) "to the extent that all nations are free to deal and interact with all others as their national interests dictate." The effect of such un-restricted dealing ought to be "such a welter of cross-cutting ties and such a shifting of friendships and hostilities that no single set of interests can create a self-aggravating and self-reinforcing division or cleavage among the nations." It follows from this set of assumptions "that anything which re-strains or inhibits free or vigorous pursuit of the separate national interest will limit the efficacy of the stabilizing mechanism. And among those ar-rangements seen as most likely to so inhibit that pursuit are formal alliances" (Singer and Small 1968, p. 249). Nations in the same alliances are restricted to some degree from competing with their allies in the alliance, and are less free to cooperate with nonalliance nations. The reader who is familiar with economic arguments will recognize that this is an extension of Adam Smith's "invisible hand" mechanism (used to justify free economic competition among producers and suppliers) to the international arena.

How much a given alliance will restrain a nation from pursuing its interests is not easily determined. Singer and Small distinguish among three types of alliances—defense, neutrality, and entente—expecting that they cause different degrees of restraint. The crux of the argument is that if each alliance somewhat reduces the interaction opportunities among nations, then as alliance commitments increase the system's interaction opportunities will diminish. The predicted result is that war will then increase in fre-quency, magnitude, or severity. "Carried to its extreme conditions, this tendency culminates in a completely bipolarized system, with interaction op-portunities reduced (theoretically, at least) to one; each nation would then have only friends or foes..." (Singer and Small 1968, pp. 249–50).

The argument is summarized in two basic hypotheses: (1) *The greater the number of alliance commitments in the system, the more war the system will experience.* (2) *The closer to pure bipolarity the system is, the more war it will experience.*

Singer and Small are not especially committed to demonstrating the argument's accuracy. It has been the subject of a great deal of rarified con-ceptual discussion and several historical examinations. The authors wryly remark, "rather than dwell any longer here on the plausible reasons why alliance aggregation *should* correlate with the onset of war, it might be more useful to ascertain the extent to which it does" (1968, p. 250). How they do so we shall see in subsequent sections.

2.2   Variables and Indicators

Most of the basic variables in the three studies are self-evident from the statements of the problems: values, party, deprivation, strife, alliance aggregation, and war. The next major issue is how each of them is conceptualized and set up for measurement. First, we require some general definitions and distinctions among kinds of variables.

Terminology

A *variable,* to expand on what was said in Chapter 1, is a characteristic or quality which people, groups, nations, events, or interactions have in different degrees. Variables are sometimes said to comprise *dimensions.*[1] "Political democracy" might be regarded as a dimension: democracy is "high" or strong in a political system with open competition for public office, considerable protection of individual rights, freedom of speech and press, and so forth. Conditions such as open competition for office, protection of rights, and freedoms of speech and press are variables, high levels of which tend to occur together. If and when they do coexist, we can say that they signify a high degree of political democracy. To say that a set of variables is, or represents, a dimension can be justified by theoretical arguments or by empirical evidence. It is most convincing if it is based on both.

We must make a clear distinction between variables and measures of them before proceeding. *Variables* are abstract properties of entities; they are concepts that we use in theoretical thinking. *Measures* are our estimates of how much of a variable a particular entity has. The height of people is a variable; a tape measure provides measures of different people's heights in inches or centimeters. The power of countries is a variable; Gross National Product (GNP) is one measure of different countries' relative power, and another is the size of their armed forces. A tape measure provides a relatively direct and complete measure of length. GNP and military strength are indirect and partial measures of power. I remarked in Chapter 1 that such indirect and partial measures of variables are called *indicators.* Unfortunately, the term "variable" is often used in social research as an equivalent to "measure" and "indicator." This usage is avoided here, for it is a bad habit for the researcher to think that because he or she has constructed an index of political participation, or some other variable, there is then nothing more to be said or measured about it. How well an indicator represents a variable is a question of its *validity,* an issue considered at more length in Chapter 3.1.

The preceding paragraphs assume that political competition, democracy, and so forth are *continuous* dimensions and variables. In other words, they are conditions which vary by degree. Organizations, cities, countries, elections, and negotiations can have more or less of them. They might also be regarded as *dichotomous* variables. These are variables that have only two possible values or positions: a quality is said to be present or absent, high

---

[1] "Dimension" also has a technical meaning in factor analysis, discussed in Section 7.2, which is similar but not identical to its conceptual meaning.

or low, but not in between. In dichotomous terms, an election is said to be democratic or not, a country has freedom of the press or it does not. It may seem too simple, or rigidly ideological, to treat the world in such black-and-white terms, but there are kinds of theory, and kinds of measurement, in which it is useful to define variables dichotomously. There also are some conditions that by their nature are dichotomous: sex is one of them, and the old jibe that "You can't be half-pregnant" suggests another. But even such "naturally" dichotomous variables are often a matter of perspective. In legal and medical terms, pregnancy certainly is an either-or condition. In social terms it is a continuous variable, and people's feelings and actions about it vary greatly according to whether a woman is two weeks, two months, or eight months pregnant. To use a political example, whether an individual is a Republican or not seems to be a dichotomous variable, and as such can be used to help predict voting decisions. More important for many political questions is *how* pro- or anti- Republican he or she is. Strong enough only to vote Republican, or to canvass for its candidates? Opposed only enough to say so to an interviewer, or enough to run for local office against Republican incumbents? Thus, whether we treat a variable as continuous or dichotomous usually depends, first, on how we have phrased a research question, and second, on how we can or want to measure it.

Types of Variables

There are many ways to distinguish among types of variables. The reader may wonder, after considering some of the many distinctions mentioned below, why we should bother doing so. A basic answer is that the investigator's choice of variables to analyze, along with his choice of cases, is decisive for his research design. He should have in mind a clear picture of his range of alternatives, so that his choice, as Galtung puts it, "may be a fruitful one, and not only a traditional one" (1967, p. 37). There are also important theoretical and technical implications behind the kinds of variables chosen for analysis; some of them are mentioned elsewhere in this book and some of them are beyond our scope. The central point here is that classification of variables can and should expand the researcher's consideration of the kinds of things he can compare to answer his questions.

LEVELS OF ANALYSIS   Variables can be distinguished by *level of analysis*, that is, according to the type of entity whose properties are being studied. The simplest level-of-analysis distinction is between variables which apply to individuals and those which apply to collectivities. Variables at one level of analysis often have analogs at another. Or, to put the matter somewhat differently, we can define variables so generally that we can identify manifestations of them at different levels. An example is "hostility toward others." At the psychological level we can ask how openly hostile are individuals toward members of other groups. A structural manifestation of hostility might be the extent to which an organization has roles and procedures for taking damaging action against other organizations. The underlying variable is the same, but its manifestations differ according to the level of analysis.

PROPERTIES OF ANALYSIS   Variables also can be distinguished according to the *properties of analysis,* that is, according to what kinds of qualities of entities are being compared. In studies of individuals a basic set of distinctions can be made among *background, personality, attitudinal,* and *behavioral* variables. Background variables are the generally permanent characteristics an individual has, by virtue of such things as his family origins, class, education, and occupation. Personality variables are relatively permanent aspects of his psyche, such as his basic beliefs, motivations, modes of relating to others, and emotional tone. Attitudinal variables are more changeable aspects of his psyche, including immediate motivations, feelings, and opinions and evaluations of his circumstances. Behavioral variables are the things he says and does. (See Galtung 1967, pp. 29–36; I distinguish attitudinal from behavioral variables here, which Galtung does not.)

Some properties are more readily observed than others, which leads some researchers to distinguish between *hard* and *soft* variables. The number of war casualties, or a political party's electoral support, are said to be "hard," objective variables. Characteristics of personality and attitudes are "soft" variables (see Holsti and North 1966). This distinction has been criticized on the grounds that it depends less on the intrinsic nature of the variables than on whether they are regularly and authoritatively measured. Thus, variables which are measured by governments, like GNP, are "hard" while those measured by private researchers are quite likely to be labeled "soft."

A CROSS-CLASSIFICATION OF VARIABLES   It is advantageous to have a classification of variables that is directly applicable to political research, and that also combines both levels and properties of analysis. A classification of this sort is shown in Table 2.1, derived from a proposal by Singer and Small (1968, pp. 247–48). Four politically relevant levels of analysis are distinguished: the *individual,* the *subnational collectivity,* the *nation,* and *international organizations* or *systems.* At each of these levels of analysis there are four properties: *psychocultural attributes, structural and physical attributes, behaviors,* and *relationships.* The cross-classification of levels and properties of analysis gives us 16 types or categories of variables.

The four levels of analysis should be self-explanatory. Each refers to an easily recognizable class of entities that are of interest for political research. For some purposes it may be useful to distinguish among three or more types of subnational collectivities. Occasionally we are interested in variable properties of *categories* of people, for example in the political orientations of different socioeconomic classes. We are more likely to be concerned

TABLE 2.1 *Variables Classified According to Levels and Properties of Analysis*

		Properties of analysis			
		Psychocultural attributes	*Structural attributes*	*Behaviors*	*Relationships*
Levels of analysis	*Individuals*				
	Subnational collectivities	Party values	Political parties	Strife events ←	(Conflict)
	Nations	Discontent / Justifications	Wealth	Magnitude of strife / War	Alliance formation
	International systems		Alliances	Magnitude of war	

with properties of *groups,* which are loosely connected sets of people like neighborhoods, cities, or provinces. Politimetricians interested in the politics of particular nations are most often concerned with comparing properties of tightly knit *subsystems* like political parties, reform movements, or government agencies. (On types of collectivities see Galtung 1967, pp. 38–40.)

Our four-way classification of the kinds of properties is somewhat more arbitrary, but not difficult to explain or use. *Psychocultural attributes* are mental properties, whether of individuals or collectivites, such as cultural values, peaceful or hostile orientations to action, and ideological commitments. *Structural and physical* attributes are external, more "objective" properties such as social background (of individuals), natural resources (of collectivities and nations), capacity for change (of all kinds of entities), and size, components, power, and durability (of collectivities, nations, and international systems). *Behaviors* are dynamic properties and actions of entities; they are likely to fluctuate markedly within an entity over time, as well as among entities. Some examples are the extent and types of change, kinds of decisions and policies, communicativeness, and attacks. *Relationships* are the ways in which individuals and collectivities are linked to one another, both across and up and down the four levels of analysis. Some relationships are *comparative*: some groups are more or less powerful than others, nations are geographically near or distant from one another. Other relationships are *interactive.* We may be concerned with the extent of coalition formation between political parties, or in flows of trade and investment among nations.

Time is used in many studies as a variable but cannot be classified according to some level or property of analysis. For example, we might study correlations between time—measured in years, months, or any other unit— and any changing attributes or behaviors of any kind of entity. This does not mean that time "causes" changes in entities, any more than we can say that time "causes" human aging. Changes in a man's ideological position as time passes are the result of changes in his experience and circumstances, not of time itself. So when we correlate time with some other variable, we are using time as a substitute for the attributes and behaviors that cause changes over time.

Some of the basic variables of the three studies we are examining are used to illustrate the variables classified in Table 2.1. No "individual" variables appear because of our concern with macropolitics. Almost all other variables are represented, however. The table also shows that some variables overlap levels of analysis and properties of analysis. "Discontent," for example, is a psychocultural property of *individuals* and *subnational collectivities*; in the "Causes of Strife" study it is aggregated (summed) to the *national* level. As another example, "magnitude of war" as defined in the "Alliances and War" study is a behavioral property of the *international system,* but is aggregated from the war activities of each *nation* in the system. Alliances are an example of connections across properties of analysis. When a nation forms an alliance it enters into a *relationship* with other nations. At the level of the international system, alliances are *structural attributes,* more or less enduring patterns of obligations and interaction among the components of the system. An international system varies across time in, say the number of alliances among its members and their degree of aggregation. Some other overlaps and transformations of this sort are mentioned below.

Variables in "American Values"

There are four (sets of) variables investigated in Namenwirth and Lasswell's study of American values. The basic set is *values*: each of the categories and subcategories of values, and each type of reference to them, is a variable, a property that varies in importance from time to time and group to group. The authors' approach to measuring the importance of these values is to develop a "dictionary" of words which are listed according to the category of value and type of transformation to which they refer. The relative frequency with which each class of words occurs in party platforms is the operational measure of its importance. The same technique could be applied to any other written documents or to speeches. Not all words refer unambiguously to values, so a number of residual categories of words are also used as variables. A total of 46 value categories/variables are used in the value dictionary and the study, plus 16 "value unspecific" categories of words.

Political party and *time* can be thought of as variables, but in this study they are not used as such but serve to generate categories across which the "value" measures are compared. The Republican (R) and Democratic

TABLE 2.2 *Comparisons in the "American Values" Study Party Plat-forms*

		Democratic (D)			Republican (R)		
Period	1844–1864 (1)	*D*1 1844 1856	1848 1860	1852 1864	*R*1 1844 1856	1848 1860	1852 1864
	1944–1964 (2)	*D*2 1944 1956	1948 1960	1952 1964	*R*2 1944 1956	1948 1960	1952 1964

(*D*) parties are distinguished, as are two time periods, 1844–1864 (1) and 1944–1964 (2). A few additional comparisons are made on an election-to-election basis (see below). Thus, for any given value variable, three kinds of comparisons are made, as shown in Table 2.2. The parties can be compared, *D* vs. *R*, and so can the two time periods, 1 vs. 2. A set of cross-comparisons can also be made: *D*1 vs. *D*2; *R*1 vs. *R*2; *D*1 vs. *R*2; and *R*1 vs. *D*2. Which comparisons *are* made depends on the researchers' substantive interests.

The fourth and last variable is the *economic wealth* of the United States, which is examined in Namenwirth's (1968) study of connections over time between party emphasis on the "wealth" value and objective economic conditions. These comparisons are made for every presidential election between 1844 and 1964, to help answer the questions of when, and how much, different kinds of economic change were reflected in the parties' platforms.

Variables in "Causes of Strife"

There are four basic sets of variables in this study. The dependent variable, i.e., the object of explanation, is magnitude of strife, which is treated as a nation-behavior variable. The three independent variables, those used to explain it, are the extent of discontent and of justifications for strife, and the balance of support and coercion between dissidents and regimes.

"Discontent" is basically an individual variable, one that can be aggregated at any collective level. It is important for strife to the extent that it is intense among members of any large collectivity. "Justifications" are also individual variables that can be aggregated to any collective level. Like discontent, they are cross-classified as psychocultural variables. "Balance of support" and "balance of coercion" are evidently structural properties, though aspects of them are subject to short-term "behavioral" change. At the subnational level of analysis, we can distinguish support for dissidents from support for regimes, and dissident coercion from regime coercion. Both can be combined at the national level in a set of "balance" variables.

All four variables are complex enough that I refer to them below as *dimensions,* i.e., as "bundles" of related variables. The component variables of "magnitude of strife" and "balance" are discussed here. Two magnitude of strife variables are listed below, with their operational definitions:

1. *Intensity* is the human cost of strife, indexed by deaths from strife per million population.
2. *Man-days of strife* is indexed for each occurrence by multiplying the number of participants by the duration; results are then summed and expressed as man-days of (each type of) strife per 100,000 population.

Each of these variables is directly measurable for each occurrence of strife. Each can also be aggregated for all occurrences of each category of strife events, and for all strife in a nation in any time span.

The "magnitude of strife" dimension has two component variables, each of which could be directly measured. The "balance" dimension has four conceptually distinct variables, identified in the following two quotations:

> Dissidents, and regimes, have *institutional support* to the extent that they direct organizations through which they obtain consistent compliance with their demands and directives without resort to coercive sanctions. Levels of institutional support are a function of the relative scope of dissident and regime organizations, and of the degree to which leaders can demand and receive sacrifices from members in the service of the organization... (Gurr 1970a, p. 277).

> Dissidents, and regimes, have *coercive control* to the extent that they can obtain consistent compliance... with their demands and directives through the use of threats of negative sanctions. The most immediately compelling of such negative sanctions is force itself... (Gurr 1970a, p. 234).

The four component variables are dissident and regime institutional support, and dissident and regime coercive control. None of these variables could be fully or directly measured, so a number of indirect indicators were used for each. These indicators are summarized below:

Dissident Institutional Support
Size of Communist parties
Oppositional status of Communist parties
Size of dissident labor unions
Number of political strikes 1955–66
Size, degree of organization, and isolation of other dissident groups
(also used to index "dissident coercive control," below)

Regime Institutional Support
Size of progovernment labor unions
Central government budget as a proportion of Gross Domestic Product
National political integration
Political centralization
Extent of voting participation
Government party seats in national legislature

Dissident Coercive Control

Frequency of military participation in antiregime strife, 1961–65
Level of foreign support for dissidents
Number of countries providing foreign support for dissidents
Size, degree of organization, and isolation of dissident groups

Regime Coercive Control

Relative size of military forces
Relative size of internal security forces
Historical loyalty of coercive forces to the regime
Proportion of population in cities larger than 20,000

Precise measures were available for less than half of these indicators. The others required the use of various judgmental scales, of types described in Section 4.2, below. Procedures by which these indicators can be combined are discussed in Section 5.2.

Note that these indicators represent many different levels and properties of analysis. Some are structural attributes of collectivities, including the size and organization of dissident groups. Others are behavioral attributes of collectivities: political strikes and the participation of coercive forces in strife are examples. Foreign support for dissidents is a relationship among nations. This sort of combination of indicators, of widely different types, reflects a decision to treat a theoretical dimension in as many empirical ways as feasible. Operational neatness is compromised in order to help meet conceptual requirements. The approach is called "multiple operationism" and is discussed at several points in subsequent chapters (see also Campbell and Fiske 1959, and Campbell 1969).

Variables in "Alliances and War"

The three variables specified in the two basic hypotheses of this study are the dependent variable, *war*, and the independent variables, the *number of alliance commitments* in the international system, and the extent to which the system approaches *bipolarity*. *Time* is also used as a variable, since comparisons are made for different years. There are various kinds of war: international, imperial, colonial, and civil. Singer and Small restricted themselves to international wars, those "in which at least one participant on each side is an independent and sovereign member of the international system, with a population exceeding 500,000 and enjoying diplomatic recognition from...Britain and France" (1968, p. 258). They also excluded very small wars, those whose battle-connected deaths total less than 1,000.

The simplest indicator of "war" is a dichotomous one: in any given year, there *is* war in the international system or there *is not*. Rather than relying on this kind of index, the investigators relied on three more variable properties of war:

1. *Number of wars begun* in a period.
2. *Magnitude of war,* the sum of the months which all nations separately experienced as participants in war. Since the relative weight of a war-month for, say, the United States is much greater than a war-month for a minor power like Greece, magnitudes were separately assessed for major powers alone, and for major and minor powers together.
3. *Severity of war,* the number of battle-connected deaths of military personnel sustained by all participants in a war. Separate indicators again were used for major-only wars and all wars.

A more complex set of "alliance" variables is specified, all of them being defined operationally, as the "war" variables were. The first hypothesis (p. 23) stipulated that as the number of alliances in the system increased, war would increase. Five measures of number of alliances were used in the segment of the study examined here.[2] For each year, the following scores were computed:

1. Percentage of all nations having at least one alliance of any class with any type of nation, major or minor.
2. Percentage of all nations having at least one *defensive* alliance with any type of nation.
3. Percentage of *major* powers having at least one alliance of any class with another major power.
4. Percentage of *major* powers having at least one *defensive* pact with another major power.
5. Percentage of *major* powers having at least one alliance of any class with any *minor* power.

The reader might ask at this point why so many different indicators of the alliance aggregation variable were thought to be necessary. Why not use just one or two? There are several good answers. One is that in the absence of strong hunches or theoretical arguments, the researchers cannot know in advance whether the alliance aggregation–war relationship holds more strongly for one type of alliance or type of nation than another. And even if they did have such hunches, they would be obliged to test them by constructing alternative measures. A second, equally compelling argument is that, scientifically, it is intrinsically desirable to describe and analyze the relative aggregation of different types of alliances. No other researchers had previously proposed and tried to validate such indicators. A third, methodological justification is the "multiple operationism" argument mentioned above. No single indicator is likely to represent a theoretical variable fully; there will be "slippage" between indicator and concept. Moreover the amount of error in a single indicator is almost never known. The researcher

---

2 Lists of these and other measures, and the information from which they are derived, are given in Singer and Small (1966b); this study also lists nations in the international system (categorized according to whether they are major or minor), alliances by dates and types, and alliance scores by year from 1815 to 1939. Additional data through 1965 are in Singer and Small 1969.

who uses multiple indicators, and analyzes them seperately, will have a much sounder basis for estimating the validity and reliability of his results. But Singer and Small did not take the final step in the multiple operationism procedure, which is to combine those measures with demonstrated similarity into a single, composite indicator.

The last variable in the Singer and Small study is "bipolarity." Measures of it are needed to test their second hypothesis that the greater bipolarity is, the more war. They simplified their operational task by limiting themselves to determining the amount of bipolarity in *defensive pacts* among *major powers*. The procedures used in making these determinations were too complex to summarize here.

The Ecological Fallacy and Some Others

Critics sometimes seek out fallacies in one another's quantitative political research in much the same spirit that medieval churchmen thundered "heresy." They enhance the virtue of their own position by denouncing their opponents' moral and intellectual turpitude. Since challenge begets response, and since social research lacks any ultimate arbiter—moral, intellectual, or coercive—"fallacies" tend to come in dialectically opposed pairs: critics of "ecological" fallacies assail critics of "individualistic" fallacies, the inductive fallacy confronts the deductive one, psychological reductionism contends with social wholism, and so on. The politimetrician may sometimes be justified in turning a skeptical eye on such debates and getting on with the job at hand. Nonetheless, there is at least one area of "fallaciousness" that he ignores at his peril: the various ramifications of the so-called ecological fallacy. It ought initially to be considered when specifying and operationalizing variables, which is why it is discussed here. It also has implications for statistical analysis and its interpretation. (For a list of fallacies see Alker 1965, pp. 101–5.)

The "ecological fallacy" takes its name from a technical problem pointed out in sociology by Robinson (1950): the correlation of variables at the individual level of analysis is usually weaker than their correlation at aggregate levels. (The problem had previously been noted and debated in economics and psychology; see Scheuch 1966). One of Robinson's most dramatic examples came from his study of the correlation between Negro population and illiteracy, as reported in the 1930 U.S. census. When he divided the country into nine large-scale *census* areas, the correlation between Negro population and illiteracy was a very high .95: increases in black population and illiteracy seemed precisely connected. But when he correlated the same measures for the 48 *states* the correlation was distinctly lower, .77, and for *individuals* it was a low .20: black individuals were only slightly more likely than whites to be illiterate. *If* the researcher had inferred from the census-area or state results that illiteracy was highly concentrated in black individuals, he would be wildly in error, a victim of the "ecological fallacy." Such inferences from subnational collectivities, like counties or voting precincts, to the individual level of analysis have been especially common in voting research.[3]

Since we are dealing with macropolitical comparisons, the reader may wonder how relevant the problem is. The answer is that we face the same problem whenever we move from one level of macro analysis to another: from census tracts to cities, cities to counties, counties to regions, regions to nations, etc. Here is an empirical demonstration by Blalock (1964a, pp. 102–14) which uses measures of two "subnational collectivities" variables for 150 Southern counties: (1) percentage nonwhite population, and (2) the differential between white and nonwhite incomes. When the 150 counties are analyzed as separate cases, the correlation between the two variables is a moderate .54. The counties were then grouped in pairs, fives, tens, and finally fifteens. Without exception, *the larger the grouping, the higher the correlation coefficients,* rising to .95 for groupings of 15. The technical explanation of these consistent differences is, essentially, that the larger the units of analysis the greater their homogeneity—purely on probability grounds—and the less the variability within them. The substantive and theoretical interpretation is that the grouping of cases controls (eliminates) the effects of unknown or unmeasured variables which decrease the strength of the relationship being studied. (The reader with a knowledge of statistics can best understand these reasons by referring to the literature on the subject. A useful general discussion is Scheuch 1966; a good technical one Blalock 1964a, pp. 102–14. Other major discussions are Robinson 1950; Goodman 1953 and 1959 and Duncan, Cuzzort, and Duncan 1961.)

We can now restate and generalize the problem: *the researcher runs the risk of systematic error when he measures or counts at one level of analysis, and infers from the results what is the case at another level of analysis.* One aspect of the problem Scheuch calls the *group fallacy,* of which the ecological fallacy is a special case: it results when we make inferences from units of observation at a *higher* level of analysis to units at a *lower* level. The obverse problem is the *individualistic fallacy,* also called the composition fallacy, which is "present when the units of observation or counting

---

[3] The discussion here and elsewhere in this chapter assumes that the reader has an approximate if not precise understanding of what a correlation coefficient (r) is. For those who do not, it is a measure of how closely related two indicators are. If they are perfectly and positively related, ("for every 1,000 houses visited in a vote registration drive, registration increases by exactly 12"), $r = +1.00$. If they are unrelated ("door-to-door canvassing has no effect on voter registration"), $r = 0.00$. If they are perfectly and negatively related ("for every 1,000 houses visited in a registration drive, registration declines by exactly 5"), $r = -1.00$. Most correlations observed in social research are in the low or middle range, $-.50$ to $+.50$ ("for every 1,000 houses visited in a voter registration drive, between 4 and 20 new registrants have been observed, depending on the area"). Chapter 6 demonstrates how to calculate and interpret some of the different kinds of correlation coefficients.

are smaller than the units to which inferences are made" (Scheuch 1966, p. 164). Both these problems can be illustrated, in practice or prospect, from the indicators used in the three studies we have considered.

The "Causes of Strife" study affords a particularly clear example of a possible group fallacy. The theoretical argument rests on the assumption that intensely discontented people who believe in violence are (likely to) rebel. But discontent and violent attitudes are indexed only in the aggregate, at the national level; as we shall see in Chapter 7, the correlations are about .50. *If* we inferred, as a result, that there was an equally strong correlation between an *individual* being discontented, holding violent attitudes, and actually joining in strife, we would be committing the group fallacy. The true correlation between an individual's dispositions and actual participation in strife is almost certainly much weaker: many are discontented, only a few rebel. What saves the study from the group or ecological fallacy is the limited, probabilistic nature of the inferences made from the measured level of analysis to the level at which inferences are drawn.

A concrete example of what might be an individualistic fallacy is suggested by the "American Values" study. The word counts which comprise the indicators for the various values cannot be uncritically assumed to represent the relative value concerns of Americans, or of supporters of the particular party, or even of the authors of the documents. The most they *directly* represent is the authors' perception of what the major value concerns of the election campaign were, and any further inference from them risks a sort of individualistic fallacy.

This discussion of fallacies has gone well beyond the immediate questions of how variables are chosen and defined. Put bluntly, the point is that the investigator who plans to infer relationships among variables up or down levels of analysis from the level at which he actually measures the variables runs an increased risk of theoretical silliness and factual error. Seen in this light, "fallacy" seems too strong a word for the problems at issue. There are many fascinating and important research questions that can be studied only, or most practically, by making inferences across levels of analysis. The researcher thus often wants to or must risk these "fallacies." The important consideration is that he or she make the conceptual leaps knowingly, and recognizing that some kinds of conclusions drawn from them can be truly fallacious.

2.3 Universe of Analysis

Many kinds of cases—men, cities, nations, time periods, events—can be studied in political research. There are also many ways to choose examples of a particular case. In practice, though, how the researcher formulates a problem and specifies its variables usually sets rather narrow limits to the kinds and ranges of cases he can study. Within these limits, the researcher often finds himself balancing two considerations when making his final decisions: (1) technical questions of how many cases are needed to make reliable generalizations, and (2) practical questions of the availability of information. This section first briefly reviews the abstract possibilities of selection among kinds of cases, and then discusses the technical and some practical issues with illustrations of how they were dealt with in our three studies.

Kinds of Cases

We earlier categorized types of variables in political research according to the properties and levels of analysis to which they referred (Table 2.1). Cases can be categorized similarly. They can be drawn from different levels of analysis, ranging from sets of roles and individuals (each role or individual = one case) to sets of nations and international blocs (each nation or bloc = one case). Cases can also be either structures or behaviors. Some representative cases at the three macro levels of analysis are shown in Table 2.3. Of these various cases, nations and subnational governmental structures are the most common in macropolitical research. Behaviors are not often chosen as cases, mainly because political scientists usually think of describing and explaining behaviors as variables of structural cases. For example, assume that we want to determine what proportion of riot violence is typically caused by protestors' actions and what proportion by police action against the protestors. The conventional practice in politimetrics would be to choose, say, 50 political structures (cities, provinces, or nations) as cases and to measure these proportions for all riots in each. But we could just as well take a set of 50 riots as cases—riots are behaviors—and estimate the proportions in each of them. As this example implies, some important questions may best be answered by taking behaviors rather than structures as cases. The opposite also is true: some questions require structures and not behaviors as cases. If we were studying the *causes* of riots, we should choose political structures not riots, for if we looked only at riots we could not identify the social conditions that made the difference between rioting and civil peace. The same difficulty faces scholars who have tried to build theories of revolution on the study of one or a few revolutions: they have no basis for saying that their "revolutionary conditions" were not also present in many nonrevolutionary times and places.

Time is another dimension of variation in cases, one which cuts across levels and properties of analysis. The conventional procedure in comparative political research has been to select a *synchronic* or *cross-sectional* set of cases, e.g., a set of elites, parties, or nations at one point in time. In a cross-sectional set of cases we do not have to worry much about the effects of unmeasured changes over time on the conditions we are studying. But quite often this is precisely what we want to know about: the processes of change.

TABLE 2.3 *Types of Cases Classified According to Macro Levels and Properties of Analysis*

	Properties of Analysis	
	Structures	*Behaviors*
Subnational: Categories	Classes Occupational groups Geographical units	(All the following behaviors are either behaviors of groups, or behaviors by which categories or subsystems acquire more ordered structures.)
Subsystems	Elites Ethnic, linguistic groups Ecological units (neighborhoods, metropolitan areas) Political units (counties, cities, provinces)	Political statements (speeches, party platforms, petitions) Subnational constitutions, laws, policies, decisions
Groups	Government agencies Legislatures Judical bodies Political parties Interest groups Businesses Schools, universities Segmental and informal subgroups of the above	Creation or amalgamation of political organizations Decay or fragmentation of political organizations Subnational movements of protest or reform Demonstrations, riots, clashes, strikes
National	Nations Colonies	Constitutions, laws, decisions, policies Elections Reform movements Revolutions, coups d'état Foreign interventions
International	Alliances Regional blocs Political blocs International organizations International systems	Charters, policies, actions of international organizations U.N. voting decisions Diplomatic exchanges Alliance formations Wars

Levels of macro analysis

If so, we should consider making what is called a *diachronic or longitudinal* study, in which we examine one or several "cases" over a long period of time. If we are studying *structures* longitudinally, the time points at which we observe the cases may be successive weeks, months, years, or even decades. In the "Alliances and War" study the cases are the state of the international system in successive years. (In this particular study, the selection of "the international system" as the focus of study made it necessary to conduct the study diachronically. Since by definition there has been only one international system of nation-states in recent history, multiple cases for study are made possible only by repeated observation of the same structure.) If *behaviors* are being studied diachronically, the time points are usually determined by the periodicity of the events, e.g., every fourth year for party platforms in the" American Values" study. Some other behaviors are neither simultaneous nor periodic, but episodic. Examples are reform movements, revolutions, and wars. Nonetheless they can be studied either in cross-section, by using as cases all such events in a limited period, or longitudinally, by selecting them from widely different periods of time. Which approach the researcher might choose depends on his research questions. If he hoped to identify the basic common denominators in all revolutions, he would examine as wide a time span as possible. If he were interested in revolutionary movements in economically developing societies only, a much more limited time frame is indicated.

A third pattern of case selection combines the synchronic and diachronic approaches: one set of cases is selected and examined at two or more time points. The "American Values" study uses this technique, comparing 1844–64 party platforms with 1944–64 platforms. The technique is relatively more common in cross-national comparisons. This kind of research design adds some of the advantages of diachronic analysis to synchronic comparison. The synchronic comparisons usually include sufficient cases to permit reliable generalization about synchronic patterns; the time-lagged comparisons permit inferences about the directions and sequences of change. Problems and procedures of time-lagged and diachronic research are discussed further in Section 7.3.

The Number and Range of Cases

Once the researcher settles on one particular type of case, he or she must decide how many, and which ones: How many countries or cities, and which ones? What revolutions? What span of years?

NUMBER OF CASES *How many* cases should be included, called the *n* of a study, involves both technical and practical considerations. Technically, the more subtle or smaller the correlations being studied are, and the greater the likely variability in cases, the greater the *n* needed for statistical analysis. This should be intuitively evident in considering the "Alliances and War" study. If the substantial majority of alliances lead to an increase in war, we should have to look at relatively few years, or alliance formations, before the pattern became evident. But if there is only a slight tendency in this direction we must examine a great many alliances and their aftermaths before we can be sure that something more than chance is at work. There is an extension of this principle: if we plan to divide the cases into subgroups for separate examination, say by type of alliance, or time period, more cases are needed to detect differences. No consistent rules seem to be applied by politimetricians in deciding on numbers of cases. As a rule of thumb, at least 10 and preferably 20 are needed for any kind of informative statistical generalization.[4] If fewer than 10 cases can be identified and studied, statistical tests of significance and correlations are only embellishments on, and not substitutes for, narrative comparison and generalization.

Beyond an absolute minimum of $n = 10$, the more cases the better, but with diminishing returns in improved precision in the upper ranges. Two rather different questions are at issue in considering maximums: whether a relationship between two variables exists at all, and if it does how strongly it holds. For the first question, one can argue that if a relationship is not apparent (statistically significant) in 50 cases or so, it is too weak to be of much substantive or theoretical interest. But if the investigator wants to determine accurately *how strong* a relationship is, he would ideally require several hundred cases. In fact, most aggregate political comparisons are based on 20 to 100 cases. The basic analyses in the "American Values" study rest on 24 cases: 12 party platforms in each of two periods. Some subsidiary analyses include 62 party platforms representing all presidential elections between 1844 and 1964. The "Causes of Strife" study discussed here uses 38 polities (nations and colonies) as cases; the larger study of which this is a special analysis includes 114 polities. In the "Alliances and War" study $n = 130$; the state of the international system is measured for each year between 1815 and 1945.

LIMITATIONS ON NUMBERS OF CASES   One practical limitation on the number of cases is lack of information for some that might otherwise be included. This problem of information availability is discussed in the next chapter.

Another limitation is illustrated by two of our three examples: given their research designs, they practically exhaust the universe of cases. The "Causes of Strife" study includes all institutionally democratic countries with a population of over one million in 1962. (On the precise basis for identifying these democratic countries, see Gurr 1969, Appendix II.) If the definitions or the population limit had been stretched, only a handful of additional countries like South Africa and Luxembourg would have qualified. But other possibilities for increasing the n would require major changes in the research design. Possibilities include (1) using regions of countries rather than nations as cases; (2) making the study longitudinal rather than cross-sectional; (3) using outbreaks of strife as cases.

The n of the "Alliances and War" study could have been increased in

---

4 In psychometrics, technical guidelines have been developed for estimating sample size (number of cases). They enable the researcher to relate sample size to his willingness to risk rejecting a true hypothesis, and to the "power" of statistical tests to be used. For discussions see most statistics tests, e.g., Hays 1963, Chaps. 9 and 10, and also Kish 1965. The paradigmatic differences in research design between psychometrics and politimetrics are sufficiently great that the applicability of the psychometricians' sampling criteria is not always clear.

two ways. One would be to use time slices smaller than a year. The results of the initial study do not justify this: the researchers found that the three-year average in alliance aggregation is more closely related to magnitude of war than shorter segments. The second would be to extend the period studied beyond the 1815–1945 era. The researchers suggest that this appears unjustified, because this era seems to differ appreciably from the pre-1815 era and perhaps also from the post-1945 one. The 1815–1945 period had a "remarkable constancy. The national state was the dominant actor and the most relevant form of social organization; world politics were dominated by a handful of European powers...the concept of state sovereignty remained relatively unchallenged..." (Singer and Small 1968, p. 251). In fact, the data have since been brought forward to 1965 (Small and Singer 1970), for a modest increase in the n. But conceptual considerations still dictate rather strongly against extending the range into the period before the Congress of Vienna in 1815.

CHOOSING CASES   In the above examples, technical and conceptual considerations limit the number of cases that can be included. But the investigator will not always confront such a restricted universe. He may instead have more cases than could reasonably be studied. This is particularly likely when the cases are subnational entities like census tracts, cities, or interest groups; and also when they are "behaviors" like speeches, decisions, demonstrations, coups d'état, or elections. The researcher then must decide how to choose among the many possible cases. He has two basic alternatives. One is to make an *expedient selection* of cases that seem most important, or interesting, or easiest to study. In this instance, results cannot be safely generalized beyond the cases actually studied. The other alternative is to choose a *sample* of cases so that some reliable generalizations to others can be made.

Expedient selection is the choice of cases without regard to how well or badly they represent some larger universe. If we found that the correlation between police expenditures and crime rates in the 20 largest American cities was +.40, we would have no *statistical* grounds for assuming the correlation for smaller cities was similar, or even that it was positive rather than negative. To take a real finding, my studies of civil strife show that in the early 1960s the more developed African countries had more strife than the less developed ones. I could not assume that the same correlation held for Latin American countries without studying them as well. In Latin America, in fact, the correlation is reversed.

It is not necessarily a bad research strategy to choose an unrepresentative set of cases. There can be good theoretical or policy reasons for wanting to know how some set of variables is related in large cities, or in Latin American countries, or in conflicts between large nations. What *is* bad research strategy is to plan to generalize to other nations on the basis of Latin American results, or to generalize from large cities to small ones. Few researchers, even beginners, are likely to make such obvious errors. The more subtle, hence dangerous trap is to select cases which are not obviously *un*-representative and to generalize from them without fully realizing how unrepresentative they might be.

The problem identified in the preceding paragraph can be called the "error of misplaced generalization." Another aspect of it is to study cases in one era and to assume that the results apply to other eras as well. This can be assumed only if there are theoretical and empirical reasons to think that the patterns identified represent *universals,* which have the same form and magnitude for all times and places. Most paradigms for "good theory" assert that we should be able to propose and find evidence for such universal patterns among variables. But most variables thus far studied in politimetrics have proven to be related differently in different regions of the world, and in different eras. The "Alliances and War" study offers one more example: the connection between alliance formation and the extent of war was distinctly negative in the nineteenth century, yet just as clearly positive in the twentieth century. The theoretical answer to such findings is to identify the additional variables that cause the difference. The prescription for empirical research, though, is that considerable evidence is needed before we generalize beyond the kinds of cases studied *or* the eras in which they are studied.

Sampling is necessary if we hope to generalize our research results with confidence beyond the cases studied. A sample is a selection of cases that in some specifiable way represents a larger universe. Probably no one has ever tried to obtain an absolutely universal sample, one which embraces all eras and regions of mankind. What is often done is to sample from a more narrow universe, choosing for example samples of local party organizations in the United States, or revolutionary movements. *Time* samples also can be made, which was done in the "American Values" study.

Samples can be chosen in many different ways; the better the sample, in the sense of providing an unbiased representation of the universe, the more reliable are generalizations from it. A basic distinction is made between *probability* and *nonprobability* samples. A probability sample is one for which we can specify the probability that each case in the total universe will appear in the sample. In nonprobability sampling there is no certainty that every case has a chance of being included. Procedures for nonprobability sampling are discussed in the texts cited below; some, at least, are better than "expedient selection," discussed above. But probability sampling is preferred. To make a *simple random sample* the investigator must accomplish the manual or computer equivalent of putting a slip of paper for every case in a raffle drum and then spinning the drum. The first *n* slips drawn out of the drum are his sample. When survey researchers speak of "drawing" a sample, the term has its literal origin in just such a procedure. A variation is the *systematic sample*: a list of all cases is made, it is entered at a randomly chosen point, and every *n*th case on the list is taken for the sample. Another type of probability sample is the *stratified random sample,* which is widely used in survey research: the cases are stratified into more or less homogeneous classes and a random sample drawn from each class. But quite often in politimetrics we do not have complete lists of our possible cases, nor can we make reasonable assumptions about the representativeness of those cases that we do know about. So probability samples in politimetrics are more often the exception than the rule. (For introductions to sampling see Selltiz et al. 1963, Appendix B, and Stephan and McCarthy 1958. A technical treatise is Kish 1965.)

Usually the most serious practical limitation on devising a sample of cases for any kind of macropolitical research is that we lack information for many of the cases, or eras, that we ideally would like to study. The next chapter describes in some detail what kinds of information are generally available, and what kinds of procedures we can use to increase the data available to us.

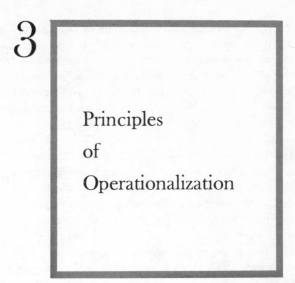

3

Principles
of
Operationalization

To operationalize is to decide how to measure variables. It requires numerous decisions about which specific data to collect, and how to treat them. There are a great many requirements for good measurement, and they are often at odds with one another. Usually there is no firm basis for saying that it is more necessary to meet one requirement than another. One result is that almost every kind of measurement, even the simplest, is subject to criticism from some technical point of view. Even if we measure the size of our desk with a yardstick, we can be criticized for not measuring other "more important" things about it, or for failing to check the yardstick for error, or for not using a more precise instrument.

Three different criteria for good measurement in politimetrics are discussed here and in the next chapter: conceptual, technical, and practical. The researcher should consider all three, but also will have to make compromises among them. The researcher who uses multiple indicators to tap all the conceptually important aspects of his variables is usually creating technical problems for his statistical analysis; and plans for using data that are both conceptually and technically ideal almost surely will run afoul of practical considerations. Politimetrics thus has at least one thing in common with practical politics in democracies: its successful practitioners must learn the art of compromise among competing demands.

3.1 Conceptual Considerations: Validity

A measure or indicator is *valid* if it is an adequate measure of what it is supposed to represent. Every researcher who uses quantitative methods must be concerned with the question of validity, and must give considerable thought to how well alternative indicators suit his conceptual purposes. If he wants to index people's political satisfaction with or alienation from their governments, for example, he might rely on data about how many of them voted for or against the governing party(ies) in the last election. "Aha!" says the critic, "but what about countries with only one party, and what about those with Tweedle-dum, Tweedle-dee parties that offer no effective choice? Your measure isn't valid for them!" If the researcher accepts the criticism, he might consider a cross-national opinion survey in which people are asked how politically satisfied they are. But the persistent critic may challenge him again, saying, "I still don't think your results will be valid. After all, most people will only give you superficial opinion, not what they really feel." At this point the exasperated researcher may ask just what it is that makes a particular indicator valid or not, and how he can possibly determine its validity.

The first point to be made is that there are no absolute criteria for judging an indicator's validity, not in political or any other research. There are only relative standards for validity, such as a consensus among scholars that a particular measure represents a variable more or less well. Two kinds of evidence help build confidence in the validity of a measure or indicator. One is a theoretically and substantively plausible argument that spells out how and why an indicator represents a significant aspect of a conceptual variable. The other is an accumulation of empirical evidence that an indicator is related to a variety of other measures or indicators in consistent, predicted ways. Evidence of the first sort contributes to *face validity*. Evidence of the second sort adds to *empirical validity*, or "construct validity" as it is sometimes called.

Face Validity

The initial source of face validity is a logical theoretical argument that gives a verbal definition of a variable, and then shows why a proposed indicator is a satisfactory representation of it. The researcher cannot be expected to use indicators that represent all possible meanings or aspects of a variable. On the other hand, he should be able to demonstrate that a measure has *some* correspondence with the variable he says it indicates, and is not wildly at odds with how other researchers think of that variable. Say that we are interested in the extent of hard-core support for political parties in different countries. We might define this variable generally as "the extent of intense support for the programs and leaders of a party." One possible indicator of such intense support is the number of members reported by each party. But we know from other research that "membership" is a very different thing from one party to another. For some parties "members" are those who pay dues. For others it is those who belong to local and regional party committees. For still others it is the total membership of trades unions and cooperatives that are affiliated with the party. Thus the face validity of an indicator based on reported party membership is not very high. We would be better advised to find other, or at least additional, indicators.

This hypothetical example suggests that the face validity of indicators depends partly on what is already known of the subject being studied. The politimetrician who is working on a subject for which there is substantial theory and evidence will have less difficulty in developing indicators that have high face validity than if he is working on an unexplored subject. This is also an argument for researchers to read widely about a subject before they attempt to devise new indicators.

A *conceptual reduction* approach to the validity problem is to reduce the theoretical distance between what the politimetrician claims to be measuring and what he is in fact measuring. As Galtung points out, "data are always valid in *some* extent, with regard to *some* latent dimension" (1967, p. 29). Instead of inferring that reported party membership is a measure of "intense support," we might claim only that membership reflects "*organized support.*" This approach has the merit of caution, and thus allows us to escape some validity criticisms. But it also usually means that we compromise on theoretical questions by studying different and less important variables.

The face validity of an indicator also can and should be assessed after data have been collected for the cases being studied. The researcher usually has a good deal of substantive knowledge about the subject he is studying which is not reflected in the data. He can use this to test his data by examining his cases—countries, parties, etc.—to see whether they are ranked the way he expects them to be. If he knows from reading a case study that party support in Mexico is weak, but finds Mexico near the top of an "intense party support" indicator, then the face validity of the indicator is in doubt. There are two reasons why caution is in order when making this kind of criticism of face validity. (1) Indicators are by definition imperfect measures, and the fact that a few cases seem misranked is not grounds for rejecting the validity of the indicators outright. (2) The critic must distingish between his unsupported preconceptions of how a case should be ranked, and his firm evidence that it ought to be ranked other than it is. An intuitive or normative expectation that Mexican party support is weak is different from *evidence* that this is the case. Evidence, not prejudice, is needed when you challenge the face validity of indicators.

Empirical Validity

Various statistical criteria have been developed, especially in psychometrics, to help test the validity of different indicators. The two somewhat different approaches to this problem are *convergent validation* and *criterion validation*.

CONVERGENT VALIDATION   The "convergent" technique is to determine whether different indicators of the same variable yield similar data. This is a kind of "up by the bootstraps" approach to validation, in which the multiple indicators of one variable are statistically compared with one another. If different measures of the same variable correlate highly, the researcher is considerably more confident that he is getting at some basic, underlying variable than if they are weakly or negatively correlated.

One question about convergent validation is *how strongly* indicators ought to be correlated for their joint validity to be accepted. There does not seem to be any absolute answer to this question, but a relative answer can be suggested: they should be more strongly correlated with one another than they are with indicators of different variables. An example will help clarify this. Suppose we are interested in the correlation between economic development and political modernization. By "development" we mean increasing economic specialization and productivity. By "modernization" we mean the growth of complex, functionally specialized, and adaptable political organizations. These are complex variables, or bundles of variables, which are not directly measurable. This obliges us to develop a number of indicators of each one. Next we collect data on each of these indicators for a large number of countries (or some other kind of case), and correlate each indicator with the others. The validity of these two sets of indicators is supported only if these two conditions held:

1. The "development" indicators are strongly correlated with one another, and the "modernization" indicators are strongly correlated with one another (*convergent validation*).
2. The "development" indicators are more strongly correlated with one another than they are with the "modernization" indicators, and vice versa (*discriminant validation*).

This pattern of results gives us confidence that our measuring instruments are good enough to distinguish two different variables, and also good enough to measure each one consistently. Now let us consider the validity implications of two other patterns of results.

1. *The indicators of both variables correlate about equally well.* This may happen because our indicators are too poor to distinguish between the two variables, *or because the two variables are very closely linked in empirical reality*. Considerably more theoretical thinking and empirical research may be necessary before we can distinguish between these alternatives. Additional indicators could be constructed, for the same set of cases and for others, to see if the same high level of intercorrelation holds. Better, we can ask theoretically what differential relations the two variables have with other variables. Ought they to have different causes, or effects? These questions can then be empirically studied. The results should provide firmer evidence for deciding whether we are theoretically justified in continuing to distinguish between two highly correlated variables.

2. The indicators discriminate the two variables, but *one or two of the indicators of one variable are only weakly correlated with the others*. The more common interpretation of this outcome is that the weakly correlated

indicators are inappropriate (invalid), and ought to be discarded. Any other interpretation requires a conceptual argument that they represent a distinct but theoretically important aspect of the variable under study. In this latter situation they may still be used in the final analyses. The "Alliance and War" study provides one example of this procedure. Three measures were constructed for the extent of war for each year: the number of wars begun in that year; the number of country-months of those wars; and the number of battle deaths in those wars. The last two measures were found to be very closely correlated, but they were only weakly correlated with "number of wars begun." The researcher decided to keep all three measures for their later statistical comparisons with measures of alliances, but to analyze them separately to see if they yielded similar results (which they did; see Chapter 8).

The foregoing examples of convergent validation are ones in which the indicators to be correlated were all devised in the same study. Another way is to correlate indicators obtained in one study, by one researcher, with different indicators of the same variable obtained by *other* researchers studying the same cases. Interpretations of the results of such comparisons are logically the same. But there is greater confidence in indicator validity if several researchers, working independently, devise different measures of a variable that subsequently prove to be strongly related.

Some important discussions of convergent and discriminant validation are Campbell and Fiske (1959) and Campbell (1969). A technical application is Bohrnstedt (1969). Caporaso reanalyzes and criticizes a politimetric study of European integration because its indicators do not meet these validity tests (1971).

CRITERION VALIDATION   This is, in many respects, the most convincing and satisfying test of the validity of indicators. Our theories and hypotheses often suggest how a variable ought to be related to other variables. If an indicator of a variable proves to be related to measures of other variables in the predicted ways, our confidence in its validity increases. The greater the number of such "tests" an indicator passes, using different sets of cases, the greater its criterion validity.

A kind of criterion validity was used when measuring "social discontent" in the "Causes of Strife" study. Social discontent could not be measured directly for more than a few nations. The operational approach therefore was to identify a number of social conditions, and patterns of change, that theory and evidence suggest are widespread causes of discontent in the contemporary world. Here is a partial list of these conditions. We distinguish between those which are relatively stable over time, and those which are likely to vary in the short run:

Persisting social sources of discontent
Economic discrimination
Political discrimination

Regional and ethnic separatism
National dependence on foreign capital
Religious cleavages
Lack of educational opportunity

Short-term sources of discontent

Short-term decline in foreign trade
Inflation
Relative declines in economic growth
New restrictions on political participation
Depriving policies of governments
Reported economic adversity

For most of these conditions, indicators were devised for both the *scope* of consequent discontent (the proportion of people affected in each country) and its *intensity* (the degrees of discontent imposed). These and other indicators of social discontent in the late 1950s and early 1960s were correlated with measures of the magnitude of civil strife in 1961–65, all for 114 countries. Almost all the indicators were correlated with strife in the positive direction predicted by the theory. This was regarded as evidence for their validity. Those listed above had the strongest correlations, and so were added to form composite indicators of social discontent. (There are several ways to treat multiple indicators of variables aside from adding them. These are discussed in Section 5.2.) This single set of correlations does not completely validate these indicators of social discontent. They should also be shown to predict to the strife criterion in other sets of cases (nations, provinces, cities) and in other time periods than the late 1950s and early 1960s before their validity can be accepted with full confidence.

CONVERGENT VERSUS CRITERION VALIDATION   Are convergent and criterion validation equally important? Should we expect indicators of political variables to meet both tests? I wish to suggest a set of answers, but you should recognize that they are not backed by a consensus among politimetricians. Criterion validation seems to be the more significant: we can have greatest confidence in an indicator's validity if it consistently predicts another variable in a theoretically expected way, more so than if the indicator "predicts" only to other indicators of the same variable. But convergent and discriminant validation are still crucial in two situations. First, the politimetrician must rely on convergent validation when criterion variables are not theoretically identified, or not measurable. Second, discriminant validation is sometimes needed to ensure that a criterion variable is substantially different from the indicator whose validity we are trying to determine.[1]

---

[1] James Caporaso of Northwestern University helped clarify the arguments of this section, without necessarily being persuaded by or responsible for them.

3.2   Technical Considerations

Validity is a conceptual criterion for good measurement. It is satisfied insofar as the researcher can demonstrate that indicators adequately represent underlying variables or concepts. Two technical criteria for good measurement are examined here: *reliability* and *precision*. A particular measurement procedure or indicator is *reliable* to the extent that it yields results that are consistent in successive measurements of the same case, and comparable among cases. A measurement procedure is *precise* insofar as we can use it to make very detailed or subtle distinctions among cases. Procedures which yield reliable results are not necessarily precise, or vice versa.

RELIABILITY

There is no such thing as error-free measurement in any of the sciences. If a physicist wants to determine the mass of a newly observed particle he will make a number of different measurements, perhaps using several different kinds of instrumentation. The values he gets will not be identical. Most will probably cluster rather closely around one point, with a few far off the mark. He is likely to discard the deviant measurements as the result of human or instrument error, and to report the average value of the others as the approximate mass. Other physicists will check his results using the same and different procedures and report their findings. None will claim to have identified the "true" mass. What they *have* accomplished in the process is to identify the range within which the "true" value is likely to be, and the margin of error that must be taken into account in any theoretical or empirical research that uses the information.

The political scientist who collects and uses macropolitical data confronts essentially the same issues and can deal with them in analogous ways. He wants to know something about the degree of accuracy he can expect if he uses a particular measurement procedure, and hence how much in error a particular datum is likely to be. For some procedures there are few reliability questions. A measure of "number of political parties represented in national legislatures" poses a modest conceptual problem about what is a "party," but once that is resolved by precise operational definition, numbers of parties can be reliably determined and compared. Procedures for content analysis (described in Section 4.2) usually yield data whose reproducibility is more suspect. But content analytic measurements can be repeated to obtain estimates of reliability: the closer are the results of two (or more) measurements of the same cases, the greater the reliability of the procedures used.[2] A third kind of data used in macropolitical comparisons are those

---

[2] Reliability tests are *intrasubjective* if the researcher repeats the measurements himself, *intersubjective* if someone else does it.

reported in statistical sources (see Section 4.1). Their reliability is often in doubt and measurement seldom can be repeated. The approach in this situation is to estimate "error margins" on the basis of what is known about the source and how its data were compiled. The politimetrician usually cannot *correct* such error, but once he knows how serious it is he can do something very nearly as good: he can determine how much and what kinds of effects it will have on his results, and hence will know better how to interpret them.

The sources and kinds of error, and ways of dealing with it, are different depending on the kind of data, as we shall see below.

Reliability of Standard Enumerations

Standard enumerations are statistical data of the sorts most often recorded in yearbooks and social-scientific compilations of indicators like the *World Handbook of Political and Social Indicators* (Russett et al. 1964). There are two distinguishable reliability problems in standard enumerations. Any particular datum, representing one case on one indicator, can be in error for reasons ranging from a typing mistake to false reporting. The most difficult problem is that the data making up an indicator may not be comparable from one case to another, not because of human frailty but because of differences of opinion and practice about collecting and reporting data. We will first examine the more serious problem, incomparability, and then that of human error.

INCOMPARABILITY   If the researcher wants to collect data on political party membership he will immediately encounter problems of incomparability: party membership is determined in different ways in different countries. We saw in the previous section that this kind of incomparability can pose validity problems, depending on what "party membership is used to indicate. The point here is that even if we impute no larger conceptual meaning to "party membership," the figures from different countries are of dubious reliability because they are compiled in very different ways. Within one country, and among units of one party, there may be conventions about how to estimate and report membership. Among countries no such conventions prevail.

A second source of incomparability is that available membership figures may represent different years. The more a condition varies over time, the more serious this kind of incomparability is. The number of parties represented in a national legislature is likely to vary only slightly over time, so a measurement for one country for 1963 is likely to be comparable to the measurement for another in 1970. But party membership—however defined —is likely to fluctuate considerably, and sometimes rather rapidly, so estimates for different parties, or countries, separated by more than a few years are not likely to be comparable.

The researcher who is making a longitudinal study of changes in the membership of one party obviously does not have to worry about comparability among parties. He *does* have to be concerned about comparability of data for the same unit over time, but this concern is less serious for two reasons. One is that the reporting practices of most organizations tend to be stable, and the other is that the researcher studying a single organization (or country) is likely to learn enough about it to know when changes in reporting practices occur and to be able to adjust for them. Substantial shifts from one basis of reporting to another are quite often evident from a casual inspection of raw data: if a statistical series ordinarily varies a few percent from one year to the next, but then shifts 20 or 30% in a single year, the researcher should look for evidence on reporting changes.

Some kinds of "temporal incomparabilities" of social data are well known. Crime indices in the United States have been compiled nationally since 1933, but are seriously inconsistent over time. There have been substantial increases in the completeness with which crime is recorded by local police and reported to the FBI, and also changes in the ways crimes are categorized and aggregated (see Graham 1969). Other such incomparabilities will be known only to specialists. The nonspecialist working with Nigerian data for the early 1960s could easily be misled by an abrupt decline in Nigerian GNP per capita. The "decline" was not due to economic depression but to the use of a new and abruptly larger population figure to weight estimates of national productivity.

The enumerations that are most subject to incomparability are those collected and reported by private organizations such as political parties, trades unions, and commercial organizations. Comparability of statistical enumerations is greatest for standard series of the sorts compiled by the United Nations and affiliated organizations. Much effort has been given by these agencies and the statistical offices of many of their member countries to developing common, or at least compatible, procedures for compiling and reporting demographic, economic, and some social indicators. Extensive references to the comparability of data will be found in the yearbooks of these organizations. The fact remains that the less-developed a country is and the more important an indicator is to the pride of development-minded leaders, the less comparability is to be expected. Underdevelopment usually means a lack of resources for comprehensive statistical services, hence less comparability and accuracy vis-à-vis an international standard. Underdevelopment also means a sensitivity about questions like economic growth rates, literacy, educational enrollment, and so forth, which induces statistical optimism even in conscientious officials. The example of U.S. crime statistics suggests that even in the most modern of nations there are sometimes reasons for doubting the indicators.

There are no technical gimmicks with which comparability can be improved. The researcher has to rely mainly on good sense and prudential lore. For example:

When there is a choice, use indicators from sources whose compilers check data for comparability.

Carefully compare definitions and notes on inclusions and exclusions when compiling data on an index from different sources.

Search for alternative sources of statistical information, and check the degree of agreement among different sources; disagreements about one estimate may reflect different reporting bases, which should be identified in order to select the most comparable estimates.

If one indicator seems likely to have serious comparability (or error) problems, try to find a surrogate indicator. For example,

  a. if party membership data are incomparable, use voter registration or party electoral support data;

  b. if economic growth rate estimates are inadequate for less-developed countries, as they often are, use fluctuations in the value and volume of countries' international trade, or changes in the market price and volume of primary crops, to estimate internal economic conditions.

ERROR   There is error in all social measurement, as suggested above. When the researcher works with standard enumerations, he has little chance of checking their reliability by duplicating the process of collecting data. The most he can usually do toward minimizing error is to rely on the compilations thought to be most accurate, and to check his own procedures to minimize the error he himself introduces. Beyond that, what he should do is evaluate the range of error in the various data he might use, and consider the potential effects of that error on his results and conclusions. The effects of error on results depend on both the extent and sources of the error, as we shall see below.

One recent study classifies error in statistical enumerations and other aggregate data according to their sources: human error, reporting error, and willful error (Merritt 1970, Chap. 2). *Human error* is pervasive. Columns of figures may be incorrectly added, coders may enter a datum in the wrong row, the fingers of typists and keypunchers slip. Even desk calculators and computer programs occasionally have hiccups. The researcher will seldom be able to check on human error in his data sources, but he should make two checks on his own handling of data:

Data and results should be checked for "glaring" errors, such as misplaced decimal points and mislabeled cases or indicators. These often are evident on casual inspection of data, which is a good argument for frequent "inspection."

The more routine a step in handling data is, the more desirable it is that it be checked in its entirety. The underlying principle is that people are most fallible when doing repetitious, routine work: such work is likely to inspire boredom, haste, or both in clerks transcribing data, typists preparing tables, research assistants doing sums, keypunchers preparing data cards, and typesetters setting articles. Hence all these processes should if possible be checked or duplicated. Even if the researcher himself has done most of these tasks they should be checked; enthusiasm for the research is no guarantee of clerical competence or accuracy.

The researcher who skimps on his obligations to check for routine human error still has an out: routine human error is usually benign error, as we argue below.

Reporting error results from the inadequacy or incomparability of data-recording and data-reporting procedures. Problems of incomparability and ways of dealing with them were mentioned above. Some errors from incomparability will still remain in almost all indicators, though. Moreover, the use of poorly trained enumerators and clerks in counting heads and votes, or classifying agricultural products or government expenditures, are sources of reporting error that can never be corrected by the researcher. But reporting error is also usually benign error.

Self-serving error is something else again. It may arise when a reporting agency reports a "firm estimate" that reflects only a consensual opinion among its officials about what the figure should be. Little better is an estimate that is the sum of figures reported on firmer grounds by district officials. The statistics of many Latin American countries have been said to be "poetry" on just these grounds. (This is no reason for rejecting such data out of hand, though, which is the conclusion usually drawn by critics of "poetic" estimates. The estimate of a Peruvian official, even if based on fragmentary information, is likely to be better than the armchair judgment of the foreign academic expert. It may be inferior relative to the accuracy of the estimates which appear on the same index for Western European countries, but not necessarily inferior with respect to the degree of accuracy the researcher needs for statistical comparisons.) This kind of self-serving error, attributing precision to "guesstimates," is also usually benign. What is definitely not benign is systematic inflation or deflation of data, such as overestimating government income and literacy to enhance national prestige, or underestimating the incidence of murder to minimize social problems. This kind of error, if widespread among the cases being studied, can make the researcher's comparisons systematically wrong in one direction or another.

The novice researcher will have asked by now how error can be "benign." It is one of the small comforts of quantitative analysis that if error is truly *random,* that is, if every estimate is just as likely to be above as below the "true" estimate, then errors will tend to cancel out. This means that when we compare indicators with random error, by correlating them or plotting them on a graph, their basic relationships will be a little weaker than if "true" estimates were used, but will be of essentially the same shape.

Several examples from analyses of *World Handbook* data (Russett et al., 1964) illustrate the principle. One critic of the *Handbook's* accuracy checked its data on "percentage of population in cities over 20,000" and found that 15 of 120 cases listed were either not listed in the sources cited or were listed but with different estimates (Banks 1965). Russett, in a reply (1965), apologized for the unnecessary errors but then pointed out that when the data were corrected, the corrected index correlated .993 with the published one.[3] "For some purposes this might indeed still have serious effects," he wrote, "but if the object is primarily to see the direction and strength of relationship between this variable and another, the conclusions should in no important way be affected; because of other problems of reliability, assumptions about 'sampling,' etc. differences of a single percetage point in squared correlation coefficients are meaningless." He then tested the effects of deliberately introducing error of the same proportion and degree as that in the urbanization index into eight other indicators. The indices were correlated with one another without error, then with error. The average difference in the r^2 obtained was less than .03; the variables with the random error usually had lower intercorrelations. In another experiment of the same sort, Russett introduced *systematic* error in some of the indicators, by deliberately increasing the estimates for all the East European countries. In this case the systematically altered indicators had r^2's with one another less than .02 higher, on the average, than the original indicators (Russett 1965). We may note if *all* of the estimates had been increased to an equal degree, there would have been no effect on the correlations: if all statistical offices inflate their estimates of GNP by the same percentage, the correlation of GNP with other indicators will remain the same. But when several different indicators are inflated in the same direction, correlations tend to increase slightly.

We have considered the effects of error on correlations among measures, and have found that, generally, a moderate amount of error is not likely to affect the results or conclusions substantially. The dangers are considerably greater when single cases are compared. Say, for example, that we want to compare the economic productivity of Tunisia, with an estimated per capita income of $173 in the early 1960s, with that of Algeria, where the per capita income was estimated at $178. The possible range of error in these estimates is ±20%, according to *World Handbook*. In other words, the true estimate of Tunisia's productivity per capita lies somewhere in the range from $138 to $208, while that for Algeria is between $142 and $214. In each case the true estimate is probably toward the center of the range, but it would be downright foolish to conclude with any confidence that Algeria was the wealthier country.

The above example suggests one approach to dealing with error in standard enumerations. Since we cannot confidently compare two adjacent —or even more remote—countries or cases on a single index without knowing something about the relative accuracy of each estimate, then *margins of error* should be estimated and examined. The *World Handbook* estimates margins of error for many of its enumerations, in some cases rather precisely and in others on the basis of guesswork. For population data, for example,

3 See footnote 3, p. 34, on the nature of correlation coefficients.

the error ranges are 1.0% for censuses taken at least decennially, 5% for sample censuses and surveys, 20% for conjectural estimates, and so forth. These error margins are based on evaluations by the United Nations Statistical Office of the accuracy of different techniques for estimating population: house-to-house censuses are more accurate than those based on sample surveys, for example.[4]

In census work, demographers can estimate the amount of error inherent in their measuring techniques by taking repeated samplings. For other kinds of standard enumerations, the politimetrician usually must make more arbitrary judgments about how adequately the data were compiled, but the principles are the same (see Gurr 1966).

Error margins can be used to estimate the reliability of any comparison of two cases on a single indicator. Another approach to the same problem is to round the data, perhaps to the nearest 00 or 000, or to group the data according to some interval suggested by the error margins (see Gurr 1966). Any arbitrary rounding of data, though, runs the risk of throwing away good data with the bad, so most researchers prefer to take their chances with enumerated data as given in the sources.

The approaches to error discussed above apply principally to enumerated data. Some other ways of dealing with the problem are more appropriately discussed in connection with content-analytic data. (Two other important studies of error in aggregate data are Naroll 1962, and Russett 1971).

Reliability of Counted and Coded Data

The problems of accuracy in counted and coded data made by the researcher (see Section 4.2) are rather different from those involving enumerated data. The investigator is either his own compiler and judge, or he sets the instructions for those who do the compiling and judging. His principal comparability problem is whether the source materials he uses give an adequate picture of the phenomena being studied. Error of the sort introduced by miscounting is a pesky problem, but a much more fundamental issue is the reliability of the procedures being used: do the procedures spelled out for coding, categorizing, and judging material produce similar results each time they are used? These two aspects of reliability are examined separately below.

SOURCE ADEQUACY   The problem of source adequacy is usually greatest for studies in which information is collected on events. Conflict studies relying on *The New York Times* or other journalistic sources are a case in

---

4 These error ranges are based on duplicate censuses taken in selected areas of a number of a countries. No "true" population figure is ever obtained for any country. The repeated measurements only give demographers an indication of the range within which the "true" figure is likely to be.

point. The most cursory examination of *The New York Times Index* demonstrates that differential attention is given to different regions and countries. The sources of differentials include formal or informal censorship, the ideological filters of newsmen and editors, the presumed disinterest of readers, and availability of space ("all the news that fits we print"). A rule of thumb is that events regarded as important by contemporary standards will be reported rather systematically in international journalistic sources, while others will not. Wars, major natural disasters, coups d'état, cabinet shakeups, and competitive national elections are among the kinds of events, mostly dramatic and violent, that seem reported with some consistency in mid-twentieth century newspapers. Lesser conflict events like demonstrations, clashes, and diplomatic protests are somewhat less likely to be reported, especially if they occur in countries that are not of great current interest. Minor outbreaks of conflict that might ordinarily be reported are sometimes ignored because they are overshadowed either by a very dramatic event or by the sheer numbers of similar events. A study of major Indian newspapers in the early 1960s has identified occurrences of turmoil more than 10 times the number reported in the *New York Times* for the same period.[5] A study of *Hispanic-American Report* for several Latin American countries identified about three times as many "instability events" in the period 1948 to 1965 as were found in a summary world news source, *Deadline Data on World Affairs* (Doran, Pendley, and Antunes 1971). In both comparisons, the small-scale and least-violent events were most often ignored by the summary sources, and accounted for most of the discrepancies in numbers of events.

Several approaches to source adequacy have been taken in recent comparative conflict studies. Counts of events such as demonstrations and diplomatic exchanges, collected in studies by Rummel and Tanter (Rummel 1963; Tanter 1966) are *prima facie* suspect, for reasons suggested above. The "Causes of Strife" studies attempted to correct for this by using measures of the *magnitude* of strife based not on number of events but on estimates of participants, duration, and casualties. The reasoning was that the larger and more serious the event, the more likely it was to be reported, and hence included; unreported events were likely to be small and hence their ommission would have little effect on the magnitude scores. This is by no means a perfect solution, however. Data on participants and casualties are themselves subject to a great deal of error, if they are reported at all. If they are misreported, the researcher must either be prepared to assume that the error is random, or to make the necessary qualifications when interpreting the results.

A second approach, taken in the Rummel and Tanter studies, was to construct *measures of possible error* and to incorporate them in the analysis.

---

[5] According to dissertation research being done by John Tannehill in the Department of Politics, Princeton University.

Censorship and lack of world interest in particular countries were thought to be likely sources of error in the reporting of conflict events. Consequently, measures were devised of the *extent of censorship* and of *degree of world interest* in each country. These indicators were included in correlation analyses. It was assumed that if, for example, world interest was positively correlated with measures of conflict, it was quite possible that conflict was underreported from low-interest countries and overreported from high-interest countries. (Other conditions could also cause such a finding, of course: world interest might be a function of conflict, for example.) They found, first, that domestic conflict measures and world interest were not positively related; instead there was a slight tendency for *more* domestic conflict to be reported from countries of *less* interest. On the other hand, diplomatic protests and expulsion of ambassadors were more commonly reported from the more interesting countries. Comparisons using these two measures are therefore suspect (Tanter 1966, p. 61).

A third approach to source adequacy, perhaps the most satisfactory one, is to rely on multiple sources. The "Alliances and War" study systematically used multiple sources. Lists of wars could be fairly easily compiled from standard historical sources. Information on alliances was obtained from the League of Nation's *Treaty Series, Great Britain's British and Foreign Papers* series, and a number of monograph studies. Once wars and alliances were identified, it was necessary to do further library research to obtain the requisite information on each of them. The number of sources cited for the study's 112 alliances, for example, approaches 100 (Singer and Small 1966b, pp. 28–31).

Source adequacy is sometimes a problem for documentary content analysis and occasionally a problem for judgmental coding as well. It may be that documents needed for content analysis are not available, in which event a case may have to be dropped from the study. In judgmental coding the researcher may have difficulty locating documents that provide enough information on a topic like decision-making in a particular political party. In fact, sensitive indicators of many important variables that might otherwise be coded judgmentally have not been constructed because of the lack or inaccessibility of information. The reseacher who prefers to plunge ahead with judgmental coding on a poorly documented topic may indeed be able to assign scores to his cases, but often on the basis of woefully inadequate sources.

RELIABILITY OF PROCEDURES   One of the essential features of the scientific process is the reproducibility of its results. The researcher who gathers or "makes" new data usually can duplicate the process and usually should. Generally, the greater the amount of judgment that enters into the scoring of an index, the more important it is that the reliability of the instructions—the measuring instrument—be checked. It is usually desirable that this be done by someone other than the person who first prepared the data, to provide a check on two important issues: (1) whether the instructions are sufficiently detailed and explicit that anyone other than the person who devised them can use them; and (2) whether the coder's biases or desire to obtain a particular result affected the coding or scoring of an index.

Reliability can be checked at different points in the research process, and in different ways. A common and desirable approach is to prepare a rather detailed coding manual at the outset of a project. If several people are involved in a study, the usual procedure is to prepare preliminary instructions and have all of them apply the instructions to the same body of material. Discrepancies in their coding show where the instructions need to be revised to reduce ambiguity. This process may be repeated several times, with different coders, materials, or both, until a comprehensive coding manual is in hand. Such a manual, and the materials to which it was initially applied, can also be used to train new coders. The standardization thus achieved in preparing the coding instructions and training several people in their use may make it seem unnecessary to do a formal reliability test of the procedures. It is still desirable that it be done, though.

A variation of this procedure is simultaneous, independent coding of all the materials by two researchers, who then compare their judgments and attempt to resolve discrepancies. The degree of agreement between the several coders working on the same matrials can be compared to obtain a measure of reliability. If the coders are regularly in communication, comparing one another's judgments, a "reliability" measure provides little guarantee that the instructions are equally communicable to others, or that the coders have not reinforced one another's biases. A truly independent reliability test is still desirable.

The crux of any reliability test is that a part of a content analysis, or count of events, or judgmental scoring be duplicated using the instructions by which the original was prepared. This does not mean that the coder who does the duplicate coding should be untrained in the procedure, any more than a physicist checking the reported mass of a subatomic particle should be unfamiliar with a bubble chamber. But the coder making a reliability test obviously should not have previously practiced on the test material.

A sample of the cases is usually sufficient for the reliability test, provided that it is a probability sample (see Chapter 2). The two codings or scorings are then compared to determine the degree of agreement, using one of the several statistical tests available. The simplest test, applicable to any kind of content coding, is the *percentage of agreement* between two coders or judges. For an example see Merritt (1970, Chap. 3).

If the categories being coded are a list of groups or types of action, a percentage-agreement test is the only way of evaluating reliability. But if the coding categories form a measurable continuum along a variable, a correlation coefficient can be computed. It requires more computation than the percentage agreement test, but it has one clear advantage: the agreement test does not take into account *how much* the coders disagree on each item, whereas a correlation coefficient does.

The final point to be made about reliability checking is that there are no generally accepted conventions to guide our decisions. It is generally thought to be desirable that coded data be checked, but formal reliability tests are reported for probably less than half the studies using coded data. When reliability tests are done, there are no generally accepted standards for what is a satisfactory level of agreement. This necessarily depends on how much accuracy is required in the comparisons to be made. If a relationship being studied is expected to be strong, then it will still be clear even if the data are quite fuzzy. If the relationship is probably weak, better quality control of the data is needed. Generally, though, a reliability correlation coefficient of at least .80 seems essential. An r of .90 seems a more appropriate minimum for precise work. No such guidelines can be suggested for the percentage-agreement test because its interpretation varies according to whether the categories represent an underlying dimension, and according to how great the discrepancies prove to be.

RELIABILITY, A SUMMARY   This section should put to rest some of the suspicions about the supposed inability of politimetricians to measure phenomena accurately. The three central points are these:

1. Absolute accuracy in social measurement is seldom attainable or necessary. Inaccuracy can obscure comparisons between two cases but must be large before it substantially affects statistical relationships among variables.
2. The politimetrician has a number of technical means for evaluating and increasing the reliability of his data. Their comparability and completeness can be enhanced by evaluation and use of multiple sources. He can check and control the quality of data he originates himself by developing precise guidelines for coding them, and by using reliability tests to determine how well the guidelines work.
3. Finally, the researcher can and should take the possible effects of error into account when he interprets results, and he should report on the comparability and error of his data so that others can better evaluate his findings.

PRECISION OF MEASUREMENT

The likely reliability of data should be thought about at the outset of a research project because it will determine how much reliance the investigator, and anyone else, can place in its results. The *level of measurement* he proposes to use will also have effects: it will determine the precision of data he collects, influence the statistical methods used in their analysis, and as a result will have some impact on the kinds of questions that the researcher can expect to answer.

Measurement has been called "the business of pinning numbers on things" (S. S. Stevens, quoted in Alker 1965, p. 18). The *level of measure-*

ment refers to the properties of the numbering system that is used. Numbers are used to denote congressional districts in each American state, for example, but in most states such numbers are no more than labels; they do not tell us, nor do we assume from them, that the 3rd congressional district is larger or more important than the 7th. The districts might as well be labeled according to their major towns or the points of the compass. In this case the numbers are said to be a *nominal* scale. A more informative numbering system is *ordinal*. Presidents of the United States are sometimes referred to by their place in the roster of presidents, as the fifth, twentieth, or thirty-first. The scale used to denote their rank is an ordinal one; from it we can determine their ordering, but not whether one served a longer or shorter period than any other. The highest, most precise levels of measurement are *interval* and *ratio* scales. The presidential vote is reported using a ratio scale, whereby one can say how much one candidate's vote exceeded another's in both absolute and percentage terms. Each of these levels of measurement is appropriate for quantitative analysis of some kinds of political questions. There are also statistical tests appropriate to each of them, and there has been some rather heated controversy between and among statisticians and politimetricians about the latter's preference for using refined statistical tools on data obtained using lower, less precise levels of measurement. What follows is a brief nontechnical commentary on the uses and limitations of each kind of measurement.

Nominal Measurement

A nominal scale in social research is any set of categories that is exhaustive (includes all cases) and mutually exclusive (no cases in more than one category). Such scales are widely used in political research, though most of the users do not think of them as forms of measurement. American political preferences can be described with a nominal scale whose categories are Republican, Democrat, independent, and other. In the "Causes of Strife" study, events were classified on a coding sheet according to whether they were "turmoil," "conspiracy," or "internal war." Each of these categories was further subdivided into a set of mutually exclusive types.

A number of quantitative political comparisons can be made with nominally scaled data. The "Causes of Strife" study offers one example. In addition to classifying the kinds of strife, I categorized the social groups that participated in each as "lower classes," "higher classes," and "regime classes," with subcategories for each of these categories. The sets of strife and group categories could then be compared against one another, to see which sets of categories were most likely to coincide. It was observed, for example, that higher class groups were more likely to participate in conspiracy than lower class groups, but in turmoil there was no substantial difference (Gurr 1969). Various statistical tests are available to determine how strong such observed differences are (see Section 6.4).

Nominal Strife Scale	Dichotomous Strife Scales		
	Turmoil	*Conspiracy*	*Internal War*
1 = turmoil	0 = no	0 = no	0 = no
2 = conspiracy	1 = yes	1 = yes	1 = yes
3 = internal war			

Other kinds of statistical comparisons can be made on the basis of nominal data. One is illustrated by the Rummel studies of conflict events, mentioned previously. For each country, the number of events in each category was counted and used as a ratio-scale measurement. That is, the number of riots per country is a ratio-scale indicator which can be correlated with ratio measures of other variables, such as countries' levels of economic development. It is not necessary to change nominal data into ratio scales in order to calculate correlations, though. A type of correlation called "point-biserial" can be used to correlate a nominal measure with an interval one. A nominal measure must first be *dichotomized*—divided into two categories —before it is statistically analyzed in this way. American party preference can be so categorized without much loss of information, but many other sets of categories cannot. The basic categories of strife again provide an example. They constitute a three-category nominal scale, as shown on the left in the accompanying table; each category can be made into a separate dichotomous scale, as shown on the right. Dichotomous scales made from nominal-scale categories are called *dummy variables*. The three examples shown here can be used to score specific strife events, or to rate cases such as cities or countries for the presence or absence of each kind of strife.

Ordinal Measurement

An *ordinal* scale, or *rank-order* scale, is one in which the researcher can order his categories along some dimension or variable, but without knowing how close together they are. One can often find some underlying dimension on the basis of which to convert nominal scales to ordinal scales. The Republican/Democratic dichotomy might be converted into a conservative-liberal scale, with several intervening categories between the extremes. But this kind of transformation is not necessarily desirable; it may be irrelevant to the researcher's questions, or worse, cause him to throw information away. A researcher may have very good reasons for retaining the Republican/Democratic dichotomy, perhaps because he wants to compare it to a separate conservative-liberal scale!

The point is that the level of measurement a politimetrician chooses is partly a function of the kind of question he has asked. Usually he will use ordinal scales when he wants to measure a continuous variable but cannot get a more precise numerical handle on it. The following chapter describes a study of governments' relative "coerciveness" or "permissiveness," which was rated on a judgmental scale (p. 82). In this instance the researchers presumably would have liked a precise measure, so that they could say that Portugal is two, three, or X times more coercive than Denmark, and so forth. Since they did not have a suitable yardstick for doing so, they chose to regard their judgments as forming a rank-order scale, with the countries grouped in six categories along it. There are a number of statistical procedures for analyzing and comparing rank-order data. Ordinal measures can be correlated with one another. They can also be compared with dichotomous measures to determine the existence and extent of significant relationships. And they can be correlated with interval data, *if* the interval data are treated as though they were ordinally measured. Statistical procedures for doing so are cited in Section 6.4.

Interval and Ratio Measurement

Most social measurement aspires to the status of *ratio scales*. A ratio scale has a standard unit of measure, like grams or meters, whereby the researcher can say that a social role has 3 units of status, or that a regime used 14 units of coerciveness in responding to a demonstration, or that 25 units of violence occurred as a result. A ratio scale also has an absolute zero point on the scale. Zero units of violence is meaningful, so is zero units of coerciveness; zero units of status is hard to imagine, though not impossible. An *interval scale* is a ratio scale that does not have a real zero point. IQ tests use interval but not ratio scales; they have no fixed zero point but are measured out in either direction from a norm. One attraction of interval and ratio measurement is the understandable desire of the researcher to want to be able to say, not merely that one group is more democratic or less militaristic than another group, but *how much* more or less. Another strong attraction of interval and ratio scales, according to orthodox statisticians, is that, they alone yield data that can be analyzed using the most powerful statistical tools. The product-moment correlation coefficient is one such tool, and so are multiple regression and factor analysis (described in Chapter 7).[6]

The Level-of-Measurement Controversy

There are two schools of thought about what kinds of analytic techniques can be applied to what data. H. M. Blalock presents the orthodox view, that held by the majority of statisticians, in this quotation:

> *The use of a particular mathematical model presupposes that a certain level of measurement has been obtained*...it is not legitimate to make use of a mathematical system involving the operations of addition or subtraction when this is not warranted by the method of measurement.... Ideally, one should make use of a data-gathering technique which permits the lowest

6 Dichotomous variables can, on certain assumptions, be treated in multiple regression and factor analysis.

levels of measurement, if these are all the data will yield, rather than using techniques which force a scale on the data (Blalock 1960, pp. 17, 20, italics in original).

This point of view derives from the logical assumptions of the mathematical systems or models that are used in statistical operations. Ratio- and interval-order statistical techniques assume that the objects or conditions have properties that can be added, subtracted, and multiplied, among other things, and that those properties have been so measured. If these assumptions are not met, the results of analysis are suspect, perhaps uninterpretable.

The opposing point of view has more support among researchers doing empirical work than among statisticians, but one of its most forceful advocates is a statistical mathematician, John Tukey. He argues that we must recognize that many crucial variables in social and political analysis can be measured at present only with ordinal, usually judgmental scales. If we therefore restrict ourselves to low-level analysis of important variables, reserving powerful techniques for precisely measured variables, the price is mathematically self-righteous ignorance. Moreover there are methodological justifications for applying the more powerful techniques in many instances. Most judgmental scales rest on the researcher's assumption that they tap some underlying property or variable which has the properties suitable for ratio measurement. The researcher usually defines his categories along a judgmental scale so that they seem to him approximately equal. If these requirements are met, it seems an excess of caution not to use ratio- and interval-scale statistical techniques. The researcher is obliged, though, to consider that he may have introduced additional error into his data, and he may have to qualify his interpretation of the results accordingly.[7]

By the loosest usage, any ordinal scale is grist for the mill of product-moment correlation, multiple regression, and factor analysis. But it is contrary to the spirit of the Tukeyesque argument to use the more powerful techniques with data that are rank-ordered without regard to their additional inequalities. If the politimetrician knows enough to rank his cases he probably knows enough, or can learn enough more, to fit them to a set of approximately equal intervals on a judgmental scale. The paramount empirical consideration is that the researcher not throw away worthwhile information merely for the sake of meeting the formal requirements of a statistical technique—which ordinarily happens when one moves from a higher to a lower level of measurement and analysis.

7 Tukey's arguments about the uses of statistics have been both unorthodox and widely influential. Some of the most telling of them circulate in unpublished drafts. A published, nontechnical statement is his 1961 paper, "Statistical and Quantitative Methodology." More technical is "The Future of Data Analysis," 1962. His most pungent comments on the inappropriateness of conventional statistical restraints for social research are to be found in the unpublished ms, "Data Analysis and Behavioral Science, or Learning to Bear the Quantitative Man's Burden by Shunning Badmandments," no date but pre-1961.

3.3   The Relative Importance of Operational Requirements

Many criteria for good measurement have been specified in this chapter. It is more important to satisfy some of them than others. Their relative importance depends partly on the politimetrician's intentions: if he is constructing indicators of a variable not previously indexed, he may be less concerned about reliability than if he is devising a more sensitive and accurate measure of a variable already indexed crudely. Their relative importance will also vary necessarily according to the dictates of the researcher's "methodological superego." The following statement of general priorities thus reflects my preferences, but is not without justifications.

Validity seems the most important of the criteria to be met in quantitative political research. If indicators do not represent what the investigator asserts they represent, at least approximately, then the whole enterprise is suspect. The only situation in which validity is not of primary initial concern is the "fishing expedition" type of analysis, in which the researcher compares a number of indicators, usually ones not previously compared, "to see what turns up." This approach postpones the validity question, but it does not avoid it: substantive interpretation of the results requires close attention to what the observed relationships signify about reality.

Comparability is ordinarily the most important of technical considerations. If data are collected on different bases from one case to another, or from one time period to another, we cannot say whether the results of comparing cases are real or an artifact of the data collection process. This problem is equally serious for standard enumerations, content analysis, and judgmental coding. The responsibility in the first instance is usually the compiling agency (and sometimes the unwary investigator) while in the second and third it is the researcher's for failure to apply consistent procedures.

Measurement error is less serious, to the extent that it is small, random, or both. It should be reduced where possible, and its approximate extent and bias estimated. Nevertheless the general pattern of results will not usually be seriously distorted unless error is substantial and systematic. Two circumstances can make error more important. One is when the researcher's primary objective is to devise a highly precise indicator; the other is when his research conclusions will be substantially affected by slight variations in results. These same arguments apply to the effects of *missing data,* the problems of which are treated in the next chapter, Section 4.3.

Level of measurement usually ought to be of least consideration, though not ignored. Certainly the researcher should not compromise on validity or comparability merely to attain some level of measurement. There is a variety of statistical techniques appropriate to each level of measurement. There are ways of converting data at one level to data at another. And there are widely accepted justifications for analyzing ordinal and interval data with the more powerful ratio-order techniques.

The reader will by now have gained a general understanding of the "official" norms and some of the effective norms that govern the collection of political data. The basic practical question is what kinds of data can be gotten from what sources, and how. This is the subject of Chapter 4, while Chapter 5 will show how some of these precepts were applied when data were collected for the three illustrative studies.

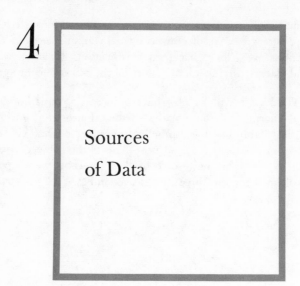

4

Sources
of Data

What kinds of data can I get on this problem? This question is in the mind of the foresighted researcher all the while he or she is thinking through a research question, specifying its variables and cases, and devising operational measures. The availability of data depends pretty much on the researcher's ingenuity and diligence. There is also a connection between the care and energy he devotes to collecting data and their quality—"quality" in the sense of reliability, completeness, and relevance to important research issues. This connection is not exact, however. Much high-quality data on key variables used in political analysis have been compiled and made generally available. Some of the principal published compilations and data libraries are mentioned below. The possibilities for *making* data, rather than relying on available collections, are considerably greater, and some of these are explored in the second section of this chapter. The third section shows what can be done when data are missing for some but not all cases on some but not all variables.

4.1 Available Data

There are a number of collections of statistical data that can be used for macropolitical comparisons. Some of them have been compiled specifically for purposes of social research, while others have been prepared by public and private agencies for more general consumption. Economic and demographic data have been collected and reported by public agencies in most Western and some non-Western nations since the early nineteenth century, if not earlier, and since the 1950s by almost all nations. Beginning in 1926 the League of Nations collated and reported much current data in its yearbooks. Since the late 1940s the United Nations and its affiliated agencies have stimulated an enormous increase in the types, accuracy, and coverage not only of economic and demographic data, but of social data as well. These official sources report relatively less aggregate social and political than economic and demographic data, though. Moreover, the farther back in time one goes, the sparser they become. The only statistical social data that seem to have been frequently and widely reported by nations before the 1950s are those for educational enrollment. The researcher who wants to measure social phenomena for nations in earlier periods must usually index them using data on population distributions, income, and so forth. The only macropolitical data that were widely and officially reported before the 1950s concerned central government budgets, the size of armies and navies, and elections.

The most convenient sources for ready-made social, cultural, and political data are the handbooks and similar compilations made in recent years by social scientists to facilitate cross-national and cross-cultural comparisons. They have two principal advantages, aside from convenience. One is that a greater degree of cross-cultural comparability of their data has usually been accomplished than is true of most official and nonacademic data. The second is that they include numerous indices of variables that would not be, and sometimes could not be, reported by other agencies. Two rather different kinds of data are used in these collections: standard enumerations and content-analytic data.

General Social Science Data Collections

World Handbook of Political and Social Indicators, by Bruce M. Russett, Hayward R. Alker, Jr., Karl W. Deutsch, and Harold D. Lasswell (Yale University Press, 1964). The *World Handbook* includes cross-sectional data on 75 indicators for as many as 133 countries and colonies. Most of the indices are standard enumerations and represent demographic, productivity, trade, budgetary, voting, and military variables, among others. Some are constructed from content-analytic data, such as measures of deaths from domestic group violence, the frequency with which chief executives are changed, and David McClelland's cross-national measures of achievement motivation. The years of reference for most enumerations are in the late 1950s or early 1960s. The *Handbook* contains a number of discussions and analyses of the indicators, and since its publication has been the most widely used and influential collection of politically relevant data.

World Handbook of Political and Social Indicators, Second Edition, by Charles L. Taylor, Michael C. Hudson, Robert Hefner, and Lester Warner (Yale University Press, 1972). This edition of the Yale Political Data Program handbook promises to be even more widely used than was its predecessor (1964). It includes a greater number of indicators—148 compared with 75 in the first edition—and more political entities are represented on most of them. About half the indicators are specifically political, including such new measures as counts of riots and armed attacks by country by year, numbers of irregular government changes, and the dispersion of party strengths in parliaments. Additional attention also is given to measures of such nonpolitical variables as cultural homogeneity and inequalities in value distribution, which are recognized as increasingly important in cross-national politimetrics.

Dimensions of Nations: A Factor Analysis of 236 Social, Political, and Economic Characteristics, by Rudolph J. Rummel (Yale University Press, 1971). This is a study of data for 82 countries for 1955, which makes use of 236 variables of the kinds reported in the *Handbooks* (above). It also includes numerous content-analytic measures of civil conflict, such as numbers of revolutions, assassinations, riots, and antigovernment demonstrations; and measures of international conflict such as presence or absence of military action against other countries, diplomatic protests and sanctions, threats, troop movements and mobilizations, etc.

A Cross-Polity Survey, by Arthur S. Banks and Robert B. Textor (The M.I.T. Press, 1963). The above four volumes contain principally enumerations; this reports data on 57 *judgmental* indicators for 115 countries. Examples are the degree to which interests are articulated and aggregated by parties and the bureaucracy; the ideological orientation of regimes; and so forth. Other variables represented in the coding include the origins of the political system (colonial/noncolonial, for example), the freedom of political opposition, types of political parties, and many others. Most of the book consists of computer printout showing the correlations among dichotomous measures of these variables. The principal criticism of the study is that its indices do not distinguish sufficiently among political systems, because either the categories on each index are too few and crude, or the information used in the coding inadequate, or both. Its undeniable merit is that it reports measures of theoretically important variables for which few if any other indicators have been published.

Society, Politics, and Economic Development: A Quantitative Approach, by Irma Adelman and Cynthia Taft Morris (The Johns Hopkins Press, 1967). This comparative study reports judgmental measures for developing countries. Political indicators are reported: degree of national integration and unity, degree of political centralization, autonomy of labor movements and parties, and so forth. Economic and social variables are also represented, and are compared statistically with the political ones to assess relationships among the types of development. The quality of the data and discrimination of the indices are somewhat better than in Banks and Textor's similar compendium, though fewer nations and rather different variables are included.

Ethnographic Atlas, by George Peter Murdock (University of Pittsburgh Press, 1967). This and the following source report information on a culture-by-culture rather than country-by-country basis, for variables of primary interest for anthropologists. The *Atlas* reports data on 44 variables for 862 cultures. Variables include class and caste stratification, jurisdictional hierarchy, and form of community organization.

Cross-Polity Time-Series Data, by Arthur S. Banks (The M.I.T. Press, 1971). This major compilation of time-series data has annual estimates for up to 155 nations and 102 variables. Basic population and political data are reported from 1815 to 1966. Measures of government expenditure, internal communications, and education are given for the 1860s to 1966. Shorter spans are covered by data on civil strife events (1919–1966), characteristics of legislatures (1946–1966), and economic productivity (1946–1966). These and other data are available on computer tape from the Center for Comparative Political Research, State University of New York at Binghamton.

A Cross-Cultural Summary, by Robert B. Textor (Human Relations Area Files Press, 1967). Coded anthropological data are reported on 42 sets of variables for 400 societies. As in *A Cross-Polity Survey,* above, the variables are dichotomized and then correlated. A computer printout of the results is incorporated in the book.

Specialized Social Science Data Collections

The above collections report data on variables that are of general, often cross-disciplinary interest. There are a great many other social-scientific sources of standardized data on specific topics. Several general ones are listed below. Articles and books on quantitative, comparative studies also report new data. To find these data the novice researcher must rely on expert advice and his own detective work in tracking down references. Such newly collected data are not always published. They may occasionally be available from the author for the researcher who has a serious interest in the subject. In political science such data are often deposited, sooner or later, with the Inter-University Consortium for Political Research (see below).

Black Africa: A Comparative Handbook, by Donald G. Morrison, Robert C. Mitchell, John N. Paden, and Michael Stevenson (Free Press, 1972). This volume reports some 170 measures for 32 black African countries. New indicators of ethnic, elite, and urban characteristics are the core of the book. Measures of basic political, social, and demographic variables are also included. The book is substantially the best collection of comparative data ever gathered for a non-Western area. It also includes a country-by-country survey of ethnolinguistic cleavages and conflicts, and a detailed discussion of techniques used in collecting the data.

The Wages of War, 1816–1965: A Statistical Handbook, by J. David Singer and Melvin Small (John Wiley, 1972). A detailed compilation of data on the wars of nations in the international system, with some related information on characteristics of the nations involved in them. The data are those used in the "Alliance and War" study described in this book.

Periodic compilations of data on elections and on military establishments are also available to political scientists; several are listed below. Data from these and other specialized sources are often used extensively by the compilers of the general collections cited above. The several editions of the *World Handbook* provide, through their footnotes, a guide to these sources.

A Review of Elections of the World, Institute of Electoral Research (London: Dillon's University Bookshop Ltd., periodically since 1954). Basic data on national elections, now issued biennially.

America Votes: A Handbook of Contemporary American Election Statistics, Richard M. Scammon, comp. and ed. (vols. 1–2, Macmillan, 1956–58; vols. 3–5, University of Pittsburgh Press, 1959–64; vols. 6–7, Congressional Quarterly, 1966–68). This is the most comprehensive printed collection of electoral data for the United States and includes data for all candidates for national offices in elections since 1952. It is expected to continue to be prepared biennially.

America at the Polls: A Handbook of American Presidential Election Statistics, 1920–1964, Richard M. Scammon, ed. (University of Pittsburgh Press, 1965). This is one of a number of historical surveys of American electoral statistics. Others include Edgar Eugene Robinson's studies of the presidential vote from 1896 to 1944, with data by party and county; Svend Petersen's *A Statistical History of the American Presidential Elections* (Frederick Ungar, 1963); and various collections for specific states.

The Communist Bloc and the Western Alliances: The Military Balance (London: Institute for Strategic Studies, annual editions, beginning 1959–60). The best continuing source of information on the size and status of military and paramilitary forces. *The Military Balance* concentrates on countries involved in East-West tensions. The Institute's *Adelphi Papers* series has included detailed studies of military establishments in developing countries, for example in Africa (No. 27, April 1966) and Latin America (No. 34, April 1967).

The *Historical Methods Newsletter* also should be mentioned as a source of information about data. The *Newsletter* has been published quarterly by the Department of History, University of Pittsburgh, since 1967. It has provided excellent surveys and reports on current research using historical data for the United States and many other countries. The existence and location of many new and previously unused bodies of data can be identified in its pages.

Data Archives

No discussion of standardized social scientific data would be comprehensive without reference to the data archives. These archives store aggregate and survey data, and make them available to students and professional researchers for secondary analyses. Some major repositories of American and international data are mentioned below. The survey data held by these archives can often be aggregated for various regional and cross-national comparisons. In the United States and some European countries, for example, comparable survey questions have been repeated over sufficiently long periods (as much as 35 years) that instructive aggregate comparisons over time can also be made.

Inter-University Consortium for Political Research, Ann Arbor, Mich. The Consortium is one of the two major institutional sources of political research data in the United States, the other being the Yale Political Data Program (see above). The Consortium does not itself collect any substantial amount of data but serves as a repository and distribution center for data collected by others, including the Survey Research Center at the University of Michigan. In 1971 the Consortium had data from about 100 studies in its three archives, including survey, historical, and international relations studies. Some of these are previously published data, such as those from the *World Handbooks*. Others are the unpublished, basic data of major research studies, deposited with the Consortium by the individual scholars who collected them. The Consortium's survey and historical holdings are predominantly but not exclusively American. Data held by the Consortium are made available on computer tape or cards, without charge to member universities, and on a cost basis to individual researchers.

The Roper Public Opinion Research Center, Williams College, Williamstown, Mass. is the world's oldest and largest repository of sample survey data. Its files include data from tens of thousands of surveys, including the surveys of almost all major commercial and academic survey agencies in the United States as well as many foreign studies. The questions in the surveys are indexed, which facilitates comparisons. The Center retrieves and processes data in response to requests from its associates, which include many universities.

The International Data Library and Reference Service, University of California (Berkeley). The Library has a more selective collection of survey data than the Roper Center. It concentrates on surveys which are methodologically adequate and relevant for cross-national comparative research. Its services and data are generally available to researchers.

Minnesota Political Data Archive, University of Minneapolis, Minn. This archive includes a substantial body of data for quantitative historical research. Time-series data on social, economic, and political variables are available for more than 60 countries, in most cases going back to 1800.

The Human Relations Area Files are a categorized and indexed set of anthropological materials on a large number of cultures, most of them "primitive." The materials have been prepared at Yale University, with duplicate sets of printed or microfilmed data available at other universities. The information is not quantified but is categorized in a way that facilitates quantitative coding. Its limitations for political scientists are that contemporary cultures and specifically political information are not fully represented.

Many universities aside from those mentioned above have libraries, centers, or offices with archives of aggregate and survey data intended principally for local use. In political science such archives typically include duplicate data from the major archives mentioned above. Often they include the specialized data collections of local scholars, which may be available for secondary analyses by students.

Official Statistical Sources

The data in the sources discussed thus far have been processed, or at least indexed, in ways that make them particularly suitable to the needs of politimetricians. The statistical data in official sources, however, are not usually collected or reported with an eye to social research. They are not necessarily less accurate, relevant, or easy to use. With the notable exception of data compiled and published by the United Nations, though, official data raises often-unanswerable questions of accuracy and comparability. Moreover, if the novice researcher plans to make contemporary cross-national comparisons, he or she will find that most of the simple and generally applicable indicators that might be constructed from official sources have already been prepared and published, either in the books cited above or by United Nations agencies or both. But if he wants to make comparisons across time, or among regions or cities, he probably will have to rely more on the official sources. These sources do afford a degree of internal comparability. They also have been little used by political scientists, so they offer novelty in compensation for their frustrations. They are "unimaginative" as well; no coded judgments on freedom of opposition or counts of violent events will be found in them—just standard enumerations and reports of birth rates, petroleum production, governmental receipts, and the like.

THE UNITED NATIONS AND SPECIALIZED INTERNATIONAL AGENCIES   The following are the major international statistical sources.

Statistical Yearbook, United Nations Statistical Office, Department of Economic and Social Affairs. Published annually since 1948, the *Yearbook* reports widely used and summary data from the more specialized yearbooks (noted below), for all countries and colonies for which the data are available. Time-series are reported on many variables. Subjects covered include population, employment and unemployment, industrial and agricultural output, education, communications, and social services.

Yearbook of National Accounts Statistics, same office as above, since 1954. Data on the components of reporting countries' Gross National Product, government budgets, external transactions, and so forth are included in this yearbook.

Demographic Yearbook, same office as above, since 1948. Each annual edition reports basic time-series demographic data and gives special treatment to a topic such as population distribution, ethnic and economic characteristics, or mortality. These special topics are repeated over a five-year cycle.

Yearbook of International Trade Statistics, same office as above, since 1950. Each annual edition has detailed information on exports and imports by country of origin and destination, as well as indices of terms of trade.

Balance of Payments Yearbook, United Nations, International Monetary Fund, Statistics Bureau, annually since 1948. Data on currency holdings and balance of international payments of reporting countries.

Statistical Yearbook, United Nations Educational, Scientific, and Cultural Organization, appearing sporadically since 1963 (7th edition in 1970). The UNESCO *Yearbook* reports data from other UNESCO publications on: education; book, periodical, and newspaper publication; and films, radio, and television.

World Survey of Education, same office as above, four volumes, 1955–66. Detailed data are reported on school enrollments in the last three volumes in the *Survey,* on primary education (1958), secondary education (1961), and higher education (1966). Time-series data from about 1930 are reported for many countries and territories.

World Communications: Press, Radio, Television, Film, UNESCO, Department of Mass Communication, published irregularly since 1950 (4th edition in 1964). Numbers of radio and TV sets in use, newspapers published and circulated, and new films produced are among the kinds of data recorded here.

Yearbook of Labour Statistics, International Labour Office, annually (with interruptions) since 1935. Data are reported on the distributions of populations by occupation and employment status, with detailed information on employment and compensation by industry. Various time-series are reported, including cost-of-living indices.

Production Yearbook, Food and Agricultural Organization, annually since 1958. Its predecessor was the (*International*) *Yearbook of Agricultural Statistics,* 1910–57. Current and time-series data are given on land use, agricultural employment, and crop production.

These are the major but by no means only international statistical sources. Historical data can be found in the League of Nations yearbooks, which appeared annually in the 1920s and 1930s, especially data on basic economic and demographic variables but also on others such as armaments. The United Nations and its agencies have published many more specialized studies and reports, some of them rich with data for specialized kinds of cross-national comparisons. A series of reports by the U.N. Secretary General on the *Progress of the Non-Self-Governing Territories Under the Charter,* for example, provides much data on African, West Indian, and some other territories during the latter days of colonial rule. A useful guide and introduction to United Nations documents is Brenda Brimmer, et al., *A Guide to the Use of United Nations Documents (Including Reference to the Specialized Agencies and Special U.N. Bodies)* (Dobbs Ferry, N.Y.: Oceana Publications, 1962).

NATIONAL STATISTICAL SOURCES   These are too numerous to list even a representative sample of them here. They include national yearbooks, "listing current officers of the government, presenting an organizational outline of the country's government and politics, giving a chronology of the year's events, and abstracting the country's most important statistics" (Merritt and Pyszka 1969, p. 88). Statistical yearbooks, censuses, and specialized statistical reports also flow in ever-increasing number into the U.S. Library of Congress and other major libraries, though only some are likely to be found in university libraries. The most detailed, comprehensive, and long-lived statistical publications come from the European countries, East and West, as might be expected. But Latin American, Asian, and some African countries also have issued them for long periods, as early as the last half of the nineteenth century in some cases. The Chinese have compiled some kinds of data for a much longer time, but only historians have made much use of them.

Merritt and Pyszka list the five guides to national statistical sources cited below. They regard the first as the most generally useful, while the second through fourth together constitute a comprehensive guide. The last is especially useful for U.S. statistics.

Foreign Statistical Documents: A Bibliography of General, International Trade, and Agricultural Statistics, Including Holdings of the Stanford University Libraries, Joyce Ball, ed. (The Hoover Institution on War, Revolution and Peace, 1967).

Statistical Yearbook: An Annotated Bibliography of the General Statistical Yearbooks of Major Political Subdivisions of the World, by Phyllis G. Carter (Library of Congress, 1953).

Statistical Bulletins: An Annotated Bibliography of the General Statistical Bulletins of Major Political Subdivisions of the World, by Phyllis G. Carter (Library of Congress, 1954).

Foreign Statistical Publications: Acssessions List (quarterly, U.S. Department of Commerce, Bureau of the Census).

Statistics Sources: A Subject Guide to Data on Industrial, Business, Social, Education, Financial, and Other Topics for the United States and Selected Foreign Countries, by Paul Wasserman, Eleanor Allen, and Charlotte Georgi (Detroit: Gale Research Co., 1965).

National, state, and local governments in the United States similarly are prolific producers of statistical material, of which two widely useful annual compilations are listed below. For a more comprehensive introduction to official publications in the United States see Merritt and Pyszka 1969, pp. 74–87.

Statistical Abstract of the United States, U.S. Bureau of the Census, annually since 1878. Includes national and state data on political variables such as elections, government finances, welfare services, the military establishment, and law enforcement as well as demographic, economic, educational, communications, and other data.

The Municipal Year Book: The Authoritative Resume of Activities and Statistical Data of American Cities (Washington, D.C.: The International City Managers' Association), annually since 1934.

REGIONAL AND LOCAL SOURCES   There are many periodical publications of local and regional governments in the United States and elsewhere. The archives of local government offices, parish records, and judicial records are other sources that might be used for comparative studies of subnational collectivities. Historians have used such sources much more than politimetricians, and provide the best guides to identifying and using them.

PRIVATE YEARBOOKS   One last important source of available statistical data—and narrative information—is the nongovernmental yearbook. The following two include a good deal of comparative statistical material useful to the political researcher; others which provide solely or primarily narrative information are mentioned in a subsequent section.

Statesman's Year-Book: Statistical and Historical Annual of the States of the World (London: Macmillan; New York: St. Martin's Press), annually since 1864. Rather detailed information on all countries and territories is reported according to a more or less consistent outline, subject to its availability, on such topics as population, government structure and finances, military forces, production and trade, religion, and education. *The Statesman's Year-Book's* value for quantitative political research is not so much its current data, most of which are reported in greater detail and comparability in United Nations sources and the social scientific compendia of data, but the possibilities of using it for cross-national and time-series comparisons for the pre-World War II era.

Europa Yearbook (London: Europa Publications), annually since 1926, in bound form since 1959. Data are listed on much the same variables as the *Statesman's Year-Book* for European and, in recent editions, for non-European countries as well. It includes data on a few subjects, e.g., trade union membership, not well-reported in other sources. Recent editions have better coverage for some little-known non-Western countries, especially Asian Communist nations. The publishers have issued a similar yearbook on the Middle East since 1948, to which North Africa was added in 1964.

Special caution is needed when using these and other private yearbooks, since little effort appears to be made by their editorial staffs to check the accuracy or consistency of statistical data reported from country sources. Both cross-national and cross-time comparisons using them are suspect as a result, though in some instances no better ones can be made.

4.2   Making Data

Available data, despite its abundance, can provide indicators for only some variables and for some units and levels of analysis. The researcher's other resource is to "make" data, that is, to look for nonstatistical materials that he can convert to numerical data. Three somewhat different kinds of data of this sort are widely collected for quantitative political comparisons:

1. *Analyses of the contents of communications and documents* are made by determining, for example, the amount of space given to particular topics, or the frequency with which particular words or ideas are used. This kind of content analysis was used in the "American Values" study.
2. *Analyses of events and interactions* are made by counting and recording other information on conflict events, international alliances, diplomatic representatives, and so forth, as reported in various news and historical sources. This was done in the "Causes of Strife" and "Alliances and War" studies.
3. *Judgmental scores* are obtained by examining a number of cases and ranking them along a varible, or assigning them to categories arranged along the variable, following precise rules set up in advance. Judgmental data were used in parts of the "Causes of Strife" study.

The researcher's ingenuity and energy are the principal limitations on the kinds of data that can be made by these procedures. On the other hand such data, as a class, are less accurate than available data and they sometimes raise serious questions of interpretation. Analysis of communication content provides, at best, indirect evidence of the effects of communications on their audiences. Counts of events and interactions are no more comprehensive than the sources from which they are drawn. Judgmental scores are frequently suspect because the researcher's expectations about how the results should turn out may have influenced the rules he formulates and the coding judgments themselves. Two indisputable advantages of data-making balance these limitations: they make it possible to index many important variables that cannot be indexed using available data; and they open up for quantitative study the whole span of documented human history.

There is no way to list or even offer a systematic sample of the sources that could be used to make data, because they depend largely on the investigator's research design and ingenuity. Diligence and luck are also required, for example in locating and getting access to a collection of documents, or in finding the complete series of an obscure handbook. A few examples below of sources used for each of the three types of data should suggest something of the range of possibilities.

Some Sources for Communications and Documentary Content Analysis

Newspapers are a major source, and so are periodicals. Soviet and American elites' social values and attitudes toward foreign policy in the years 1957–60 have been studied through content analysis of elite journals and newspapers in the two countries (Angell, Dunham, and Singer 1964). Another well-known study examined American, British, French, German, and Russian newspaper editorials for the years 1890 through 1949 to determine how, and how favorable, "democracy" was regarded (Pool, Lasswell, and Lerner 1952). In an examination of American colonial newspapers, 1735–75, the frequency of place names was tabulated to determine when the colonists began to be more concerned with American rather than British affairs and to feel an American rather than Anglo-British identity (Merritt, 1966).

Personal statements and communications have also been analyzed. Themes of hostility were studied in the internal and international communications (diplomatic notes, memos) of the key decision-makers of the European powers during the 1914 crisis that led to World War I (Holsti, North, and Brody 1968; Zinnes 1968). The wartime diaries of Nazi Propaganda Minister Joseph Goebbels have been analyzed for types of content, and the relations among the types have been plotted to show how various themes in his thinking were likely to be connected to others (Osgood 1959).

Public appeals such as speeches, pamphlets, and programmatic statements are also grist for the mill of content analysis. The speeches of John Foster Dulles during his incumbency as U.S. Secretary of State have been studied to determine how he thought of Communism and how he interpreted the policies and actions of Communist regimes (Holsti 1967). The kinds of appeals used by revolutionary movements at various stages in their development have been studied in the pamphlets, newspapers, and other records of the American colonialists 1760–76; of the Indian Swaraj (independence) movement 1925–45; and of the anti-Peronists before the Argentine revolution of 1955 (Shubs 1969; de Hoyos 1969).

Popular culture is another source of material for content-analytic research on social and political questions. One example is a widely known analysis of the extent to which children's readers from a large number of countries (23 as of 1925, 41 for 1950) emphasize the desirability of personal achievement (McClelland 1961). Television's presentation of violence in the United States has been widely analyzed, but seldom with specifically political questions in mind (see Baker and Ball 1969, Part III). The socio-political themes and contents of popular fictions, songs, plays, and comic strips have very seldom been quantitatively studied. They should not be ignored, however, because they have considerable potential as sources of information on popular attitudes, especially for places and times where opinion poll data are not available. One drawback to the political analysis of popular cultural materials is that they are low-grade ore: ordinarily much text must be processed to obtain a given quantum of relevant information.

Some Sources of Event Data

Historical studies have sometimes been used as primary sources when researchers collect information on events. Data on the occurrence and extent of wars and civil disturbances have been collected for 12 European states and empires over the period from 500 B.C. to 1925, relying only on the information contained in standard histories (Sorokin 1937). More detailed and exhaustive quantitative studies of wars have used information from more specialized historical sources (Wright 1942; Richardson, 1960; Singer and Small 1972). Historical monographs are usually the best sources for detailed information on specific events, but they are more often used as a supplement to event information obtained from chronicles—newspapers and yearbooks—than as a primary source. There are two reasons for this, the first being efficiency. We would have to plough through an enormous amount of historical literature to obtain information on all the wars of nineteenth-century Europe, or to determine the frequency and scope of elections in the Austro-Hungarian Empire, unless we were lucky enough to find a monograph on that specific question. In either case the second issue would arise, that of completeness. Most historical studies written in the twentieth century are to varying degrees selective and interpretive, not mere lists or chronicles of events. But from the viewpoint of the counter of historical events, the chronicle is usually more valuable because the chronicler ordinarily includes all events of a particular type. He may not be complete, but he is at least likely to be rather consistent in what is included and what excluded. A parallel problem arises for the data collector working with "contemporary history" (that of the last decade or two): adequate interpretative histories of recent events often are not available. Thus historical sources are most often used in politimetrics as supplementary sources of information.

Yearbooks and almanacs of various kinds have been prepared by some agencies and governments since the late eighteenth century, and can be used to identify major, recurring events. The *Statesman's Year-Book*, mentioned above, contains some narrative as well as statistical information. Other useful annuals are listed below.

Almanach de Gotha (Gotha, Germany) from 1764 to 1944 provided diplomats and other observers of international affairs with basic, annual information on kings and rulers, noble lineages, diplomatic and consular services, and some statistical information. It is a good source for historical studies of the international system.

The Annual Register of World Events (London: Longmans, Green) has provided annual surveys of current events since 1758, with special weight given to topics and regions of interest to the United Kingdom. It is based largely on *The Times* of London.

News Dictionary: An Encyclopedic Summary of Contemporary History, formerly *News Year* (New York: Facts-on-File), has appeared yearly since 1964. It contains alphabetically listed information on current affairs with a strong emphasis on the United States. The publisher also periodically issues special volumes that provide chronologies of such events as the civil rights movement and the war in Vietnam.

Political Handbook and Atlas of the World: Parliaments, Parties and Press (New York: Simon and Schuster for the Council on Foreign Relations), since 1927, lists government officials and provides information on party programs and leaders, the press, and political events for most of the world's countries. Information on the less-developed and newer countries tends to be sparse.

The International Year Book and Statesmen's Who's Who (London: Burke's Peerage), since 1953, provides information on international organizations and the nations of the world, including organizational charts of foreign ministries of many countries, as well as statistical and biographical information.

Congressional Quarterly Almanac (Congressional Quarterly Service), has provided since 1947 the most thorough periodic information on the U.S. Congress, including data on the background characteristics of Congressmen, information on major items of legislation, tabulations of roll-call votes, and a survey of political developments.

The Americana Annual (New York: Americana Corp., since 1923) and *Britannica Book of the Year* (Chicago: Encyclopedia Britannica, since 1938) are two of a number of encyclopedia annuals that provide surveys of current affairs. *The Americana* has particularly useful surveys of current governmental, political, and economic activities for a substantial number of countries.

The World Almanac and Book of Facts (New York: Newspaper Enterprise Association, since 1868) and *Whitaker's Almanac* (London:

Whitaker's Almanac, since 1869) are two among several general almanacs that provide a potpourri of information including reviews of the year's events. They can be relied upon for a quick overview but seldom for much else.

Newspapers and news digests have been most often used to compile event data. Contemporary measures of civil conflict like numbers of events of various categories, numbers of participants and casualties, and duration have been obtained from such sources as the *New York Times,* its *Index,* and *Facts-on-File* (Rummel 1963; Gurr with Ruttenberg 1967). Regional news digests like *Hispanic American Report* have been used to make lists of acts of collective violence, governmental changes, and acts of repression (see Bwy 1968). Historians (but few other social scientists) have made detailed use of the local press in compiling information on political events; a major example is Tilly's study of collective violence in French history, relying on many local and national papers (Tilly 1969). Some of the most useful general and regional news sources are listed below.

The New York Times, published since 1851, and its cross-referenced topical *Index,* 1851–present, have been the news sources most widely used to compile data on events. The relative detail with which the *Times* provides news coverage, and the quality of its *Index,* make it an invaluable resource for political research, especially from the World War II era to the present. The farther back in time the researcher goes, however, the less adequate the reporting and indexing. The problem is least serious for American news, most serious for the domestic news of foreign countries.

The Times of London was privately indexed from 1790; beginning in 1906 the *Index to the Times* was published by Times Newspapers Ltd. Compared with the *New York Times* this newspaper offers the advantages of longer span and somewhat different perspective on comparative and international politics. The quantity, though not the quality, of its reporting seems to have declined in the 1960s. Like the *New York Times,* its index volumes for the nineteenth and early twentieth centuries leave much to be desired by contemporary standards.

Other Newspaper Indexes include *The Wall Street Journal Index* (New York: Dow Jones & Co., since 1958); *Annual Index of The Christian Science Monitor* (Corvallis, Ore.: Helen M. Cropsey, since 1960); and *Le Monde, Index Analytique* (Paris: Le Monde, since 1965). In preparation are index volumes to *Le Temps* (Paris) for 1861 to 1942 (*Table du Journal Le Temps,* Paris: Institute Française de Presse, Section d'Histoire: Éditions du Centre National de la Recherche Scientifique, 1966–).

Keesing's Contemporary Archives: Weekly Diary of World Events (London: Keesing's Publications Ltd., since 1931) is the most extensive of general news digests. It provides some election and statistical data, documents, and speeches as well as news summaries. An index is also prepared.

Facts-on-File: World News Digest with Index (New York: Facts-on-File, since 1940) is a weekly digest of current affairs and topical information classified by subject. The material is compiled in an annual *News Dictionary* (above, p. 79).

Deadline Data on World Affairs (Greenwich, Conn.: Deadline Data, since 1948) reports current-affairs information by country and subject on 5″ × 8″ file cards, cumulated since 1968 in a monthly publication, *On Record* (McGraw-Hill). *Facts-on-File* and *Deadline Data* have both been used to compile data on conflict events, despite questions about their comprehensiveness.

Africa Research Bulletin: Political, Social and Cultural Series (Exeter, England: Africa Research Ltd., since 1964) are goldmines of detailed, indexed information based on a comprehensive survey of current documents and many news sources. Another more discursive and less detailed African source is *Africa Diary: Weekly Diary of African Events with Index* (New Delhi: Africa Publications, since 1961).

Asian Recorder: A Weekly Digest of Asian Events with Index (New Delhi: New Age Printing Press, since 1955) reports political and governmental information by country. Despite its inadequacies it has no competitors.

Hispanic-American Report (Stanford: Hispanic-American Institute) provided an excellent, indexed summary of the Latin American press from 1948 to 1964 but ceased publication for lack of funds and has not been replaced.

Indexed excerpts from the press of the U.S.S.R. and the People's Republic of China appear respectively in *Current Digest of the Soviet Press* (Washington, D.C.: Joint Committee on Slavic Studies, since 1949) and *Survey of China Mainland Press* (Hong Kong: U.S. Consulate General, since 1952). These digests are probably more useful for content analysis of themes and symbols than for obtaining reliable data on most kinds of events.

Sources of Judgmental Data

All the sources mentioned above can be used in obtaining the information needed for making coding judgments. At least three approaches to judgmental coding can be distinguished in politimetrics; they differ mainly in how systematically the information in such sources is used.

SOURCE-DETERMINED JUDGMENTS   These are made on the basis of information collected according to predetermined categories, and from one or two standard sources. Two illustrations suggest how this is done. In one recent study an attempt was made to index the "efficiency" with which governments maintained their authority. *The Annual Register* and *New York Times Index* were used to compile information about political processes for 12 countries for 1927–36 and 1957–66. When national elections were scheduled, for example, information was recorded on whether they were held, whether prescribed or new procedure were used, and how much serious elite conflict occurred before the elections. Similar information was recorded about the formation of new governments and how they maintained themselves in power. This information was used to devise and code a series of five-point scales of how smoothly and legitimately each of these processes was managed. The scores were combined into a summary indicator of governmental efficiency in maintaining authority (Gurr and McClelland 1971).

As a second example, 28 kinds of political instability were categorized, ranging from resignations of cabinet ministers to political arrests to civil wars. *Deadline Data on World Affairs* and the *Encyclopedia Britannica Yearbooks* were used to collect data on the frequency of these events in 84 nations between 1948 and 1965. A seven-point scale of political instability was devised: elections were scored 0, for example, sabotage 3, and civil war 6. The scores for all events in each country were combined in several different ways to give summary instability scores to each country (Feierabend and Feierabend 1966).

SCALE-DETERMINED JUDGMENTS   The crux of this approach is usually "less data and more judgment." The researcher does not rely on large amounts of carefully categorized data from particular sources. Instead he devises a precisely defined scale on which cases can be simply coded, using information from whatever sources seem appropriate to each case. One illustration is a six-point scale used in a recent study to measure the relative coerciveness or permissiveness of contemporary political systems. The "most permissive" category of nations included those with such characteristics as the presence and protection of civil rights and political opposition, regular and free elections, the existence of independent and effective legislative and judicial bodies, and so forth. The "most coercive" category of nations included those with no protected civil rights, no political opposition, "showcase" elections only, and legislative and judicial bodies entirely dependent on an autocratic executive. The scale categories between these two extremes are similarly defined in terms of specific characteristics. To code countries using the scale, various sources dealing with each country were read independently by several coders, who then decided which of the categories was most appropriate. Discrepancies in coding judgments were worked out in consultation (Feierabend and Feierabend, 1966).

For the "Causes of Strife" study, the potential loyalty of military establishments to civilian regimes was measured using information about how recently, before 1960, the military or police had attempted overtly to seize power. The highest "loyalty" score on a five-point scale was given to long-independent countries that had experienced no such military intervention since 1910; the lowest score was given to countries which had military interventions between 1958 and 1960. Since overt attempts to seize power are usually easy to identify, it was a fairly simple matter for a coder, relying on standard histories and country studies, to identify the date of the last such attempt in a country (if any) and hence to assign a score. An alternative, requiring more information from similar sources, would have taken into account *how frequently* the military had intervened over some specified period (Gurr 1968).

The difference between source-determined and scale-determined judgments coding is one of degree. The detailed data collection involved in source-determined judgments may be used as a preliminary step to constructing a scale whose data requirements are much less complex. One example is a reanalysis of the Feierabend data on political violence, 1948–65 (see Nesvold 1969).

EXPERT OPINIONS   These are the third source of judgmental data. In some cases, for example in preparing *A Cross-polity Survey* (see pp. 68–69), experts on a country or region are asked whether they agree with preliminary scoring judgments made by the researcher. In other cases an entire comparative project may be based on expert opinion.

One illustration is an expert assessment of Latin American countries' relative progress toward democratic institutions and practices. At five-year intervals, from 1945 to 1960, the researcher sent questionnaires to 10 to 40 experts. He asked them to use five-point scales to rate each of 20 Latin American countries on 15 separate dimensions of "democracy." The dimensions included "free and competitive elections—honestly counted votes," "civilian supremacy over the military," and "fairly adequate standard of living." The average ratings on the dimensions were combined in summary indices, used for comparing democratic developments among and within countries over time (Fitzgibbon and Johnson 1961).

In another example, four journalism experts and an area expert were asked to rate the freedom of the press in almost every country and major colony of the world. They used a scale ranging from $1 =$ free press system, without qualifications, to $9 =$ controlled press system, without qualifications (Nixon, 1965).

There are three general difficulties with using expert judgments for quantitative political comparisons. (1) One is that, in practice, they have been largely limited to static and general country comparisons—except where a panel is asked to judge the same phenomenon over and over again, as in the Latin American example above. It would be more difficult to find experts with sufficient knowledge to judge year-by-year changes in a country, or to judge smaller units like regions or groups. (2) A second difficulty is that the researcher seldom knows to what extent the judgments reflect biases and misinformation. The use of a number of judges is only a partial control for this factor. The judges may all share common biases, as one might expect among the judges in the Latin American example above (almost all of the judges were American academic experts). (3) The third difficulty arises from the fact that many, probably most, area and country experts intellectually resist making summary quantitative judgments because they think their subjects have subtleties that no set of scales could take into account. All of these obstacles can be overcome, in principle, and for some research projects it may be well worth doing so. The "expert judgment" approach seems especially desirable when a researcher has a set of variables that are very difficult to index using other means, and when there are a number of experts on the subject whom he can readily consult.

4.3   Missing Data

The researcher who is concerned, say, with tracing postrevolutionary political mobilization in Turkey may well find much information on party membership and voting participation in the 1960s. Its availability is no guarantee that similar data can be found for the 1920s or 1930s. The politimetrician making a cross-national study of the contemporary connection between inflation and political instability will find good national and regional data for most European cases; he should not expect to find it for Nepal, Malawi, or Paraguay. A lack of data for a few cases for some indices is tolerable in most research designs, but if data are missing for *many* cases in a cross-sectional study or for substantial periods in a longitudinal study, the study usually will have to be substantially modified and sometimes abandoned. Thus the researcher planning his study needs a good deal of knowledge about the availability of data, and should consider how he will deal with cases and indices for which data are missing.

Some Causes and Effects of Missing Data

The problems of missing data vary with the research design. For some studies data will be complete by definition. If the study is a content analysis of newspaper editorials, for example, some newspapers may be difficult to locate but once they are obtained and analyzed the data are "complete." If a comparative study is being done with available data from standard collections, the researcher may choose at the outset to restrict himself to those cases with complete information. Aside from this, here are a few generalizations about missing-data problems. Data are likely to be more complete for:

> *contemporary rather than historical studies,* because statistics and documentation tend to decrease as one goes back in time;
> *cross-sectional rather than longitudinal studies,* for the same reason;
> *studies using European and American rather than Asian and African*

cases, because statistical, chronological, and narrative materials used in quantitative, comparative studies are available in approximately the following declining order: Western Europe, North America, Eastern Europe, Latin America, Asia (except China and Japan), Africa;

studies including larger countries rather than very small ones, because available statistical and narrative materials are scanty for most contemporary countries with populations less than one million;

studies using judgmental coding rather than standard enumerations, because narrative materials are more widely available than statistical compilations;

studies making cross-national rather than cross-regional comparisons, because statistics and chronologies are more often compiled on national than regional bases—except for census data, and except for federal political systems.

This should not discourage the researcher from undertaking historical or cross-regional or African studies. On the contrary, they are likely to be substantively more rewarding because relatively few of them have been done. But the researcher setting out in these directions should expect to have to be more ingenious in devising measures and more diligent in searching out data sources than the researcher who keeps to easier ground.

Missing data are not an absolute evil. They can be tolerated just as error can be tolerated, and for much the same reason: their effects are comparable to those of error (see Section 3.2). If missing data are randomly distributed through a data matrix, they will decrease the precision of results and conclusions but are not likely to seriously mislead the investigator. But if missing data are clustered on particular variables or among distinctive kinds of cases, results can be seriously distorted. For example, several comprehensive studies show that political strife and instability are, on the average, greater in developing countries than in either the most traditional or most modern ones (see Adams 1970). But most kinds of enumerated data are not available for traditional countries like Nepal and Afghanistan, so they are often excluded from comparative studies. If we therefore excluded them from a cross-sectional study of the relation between economic development and instability, we would come to the erroneous conclusion that the higher is economic development, the greater is stability. In fact, the early stages of development seem to cause *in*stability. (A longitudinal research design offers a better approach to this question.)

The distorting effects of missing data on results are seldom as great as in this example, but they can be serious. The researcher has two ways of minimizing the likelihood of distortion. One is to give special attention to including cases that represent the full ranges of his variables. The other is to examine extreme cases on the basic variables as a separate group, to see whether different relationships seem to be at work in them.

Solutions for Missing Data

There are several solutions for the problems of missing data. *Deleting cases with missing data* is one of them. If a large number of cases are available and only a few have any missing data, all the latter may be discarded. More commonly, though, only those cases with missing data for a number of indicators are deleted (assuming that a number of indicators have been included). *Deleting indicators with missing data* is a more puritanical approach, but can be justified if the indicators have a large missing-data component and are conceptually expendable. Data loss is one drawback to deleting case and/or indicators, though if any cases have more than 50% missing data they almost certainly should be discarded. The other drawback is the possibility, noted above, that the deleted cases are in fact significant to the analysis. This is particularly a problem with synchronic cross-national studies in which the missing-data cases are usually the least-developed nations. Deleting most of them from analyses tends to reduce the range of variation on many indicators, not only the economic ones.

Inserting means, another approach to missing data, avoids information loss at the cost of introducing random error. If a case has no score for one indicator, the average score on that variable is used instead. The technique is appropriate if error is randomly distributed among cases, and if cases with more than 50% missing data have already been deleted. (It would make little sense to insert six erroneous values—means—for a 10-variable case in order to save four correct estimates.)

Interpolation is a method suitable for handling missing data in some kinds of time-series. The researcher may need annual estimates of the size of the military, but find several years missing in published estimates. The missing years can be estimated by straight-line interpolation (averaging) between the reported years. Interpolation is justifiable for variables which seldom are subject to abrupt fluctuations, like population, government expenditures, and so forth. The researcher ordinarily can determine whether interpolation is justified by considering both contextual information (was the missing period normal by other indicators, or a time of crisis?) and the trends in the data before and after the missing estimate (does a smooth line or curve fit the data, or is there an apparent change in the trend at that point?).

Estimating values is the most sophisticated approach to missing data. The basic procedure is to use other information, either contextual information or data from the matrix itself, to estimate a missing score with less error than is likely from using the mean. The use of *contextual information* is illustrated in the "Causes of Strife" study. "Numbers of participants" had to be estimated for some demonstrations, riots, etc. In one stage of analysis, average numbers of participants were calculated for each type of event and were plugged in where data were missing. But the results were unsatisfactory. Most of the "missing-data" events seemed much smaller in scale than those from which we calculated the means. So we examined the available data for these small demonstrations—such as where they occurred, their objectives, and the type of groups involved—and interpreted them in light of general knowledge about the country's politics. This information made it possible to "guesstimate" the number of participants.

A more systematic use of contextual information is to identify a small group of complete-data cases similar to one with a missing datum on variable Y, and to use the average score of variable Y from the similar cases as the estimate. It is also possible to make systematic *matrix-based estimates* of missing data, using data in the otherwise-complete matrix. This requires multiple regression techniques, a topic best discussed in more advanced texts.

Which, if any, of the missing-data techniques should be used, and when? "When" can be more easily answered. Missing data for standard enumerations are best estimated after all available data have been gathered. In this way the researcher does not waste time estimating data for cases that later must be discarded, and also maximizes the information available for estimation. But if data are missing for coded events and are to be estimated from contextual information, then the estimate is best made when the contextual material is at hand, i.e., when coding.

Which technique to use depends on a number of factors, a few of which can be suggested here. First, if data are missing for a dependent variable—one which is to be "explained" or "predicted" in the study—they should be estimated only on the basis of contextual information, if at all. It is much better to discard cases with missing dependent-variable data than to confound the analysis by using matrix data on independent variables to estimate what is supposed to be explained. Second, it is more appropriate to estimate missing data on structural variables than to estimate data on events and interactions. There are likely to be more or less regular relationships according to which the researcher can roughly estimate, say, the approximate size of a locale's police force from the amount of money budgeted for it, or income growth rates from changes in agricultural production. There are no similar bases from which he could make a reliable inference that riots occurred in a particular place at a particular time, or guess the proportion of people participating in an election.

Generally, a good deal of caution should be exercised in estimating missing data. If many data are missing, or if many have been estimated, the researcher who has access to a computer should consider duplicating his basic analyses. One analysis should be done for cases with the most complete and accurate data, a second for all cases. If relationships are stronger for the smaller set of cases, and if the extremes of the variables are well represented, it is probable that the other cases contain more error than information.

4.4 Planning for Data Collection

The novice investigator may have decided at this point to rely largely on available data and to concentrate on improving the validity and comparability of his indicators. All of these are reasonable decisions. One other practical compromise also is open to him, and to more experienced researchers as well: to limit the number of cases studied. It is commendably universalistic to want to test whether a relationship holds among all 137 U.S. urban areas of 100,000+ population, or among all 85 or 119 or 130 countries, or for every year in the post-Revolutionary history of France. But significant results can be equally well obtained from a representative sample of places or years, or from an analysis of a distinctive subgroup of countries or cities (see Chapter 2). A successful study of part of a universe of analysis, carried to its conclusion, can serve as a pilot study for a more ambitious one. If its results are unpromising, much effort is saved.

Data collection, and analysis, usually prove more time-consuming than planners estimate. Apprentice researchers are not unlikely to underestimate the requirements by ratios of three or four; journeymen often invest twice as much effort as first proposed. Students planning politimetric research need not necessarily be cautious in what they propose to accomplish, but they should build one or two fall-back positions into their research design. A priority order can be given to indicators for which data is to be collected, with the most important done first. Cases can be set out in blocs or clusters, and data collected for them in sequence. The researcher who faces an imminent deadline will be able to take great practical comfort from being able to cut off data collection at variable j or case p, knowing that he has enough data for meaningful analysis.

5

Collecting Data and Constructing Indicators: Three studies

The researcher evidently should do a great deal of thinking and make many decisions before setting out to the library or archives to record information. He has had to think through the theoretical problem, define and operationalize variables, and evaluate the sources of data. Some data probably were collected, or at least examined, in these initial stages of research, perhaps as a check on its availability and reliability, perhaps to help in the construction and validation of judgmental scales. It is the norm, and the best prescription for good research, that the investigator ought to be equipped with a careful set of specifications before collecting and processing most of his data. But we must recognize that some researchers choose to begin by collecting data on a vaguely formulated question, working out the conceptual and methodological problems as they go along, or even after the fact.

The purpose of this chapter is to show, in some detail, how data are collected and how indicators are constructed from them. The discussion assumes that the basic theoretical and methodological issues have been decided. We shall see, though, that some of their details are best worked out with some data in hand. The three studies are used to provide detailed illustrations. One subject not dealt with here is how data are mechanically prepared for statistical analysis; this is a technical subject for which other good introductions have been written (see Janda 1969).

5.1 Procedures of Data Collection

The data collector requires two basic tools: a set of *data specifications,* and some kind of *recording form* for summarizing and storing information in orderly fashion.

Data Specifications

A single phrase may suffice as a data specification. Examples are "provincial population, 1970"; "number of national elections, 1950–75"; or "annual defense budget by year, 1920–40." Usually, though, some contingent distinctions and definitions are needed even for apparently clear-cut indicators such as these. In recording the populations of provinces, for example, guidelines probably will be needed to deal with provinces whose populations are given only for other years. Determining the number of national elections requires careful definition of "national elections": does one include nationwide elections for   local offices? elections in which national representatives but not the chief executive are elected? national referenda? uncontested elections for national officials? An arbitrary definition can settle these questions for data-collecting purposes, but they are best resolved by reference to what the concept "elections" means to the investigator, and what he expects to do with the "number of elections" index. Recording "annual defense budget" estimates for a country over time can pose a host of problems requiring specifications. What to do about differences between *budgeted* and *actual* expenditures? Should we try to include the costs of internal security forces? How can we adjust for inflation, since it makes the figures incomparable from one year to the next? Shall we adjust the estimates to a calender-year basis, or stay with the fiscal year? Most of these issues are technical, and require solutions that maximize the comparability of the data. The technical problems of data specification, and sometimes some conceptual ones, may not occur to the researcher until he begins recording data. When they do occur, they require a considered, theoretically justified decision that is added to the data specifications and henceforth followed consistently.

When the investigator is recording information on events, detailed coding guidelines are usually required. These may be a set of questions requiring verbal or numerical answers: "Which group(s) initiated the action?" "How many hours/days did the clash last?" The information initially collected in this manner may be entirely verbal, or it may be narrative. In the latter case the numerical coding or scaling is done later. When a numerical answer is indicated, a set of alternative responses can be listed: "less than $\frac{1}{2}$ hr."; "$\frac{1}{2}$ to 1 hr."; "1 to 2 hrs."; "unspecified but less than $\frac{1}{2}$ day"; "unspecified, no basis for judging"; and so forth. Judgmental coding, described on pages 81–84 requires a set of carefully defined categories to which cases can be unambiguously assigned.

In practice the data collector may find events and conditions for which the initial coding guidelines do not seem to provide. Such occasions are usually cause for thought, consultation, and adjustments in the guidelines. If such questions arise late in the data collection process, though, it is risky to modify the guidelines. Any new distinction or qualification must be retroactively applicable to cases already coded—otherwise comparability is lost. Thus, a practical recommendation when applying a complex set of coding guidelines is to code some "sticky" cases first, as a way of getting ambiguities out of the instructions.

Recording Forms

Forms for recording data vary according to how much and what kinds of information are being gathered. When simple aggregate data are being recorded—like population, number of elections, defense budget—it is usually sufficient to use mimeographed sheets or ruled notebook pages. The cases (provinces, countries, years, whatever) are listed down the left-hand side, and column labels for the indicators are added across the top. It is often useful to have a space next to each datum for recording supplementary information such as the source (if different sources are used for the index) and qualifications about the datum (year of reference, changes in inclusions, alternative estimates, apparent reliability, etc.). Sources always ought to be listed on the recording forms.

Forms for recording event information and for judgmental coding are usually quite detailed. Questions, coding categories, and space for recording the information on each case may be many mimeographed pages in length. The detailed coding guidelines are usually the subject of a separate coding document. One practical consideration in preparing forms is that they be suitable for later processing and storage. If data are to be punched onto computer cards from complex coding forms, for example, it is useful to align the quantified information along one margin or column, and to indicate the computer card location in which each datum is to be punched. An example from the "Causes of Strife" study is described and illustrated below. Original data forms also should be regarded as semipermanent records, even if the information and data are to be otherwise summarized or key-punched.

"American Values"

We referred previously to this study's use of a "value dictionary," a list of words which the authors compiled in advance to represent aspects and transformation of specific values. This dictionary constitutes the study's "data specifications." It was applied to the full texts of party platforms recorded in Porter and Johnson's *National Party Platforms 1840–1960* (1961). The 1964 platforms were obtained from periodical and party sources. The words of each platform were counted by category. The count could have been done manually, but instead the texts of the platforms were punched on computer cards and later stored on computer tape for analysis. The counting and basic statistical analysis were accomplished using the "General Inquirer" computer program, which is designed for this type of analysis (see Stone et al. 1960). Thus, once the "value dictionary" was prepared, data collection in this study required very little effort by the researchers.

"Causes of Strife"

Data collection for this study was complex, time-consuming, and was accomplished in three distinct phases that extended over several years. In each of the first two phases, analyses were carried through to their conclusion and the results published, before we embarked on a new phase of data collection suggested by the outcome of the previous round. The collection of data on *civil strife 1961–65* is discussed below because it illustrates many of the problems and procedures of "making" macropolitical data from news sources.

Our central purpose was to obtain comparable information on the number of *participants, casualties,* and *duration* of reported strife events. Since this required examination of many detailed sources we decided to compile at the same time additional information on such questions as the form of strife, kinds of people involved, their motives, and the kinds of coercive regime responses to strife.

THE CODING SHEET AND MANUAL   We began with a list of "interesting" properties of strife events about which comparable information seemed useful and obtainable. What is "interesting" is a matter of paradigmatic assumption or theoretical specification, at least in a well-established field of inquiry. Some of the strife properties that interested us were theoretically specified; the others were chosen because they were commonly discussed in historical and comparative case studies. Each of the properties was operationally defined, some as continuous variables, others in terms of specific categories. The final list of variables and categories is shown on the coding sheet reproduced on pages 94–97. The sheet is illustrated with the coding of a particular event, a general strike in Liberia. The text of the account, from the *New York Times,* is given in Figure 5.1, which also shows the basis for each coding judgment. A detailed coding manual used with the coding sheet provided general instructions on coding and definitions of the categories. The manual is quite long and has been published elsewhere (Gurr with Ruttenberg, 1969, Appendix A). Here is a representative set of instructions for recording information on numbers of participants.

> *Cols. 22–26: Number of Initiators, Proximate:* Those who carry out the reported event are counted here, not their victims or police who attempt to suppress them. If the report distinguishes between continuously and sporadically active initiators, use the total figure. People said to give frequent assistance to initiators are also counted as initiators. If two private groups engage in a riot, each attacking the other, the total membership of both groups is used.
>
> Code the proximate-scale interval designation in which the estimated number of initiators of the events falls, if sufficiently precise. If more than 110,000 persons are said to be involved, record their approximate number.
>
> If you are unable to distinguish the number of initiators as closely as this scale requires, check "00000" for cols. 22 to 26 and code instead the *estimate-scale* interval, cols. 27–30, which in your judgment is most likely to

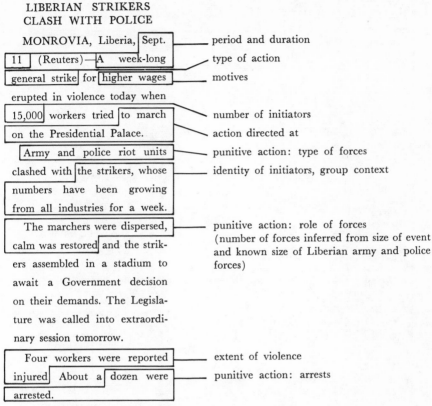

FIGURE 5.1. Text of news account used to code sample coding sheet (from the *New York Times*, September 13, 1961, p. 21).

comprise the number of initiators.... (Note: The proximate scale is a rounded geometric progression with a base of 2. Multiplying the interval designation by 20 gives the approximate mid-point of the interval.)

Cols. 27–30: Number of Initiators, Estimate: If the estimate has been fitted to the proximate scale (see cols. 22–26, above), code "0000 (previous heading coded)" here. If there is no basis for even a rough judgment about the number of initiators, code "bbbbb" for cols. 22–26 and "bbbb" for 27–30. In most cases, however, it should be possible to make an informed guess.

The format of the coding sheet was dictated by our intention to punch computer data cards directly from the coded sheets. The column numbers refer to the 80 columns of the standard computer data card. The numbers shown for each scale or category are those to be punched if that category is circled. Note that some of the sets of categories are only *nominal scales,* like "identity of initiators" (cols. 17–21) and "motives" (cols. 49–51): they are not measures in the conventional sense, but are categories to which numbers are assigned arbitrarily for the purpose of recording the informa-

Polity _Liberia_

Coder _TG_   Month and Year of Coding _7/66_

Source(s) _N. Y. Times_

Issue and pages _9/13/61 p. 21_

Summary _Clashes with police in general strike_

col. num.	contents of columns	col. num.	contents of columns
1-3	Polity I.D. Number _0 6 0_	(18)	8 some, undifferentiable 9 other
4-7	Polity Population (100,000's) _0 0 1 0_	19	Regime Classes ⓪ none or insignificant
8	Character of Report		1 military/police
	1 single report, current period, continuing event		2 public employees
	2 single report, all of continuing event, to date		3 political elite 4 military/police, employees
	③ single report, concluded event		5 political elite, employees 6 military/police, elite
	6 cumulative report, current period, continuing event		7 all three 8 some, undifferentiable
	7 cumulative report, continuing event, to date		9 other
	8 cumulative report, concluded event	20	Domestic Initiators, Summary 0 none or insignificant
9-10	_6 1_ (Year Event Began)		① lower classes only 2 middle classes only
11-16	Period Covered by Report from (_9/5/61_) to		3 regime classes only 4 lower and middle classes
	_6 1 0 9 1 1_ Year Month Day		5 lower and regime classes 6 middle and regime classes 7 all domestic classes
	I. IDENTITY OF INITIATORS	21	Resident Alien Initiators ⓪ none or insignificant
17-21	bbbbb no basis for judging		1 pastoral migrants 2 foreign workers
17	Lower Classes		3 foreign students
	0 none or insignificant		4 refugees
	1 farmers/peasants		5 political exiles
	2 rural wage laborers		6 foreign clandestine group
	③ urban wage laborers		7 several of the above (ck.)
	4 unemployed		8 other
	5 farmers, wage laborers	22-26	Number of Initiators, Proximate
	6 wage laborers, unemployed		00000 (go to next heading)
	7 farmers, laborers, unemployed		bbbb1 1 to 40
	8 some, undifferentiable		bbbb3 41 to 80
	9 other		bbbb8 81 to 240
			bbb16 241 to 400
18	Higher Classes		bbb32 401 to 900
	⓪ none or insignificant		bbb64 901 to 1,700
	1 students		bb128 1,701 to 3,500
	2 petite bourgeoisie		bb250 3,501 to 6,500
	3 professionals		bb500 6,501 to 14,000
	4 students, bourgeoisie		ⓑ1000 14,001 to 27,000
	5 students, professionals		b2000 27,001 to 55,000
	6 bourgeoisie, professionals		b4000 55,001 to 110,000
	7 all three		bbbbb no basis for judging

94

col. num.	contents of columns	col. num.	contents of columns
27-30	Number of Initiators, Estimate ⓪⓪⓪⓪ (previous heading coded) bbb4 less than 100 bb40 101-1,000, "hundreds," "many" b400 1,001-10,000, "thousands" 4000 10,001-100,000 bbbb no basis for judging other_____	37	Conspiracy Events ⓪ none 1 plot 2 purge 3 assassination 4 bombing 5 small-scale terrorism 6 small-scale guerrilla war 7 coup/putsch 8 mutiny
31-32	II. GROUP AND SOCIAL CONTEXT Initiators Acting as Members of b0 unstructured crowd b1 territorial group b2 ethnic/linguistic group b3 religious group b4 communal group b5 apolitical student group b6 political group ⓑ⑦ economic group b8 governing hierarchy b9 clandestine group ____ ____ clash between two of above; specify categories other_____ bb no basis for judging	38	Internal War Events ⓪ none 1 large-scale terrorism 2 large-scale guerrilla war 3 civil war (secessionist) 4 private war 5 large-scale revolt 6 turmoil/conspiracy event is part of internal war
		39	Summary of Form of Event ① turmoil 2 conspiracy 3 internal war 4 turmoil and internal war 5 conspiracy and internal war 6 other_____
33-35	Social Area bb1 rural village or county bb3 several villages, counties or a small town bb5 a large town b10 several towns, or a city, or a small state b20 large state, or part of the capital city ⓑ④⓪ several large states or several cities, or entire capital city b60 several states or cities and the capital city b80 almost the entire polity 100 the entire polity other_____ bbb no basis for judging	40	Number of Actions ① single occurrence 2 two, "several" 3 three, "some" 4 4-6 5 7-11 No. Reported 6 12-20 7 21-35 _____ /_____ 8 36-60 9 61+
		41	Incidence of Action ① single occurrence 2 multiple sporadic 3 multiple simultaneous
36	III. TYPOLOGY OF ACTION Turmoil Events 0 none 1 demonstration ② political strike 3 riot 4 localized rebellion 5 banditry/raiding 6 political clash 7 nonpolitical clash	42-45	Duraction of Action bbbb no basis for judging bbb1 1/2 day or less bbb3 1/2 to 1 day bbb5 1 to 2 days bb10 2 to 4 days ⓑⓑ②⓪ 4 days to 1 week bb40 1 to 2 weeks bb80 2 weeks to 1 month b160 1 to two months b320 2 to 4 months b640 4 to 9 months 1217 9 to 15 months 2000 15 months to 2 years 4000 2 to 4 1/2 years other_____

col num.	contents of columns	col. num.	contents of columns

IV. ACTION DIRECTED AT

46-48 bbb no basis for judging

46 Property Targets
- ⓪ none or negligible
- 1 foreign public
- 2 foreign private
- 3 all foreign
- 4 domestic public
- 5 domestic private
- 6 all domestic
- 7 foreign and domestic

47 Political Actor(s)
- 0 none or negligible
- ① major domestic
- 2 minor domestic
- 3 military/police, domestic
- 4 private political group
- 5 several of the above (ck.)
- 6 undifferentiable domestic
- 7 foreign public
- 8 foreign military
- 9 domestic, foreign actors (ck.)

48 Nonpolitical Actor(s)
- ⓪ none or negligible
- 1 random actors
- 2 ethnic actors
- 3 religious actors
- 4 communal actors
- 5 economic actors
- 6 several of the above (ck.)
- 7 undifferentiable
- 8 foreign nonpolitical actors
- 9 other_____

V. STATED OR APPARENT MOTIVES

49-51 bbb no basis for judging

49 Political Motives
- 0 none or minor
- 1 retaliation
- 2 seize political power
- 3 increase pol. participation
- 4 injure/suppress competing political group
- ⑤ promote/oppose specific domestic policy
- 6 promote/oppose specific domestic political actor
- 7 oppose foreign nation's policy or actors
- 8 several of the above (ck.)
- 9 diffuse political motives other_____

50 Economic Motives
- 0 none or minor
- 1 retaliation
- 2 seize economic goods
- ③ change distribution patterns
- 4 oppose economic actor
- 5 several of the above (ck.)
- 6 diffuse economic motives
- 7 other_____

51 Social Motives
- ⓪ none or minor
- 1 retaliation
- 2 promote/oppose belief system
- 3 promote/oppose community
- 4 increase social goods (status, education, etc.)
- 5 several of the above (ck.)
- 6 diffuse social motives
- 7 other_____

VI. PUNITIVE ACTION

52 Role of Punitive Forces
- 0 not committed or committed after end of action
- 1 victims
- 2 present but passive
- 3 defensive action
- ④ moderate suppressive action
- 5 extreme suppressive action
- 6 provoke action
- b no basis for judging

53 Type of Punitive Forces
- 0 none
- 1 police
- 2 domestic military units
- ③ police and domestic military
- 4 foreign military units
- 5 domestic and foreign
- b no basis for judging

54 Number of Punitive Forces
- 0 none
- 1 1 to 10
- 2 11 to 100
- ③ 101-1,000
- 4 1,001-10,000
- 5 10,001-100,000
- 6 100,001-1,000,000
- b no basis for judging

55 Arrests and Detentions
- 0 none
- 1 1 to 10   No. Reported
- ② 11 to 100   *a dozen*
- 3 101 to 1,000
- 4 1,001 to 10,000
- 5 no basis for judging

col. num.	contents of columns	col. num.	contents of columns
56	Executions ⓪none 1 1 to 10 No. Reported 2 11 to 100 3 101 to 1,000 _____ 4 1,001 to 10,000 b no basis for judging	69-72	Number of Injuries bbb0 none, none likely (bbb4) 10 or less, "few" bb40 11 to 100, "scores," "many" b400 101 to 1,000, "hundreds" 4000 1,001 to 10,000 bbbb no basis for judging No. Reported _____ Other _____
	VII. EXTENT OF VIOLENCE		VIII. EXTERNAL SUPPORT
57-58	Damage in Affected Area ⓪⓪ none or presumed neglig- able 01 slight 03 moderate 07 extensive 10 massive bb no basis for judging	73-76	bbbb no basis for judging ⓪⓪⓪⓪ none apparent

59	Who are Casualties?
	0 none, none likely
	① initiators
	2 victims
	3 punitive forces
	4 initiators, victims
	5 initiators, punitive
	   forces
	6 victims, punitive forces
	7 all three
	8 some, unspecified
	b no basis for judging
		73	Degree of Support for
			Initiators
			0 none apparent
			1 arms and supplies
			2 provision of refuge
			3 provision of facilities,
			   training
			4 military advisors, mer-
			   cenaries
			5 military units

		74	Degree of Support for Regime 0 none apparent 1 nonmilitary aid 2 military materiel 4 personnel, facilities 5 military units
60-64	Number of Deaths, Proximate 00000 (go to next heading) (bbbb0) zero, none likely bbbb1 1 to 2 bbbb3 3 to 6 bbbb8 7 to 16 bbb16 17 to 32 bbb32 33 to 64 bbb64 65 to 130 bb128 131 to 250 bb256 251 to 500 bb500 501 to 1,000 b1000 1,001 to 2,000 b2000 2,001 to 4,000 b4000 4,001 to 8,000 b8000 8,001 to 16,000 other bbbbb no basis for judging No. Reported _____	75	Number of Nations Supporting Initiators (identify) _____ (USA; China; USSR; UK; No. _____ ; _____ ; _____ ; _____ .
		76	Number of Nations Supporting Regime (identify) _____ (Metro. power; France; No. USA; UK; _____ ; _____ ; _____ .
		77	Reliability of Report ⓪ unclassified 1 unknown 2 questionable

65-68	Number of Deaths, Estimate
	(0000) (previous heading coded)
	bbb4 10 or less, "few"
	bb40 11 to 100, "scores,
	   many"
	b400 101 to 1,000, "hundreds"
	4000 1,001 to 10,000
	bbbb no basis for judging
	No. Reported _____
		78-80	Event Identification
			
			  G F T

			COMMENTS, OTHER INFORMATION

tion. Others, like "social area" (cols. 33–35) and "punitive action" (col. 52), form *judgmental scales* which can be treated as ordinal or interval-like measures—averaged, correlated, and otherwise manipulated statistically. Finally, some are *ratio scales,* including those for recording numbers of initiators (cols. 22–26, 27–30), duration (cols. 42–45), and deaths (cols. 60–64). The reported data for these ratio scales are usually imprecise. To avoid recording fictitiously precise numbers, the more precise scales for these three variables are *geometric scales.* Each interval in these scales is approximately twice the width of the next-lower one (5–10, 10–20, 20–40, etc.). Some researchers record this kind of imprecise quantitative data using base-10 logarithmic scales, in which each interval is ten times the preceding one (1–10; 10–100; 100–1000; etc.).

Researchers are seldom foresighted enough to devise ideal coding procedures, especially when working in a new field. In the strife study we later became aware of both conceptual and technical inadequacies in our procedures. *Conceptually,* we neglected to include two important sets of variables in the coding: the kinds of events that precipitated violence, and the immediate social and political consequences of strife. We also failed to distinguish between casualties and damage caused by "initiators" and casualties and damage caused by "coercive forces." This later made it impossible to distinguish adequately between the intensity of *initiators'* actions and the intensity of the regime's response to them, a distinction which is important to the theory. One *technical* inadequacy was that the coding categories for "motives" and "targets" were set up so that events with several motives of one type were punched on computer cards only as having "several of the above." As a result our computer analyses could not answer such questions as how many of all strife events included attempts to "seize political power," since some events so motivated were indistinguishably lumped in the "several of the above" category.

COLLECTING THE DATA   The *New York Times* was the basic data source because of its relatively comprehensive coverage of civil strife events. We supplemented it with summary regional sources like *Africa Digest* and *Hispanic-American Report,* and a few monograph studies. The first step was to identify events by scanning the *Times Index* for all countries and years in the study, and recording all entries that seemed to indicate strife. The next step was to take these lists, one country at a time, and locate each article in microfilmed copies of the *Times.* The coder then had to decide whether each reported event met a general definition of "strife" and whether it was one or a set of similar events, or part of a larger event described in a number of articles. Both decisions were usually easy. If a single event or set of related events was described, a coding sheet was filled out with all available information. If the report dealt with part of a larger event, the coder usually noted salient new information on a worksheet and went on to other reports of the same event. For complex events like guerrilla wars and waves of terrorism, coders quickly developed a knack for selecting the *Times* articles that provided periodic summaries. The information thus obtained was not "complete," but we felt that we obtained approximately accurate information on the more intense and serious occurrences of strife in the first half of the 1960s. A total of about 1,100 coding sheets[1] were prepared by four coders working during the three summer months of 1966. Thus about one man-year of effort was required for the basic coding, with additional time given later to corrections and estimates of missing data.

"Alliances and War"

Singer and Small's compilation of systematic information on alliances provides our last example of data collection procedures. The "alliance" data procedures differ from those used for "strife events" in two noteworthy respects. (1) An exhaustive compilation of alliances was made at the outset of the study, whereas no exhaustive listing of strife events was attempted. (The number of alliances was relatively small, hence it was highly desirable to have as complete a listing as possible; but the omission of some small-scale events in a much more populous universe of civil strife probably would not seriously distort the pattern of results.) (2) The second substantial difference was that, for each alliance, an intensive search was made for texts and histories, whereas for the great majority of strife events a single source was used. (Since information on a relatively few alliances would provide data for an approximately equal number of annual "cases," full and precise information was essential, whereas for strife events cross-checked information was desirable, and feasible, for only the larger and more complex occurences.)

LISTING ALLIANCES   Two kinds of sources were available for compiling a catalog of formal alliances and their texts: official publications such as the League of Nations' *Treaty Series* and Great Britain's *British and Foreign State Papers* series, and historical monographs. The two named sources provided texts for most of the 112 alliances finally included, the League series for the era 1920–39 and the British series for the entire period 1815–1939. The one major failing of these sources, Singer and Small note, "is the absence of secret treaties whose existence only comes to light years or decades later" (1966b, p. 2). A few other treaties did not appear in the above two sources because of oversights or compilers' judgments that they were inconsequential. Secret and overlooked treaties were later identified in historical monographs and the treaties series of other national governments.

---

1 This does not mean that we identified only 1,100 strife events, though. If a number of riots or demonstrations over a single issue occurred in a country at the same time, we cumulated the information from them and recorded it on a single coding sheet. In the United States in 1965, for example, there were an estimated 57 antiwar demonstrations; all were summarized on a single coding sheet.

CHARACTERISTICS OF ALLIANCES   Three characteristics of each alliance were determined in the coding process: the status of its members, the type of alliance, and the effective dates.

(1) The *status of alliance members* determined the inclusion or exclusion of a particular alliance from the study: at least two of the alliance partners had to be qualified, independent nation-members of the international system. The researchers thus had to specify criteria for membership in the international system and compile a list of nations meeting them, indicating the years in which each nation joined (and left) the international system. To qualify for listing, a political entity had to be politically autonomous, have a population of more than half a million, and be granted *de facto* recognition by Britain and France—the two nations generally regarded as the "legitimizers" of the international community during these one-and-a-quarter centuries. Compiling such a list itself required a considerable data-collection effort, described in Singer and Small 1966a. Use of this list enabled the researchers to determine that literally hundreds of the treaties listed in their sources were not "alliances," because only one or neither of their signatories were sovereign nation-members of the system.

A comparison with the "Causes of Strife" study is useful here. That study included all territorially discrete political entities—colonies and nations —which had populations of more than one million in 1962, a determination made simply by reference to the United Nations *Demographic Yearbook*. This selection of cases was justified on grounds that the causes of strife were universals that should be manifest in any large population. In the "Alliances and War" study it was necessary to determine which nations were *de facto* actors in the international arena. This is quite a different and more demanding question, the answers to which are by no means self-evident, even to a diplomatic historian. A total of 82 nations qualified at one time or another between 1815 and 1939, 23 of them being members at the beginning of the era and 64 at its conclusion. The point is that what seems at the outset a simple task of operationalizing a simple variable may require much subtlety and effort. The reader might also be surprised, and enlightened, to know that there was no standardized historical list of nations *qua* international actors before Singer and Small's efforts.

(2) *The nature of the treaty commitment* for each alliance was coded from the treaty texts and the monograph literature on that segment of diplomatic history. Three classes of relationship were specified, depending upon what the members obliged themselves to do in response to hostilities affecting one or more members:

1. *Defense Pact:* Intervene militarily on the side of any treaty partner that is attacked militarily.
2. *Neutrality and Nonaggression Pact:* Remain militarily neutral if any co-signatory is attacked. (The neutrality pact is usually more specific than the more sweeping nonaggression pact.)
3. *Entente:* Consult and/or cooperate in a crisis, including armed attack.

(3) *The life-span of each treaty* had to be specified, since the ultimate operational objective was to construct measures of the extent of alliances in force in the international system in any given year. The texts of treaties (or historical studies, in the case of secret treaties) provided initial dates, and in some cases the formal termination date was reported in official compilations and papers. However, informal terminations had to be judged from monograph sources.

To summarize, there were three operationally discrete steps in obtaining the alliance data. One was to identify the member states of the international system; the second was to list and obtain the texts of all possibly relevant treaties; and the third was to screen these treaties and code them according to their type and operative dates. All these steps required a great amount of effort in identifying, obtaining, and evaluating sources. One set of sources was needed to determine system members; another, largely independent set was needed for listing and coding the treaties. Throughout the study, then, the adequacy of the monograph sources in particular was of great importance to the researchers, for on these sources depended the reliability and validity of their data.

5.2   Constructing and Transforming Indicators

It should be evident that the numerical data which are collected, coded, or scored by procedures of the kinds just described are not always directly usable as "indicators," if we mean by "indicator" a single set of numbers for each variable, one per case, that can be compared statistically with other indicators. The fruits of data collection are often only the raw ingredients of indicators. Two different treatments may be applied to raw data, for rather different reasons. The first is *index construction,* in which raw data are variously weighted, aggregated, or combined with other data to form summary indicators of variables. The term is used here to refer to all such manipulations of raw data. In a narrower sense the term refers to ways two or more measures of different aspects of a variable are combined in what are described below as "composite" indicators. The second treatment is *data transformation,* in which either raw measures or summary indicators are fitted to a different numerical scale.

Index construction is essentially a data-reduction process, one in which a large amount of quantitative information is expressed in more summary and theoretically appropriate form. There are technical limitations on how index construction ought to be done, but the basic criteria are conceptual ones: the researcher wants above all to construct indicators that are adequate representations of underlying variables. On the other hand the reasons for *data transformation* are mainly technical. Many techniques for comparing indicators give valid, interpretable results only if the indicators have certain characteristics, such as a normal distribution of cases, no way-out cases, stable variance, or a linear relationship with one another—depending on the kind of comparisons being made. Data transformations help satisfy such requirements.

There are a great many ways to construct and transform indices, and a substantial general literature on the subject, especially index construction.[2] What follows is a brief review of the approaches illustrated by the three studies, suggesting why the investigators chose the methods they did. Some alternative methods of index construction are also mentioned.

Index Construction

Some kinds of raw data, as collected, constitute adequate indicators of theoretical variables—according to the researcher's conceptual scheme of things—and require no further treatment. Say that we wanted to determine the relative effects of geographical and demographic size of counties on the amount of funds allocated to them under a state program. The variables are easily made operational in ways that do not require any index construction:

> Geographical size = square miles
> Demographic size = population
> Funds allocated = amounts granted in dollars

No combinations or weightings of these measures seem necessary before we analyze them.

Another example is Rummel's study of levels of domestic conflict in 69 nations. His measures of conflict were the number of events of each type—riots, coups, deaths, etc.—that occurred in each nation during a three-year period. Once the data were recorded from the *New York Times Index* it remained only to sum and then analyze them (Rummel 1963). Similarly, the researcher who compares nations using the indices reported in the *World Handbook of Political and Social Indicators* need not do any further index construction. Judgmentally coded measures ordinarily do not need to be further processed either.

2 Most literature on index construction deals with the more limited problem, and particularly with the ways in which individuals' answers to particular questions, in survey and social psychological research, can be used to construct summary indicators of their attitudes, background characteristics, etc. The logic and procedures of this kind of index theory have important applications to macropolitical research. Some general treatments are Lazarsfeld and Rosenberg 1955, Section I; and Zeisel 1957, Chap. 5. More technical discussions are Coombs 1964; Galtung 1967, Chap. 3; and Torgerson 1958. The reader accustomed to the language of quantitative political research is warned that he may find the frame of reference in these studies unintelligible and the applicability of their dicta and procedures to his own data problems obscure. The problem is essentially one of the thus-far imperfect translation of language and method from one substantive field to another.

WEIGHTED MEASURES   It is often desirable to express one measure as a ratio of another; for example, nations' Gross National Product *per capita*; voting turnout in elections *as a percentage of* eligible voters; the *frequency* with which countries' chief executives leave office; and so forth. The computational procedure is simple enough. The primary measure—GNP, voting turnout, and number of executive changes in these examples—is divided by the base measure—population, eligible voters, number of years. The central reason for such weighting is to increase comparability among cases by eliminating some conceptually irrelevant source of variation. In statistical terms, it is equivalent to controlling for the effects of the base variable.

The "American Values" study offers a simple example. The raw data consisted of counts of the frequency with which words of various categories appeared in party platforms. The platforms were of widely varying length, however, from 360 to 16,331 words. Thus the frequencies depend so much on platform length that no other patterns among them can be seen. The simple solution is to express the frequencies as percentages of all words in a platform. The score for a 2,400-word platform with 12 words in the "power-doctrine" or ideology category is 0.50%, which can be compared directly with the percentage score of 0.20% obtained for a 10,000-word platform with 20 such words. In this instance relying on word counts alone would be highly misleading. To compare *groups* of platforms, Namenwirth and Lasswell averaged such percentage scores for each group. They found that the average percentage frequency of these ideological words for the twelve 1844–64 platforms was 0.22%, while for the 1944–64 platforms it more than doubled to 0.46%.

Weighting is easily accomplished. The problematic questions are *whether* to weight an indicator, and if so by what. Answers to these questions depend on technical and conceptual considerations to which the researcher must give careful thought. Not all irrelevant variation can be controlled by weighting. Failure or inability to weight an indicator is not fatal, either, because the researcher can later introduce one or more control variables in his analysis. If he suspects that population, or country size, or level of economic development, or some other background variable is systematically distorting his results, a measure of it can be separately included in statistical analysis and its effects determined (see Section 7.2).

CONSTRUCTING INDICATORS FROM "EVENT" DATA   Raw data on the properties of events and conditions often have to be aggregated or otherwise manipulated to construct basic indicators. Some event data can be aggregated simply by addition. In the "Civil Strife" study the number of strife participants in each country was determined by adding the numbers of participants in all coded events 1961–65 (using "guestimates" where necessary); total deaths were similarly computed. Separate subtotals were calculated for turmoil and rebellion as well.

TABLE 5.1. *Number of Strife Events 1961–65 Having Various Political Motives, Selected Countries*[a]

Apparent political motives	Great Britain	France	All democracies (38)	All authoritarian polities (33)
1) None	1	0	26	22
2) Retaliation	1	1	6	13
3) Seize political power	0	0	17	17
4) Increase political participation	0	0	2	3
5) Harm competing political group	1	0	15	7
6) Promote/oppose policy	4	7	57	51
7) Promote/oppose actor	0	7	28	14
8) Anti-foreign	2	0	53	15
9) Several of the above	1	7	69	53
10) Diffuse	0	0	7	15
11) No basis for judgment	0	0	19	10
Total events	10	22	299	220

[a] Tabulation from "Causes of Strife" study..

Data also were coded on a number of nominal scales such as that for "political motives," whose coding categories are shown on the coding sheet, p. 96. Coding on such nominal scales can be aggregated to form interval scales, as shown in table 5.1. The number of strife events with political motives of each type can be aggregated for each form of strife (not shown); for each country (illustrated by France and Britain); and for various groupings of countries (democratic and authoritarian in this illustration). The variables in this illustration are the categories listed down the left margin: each country's score on "promote/oppose policies" is the number of its strife events motivated by that objective, 7 for France and 4 for Britain. (Such scores could also be weighted, by expressing them as proportions of all events in the country: $7/22 = .32$ for France, $4/10 = .40$ for Britain. This would facilitate visual comparison.) Composite indicators could be constructed by combining categories. For example, we might combine the data for categories 2, 4, 6, and 7 into a composite measure of "strife with limited political objectives." Percentage comparisons would show that 50% (5 of 10) of all strife events in Great Britain were of this type, compared with 68% (15 of 22) in France. Note that all these composite indicators are ratio measures, hence a researcher would be fully justified in using the most powerful statistical techniques in his analysis.

The "Alliances and War" study provides one last example of how

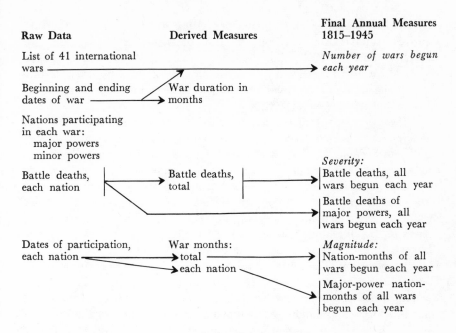

Raw Data	Derived Measures	Final Annual Measures 1815–1945
List of 41 international wars		*Number of wars begun each year*
Beginning and ending dates of war	War duration in months	
Nations participating in each war: major powers minor powers		
Battle deaths, each nation	Battle deaths, total	*Severity:* Battle deaths, all wars begun each year
		Battle deaths of major powers, all wars begun each year
Dates of participation, each nation	War months: total each nation	*Magnitude:* Nation-months of all wars begun each year
		Major-power nation-months of all wars begun each year

FIGURE 5.2. Construction of annual extent-of-war indicators, 1816–1945, from raw data on 41 wars. "Alliances and War" study, Singer and Small 1968.

data on events can be combined to form indicators. The raw data on wars was a list of all 41 international wars identified between 1815 and 1945, with information on their participants, duration, and battle casualties. This information was used to construct five measures of the number and extent of wars begun in each year, 1816–1945, as shown in Figure 5.2. In 1935, for example, the only war begun was between Italy, a major power, and Ethiopia, which was not. The war lasted from October 3, 1935, to May 9, 1936. The "number of wars begun" score for 1935 is 1; major-power battle deaths for war begun that year = 4(000); all battle deaths = 20(000); major-power war months = 7; all nation war-months = 14. Note that although the war continued into 1936, the scores for 1936 are all 0 since no wars *began* in that year.

COMPOSITE INDICATORS   The most difficult problems of index construction usually arise when a researcher has several different measures for a single variable. Such measures can be analyzed separately, as was done in the "Alliances and War" study: the five measures of "extent of war" were separately correlated with measures of "alliance aggregation" and "bipolarity." In this instance the results were all consistent with one another, thus supporting the same substantive conclusions. When different measures of variables give similar results, greater confidence can be placed in the substantive results than if only one measure of each variable is used (see Campbell and Fiske 1959). But there are many circumstances in which the investigator wants to combine different indicators of the same variable into a composite indicator. We will review here some approaches to doing so, with examples from several studies.

Two somewhat different approaches to index construction are the *inductive* and the *deductive*. We touched on the difference when discussing validity in Section 3.1. The "inductive" approach relies principally on the similarities observed among measures: empirically similar measures are combined, dissimilar ones are not. The "deductive" approach relies on prior theoretical assumptions about the relationships among measures: dissimilar measures may be combined on grounds that they tap different, uncorrelated aspects of the same underlying variable. The approaches are not absolutely distinct because there is always some element of deduction in "inductive" index construction. The initial choice of measures whose similarities are to be examined in an inductive procedure is based on some implicit or explicit theoretical notions about what things are alike and what are different. But there is a substantial difference in emphasis from one study to another, and from one researcher to another, on how much deduction versus induction is used when constructing composite indicators. Several approaches and examples are examined here.

(1) *Adding and multiplying measures.* Sometimes there are straightforward conceptual grounds for adding two or more different measures into a composite indicator, or for multiplying them. *Adding* is most clearly appropriate when the measures are of different components of what is conceptually the same variable: numbers of cherries, pears, and pineapples *can* be added if the researcher wants to generalize about "fruit." We saw above how strife data on the political motives of different events could be added in this way. Events motivated by desires for political retaliation, for increased participation, and for changing policies or politicians could reasonably be counted together on the theoretical grounds that all represent "limited political" sentiments. There is no theoretical reason for expecting additive components to be strongly correlated with one another in this example, but there may be in some others. The approach is essentially deductive.

Multiplying measures is justified if they represent two different but interacting variables which magnify one another's effects on some other variable. At one stage of the "Causes of Strife" study we used separate measures of the total *duration in days* of all strife in each country and of total *participants in strife per 100,000 population*. There is no mathematical logic by which both people and days can be measured on the same scale: they are nonadditive properties of civil strife. But if participants and duration in days are *multiplied* for each strife event, we obtain a combined measure of *man-days of strife*, which can be summed for all strife events in a country. The two separate measures are multiplicatively related to the composite "man-days" measure. Multiplicative relationships are seldom so substantively obvious. The existence of such relationships is often treated as an empirical question. If two measures when multiplied are more strongly correlated with a third, criterion measure than they are separately, a multiplicative relationship may be said to exist, and the multiplicative combination of the measures can be used as a composite indicator in further analyses.

(2) *Correlation approaches to nonadditivity.* Different indicators are seldom directly additive or multiplicative. One common, primarily inductive approach is to correlate the multiple indicators and, on the basis of the results, to add those which are strongly correlated. Another is to correlate multiple indicators with a criterion measure, and to add those indicators that are related to it in a similar way. The "Causes of Strife" study offers two examples.

Magnitude of strife was indexed in the study reported here by two nonadditive measures, one of man-days per 100,000 population (described in the preceding section) and one of deaths per 1,000,000. Both measures were badly skewed (with many low scores, a few very high ones), and so were logarithmically transformed (discussed in the next section). Their correlation for all 114 cases was .55, which supported the decision to combine them. The range and distribution of the two sets of scores were different, however, so they could not be directly added. *Standard scores* were calculated for each case (described in Section 6.2) and added. Adding standard scores has the advantage of giving precisely equal weight to the measures so treated. Any number of measures can be so added, if the researcher has conceptual or empirical grounds for ignoring their mathematical nonadditivity. There also may be theoretical grounds for regarding one measure as more important than another. The standard scores of the "more important" measure can then be weighted, i.e., multiplied by some factor like 1.5, 2, or whatever is thought appropriate.

Legitimacy refers to peoples' attitudes about the appropriateness of their governments and is very difficult to measure in any direct way. Our approach was to identify one measurable *cause* of high legitimacy and one measureable *effect* of it. The inferred cause was the extent to which a country's political institutions were developed indigenously, the effect was the length of time those institutions had endured, up to 1960, without abrupt, major changes. Judgmental scales were devised for each of these variables and coded for 114 countries. There was no reason to expect a strong positive correlation between these two measures. The argument for their construction would be contradicted only by a substantially negative correlation—$r = +.17$. The argument would be supported if both measures correlated in the same way with magnitude of strife 1961–65. This was the result: the r's were $-.30$ and $-.26$. This kind of criterion validation justified our adding the two measures into a composite index. Both judgmental scales had the same number of categories, and cases were distributed on them in an approximately "normal" manner, so they were directly added, rather than transformed as in the above example.

In the two preceding examples only two measures were combined in the composite indicators. Any number of separate measures or indicators may be collected, intercorrelated, and a composite indicator constructed by adding those with the highest intercorrelations. But the most efficient and most purely inductive technique for constructing composite indicators from a number of measures is *factor analysis,* described below.

(3) *Index construction by factor analysis.* Factor analysis is a data-reduction technique to be described at more length in Section 7.2 Briefly, the researcher begins with a number of measures of one or more variables. They should be ratio, interval, interval-like, or dichotomous measures. Factor analysis identifies the underlying "dimensions" of common variation in these measures. The more closely related they are to one another the fewer the important dimensions. Each major dimension then provides the basis for constructing a "factor score" for each case, which is a weighted combination of the measures related to that dimension. Each set of factor scores for a set of cases is a composite indicator, suitable for use in all kinds of statistical analysis.

(4) *Other approaches to composite indicators.* There are also other inductive methods for constructing composite indicators. They have been devised for analyzing data on individuals but are applicable to macropolitical comparisons as well. One of them is Guttman or cumulative scaling (see Guttman 1944). An innovative application to country data on political instability is Nesvold 1969. Sigelman has recently applied the technique to the cross-national measurement of political development (1971).

There are also various judgmental ways of combining different measures into a single scale. Two of the best-known techniques were devised by Likert and Thurston. Each employs panels of judges to determine how questionnaire items (one item = one measure) can best be combined to represent a single attitudinal variable. Some of these techniques seem adaptable to macropolitical analysis, particularly for combining the categories of different judgmental scales into a single index. A useful reference on psychometric scale construction is Edwards 1957.

Data Transformations

We have referred at several points to the need for transforming data, and to measures in the three studies that were transformed. There are three principal reasons for transforming data in macropolitical research.

(1) One is to *normalize* them, that is, to make the distribution of scores approximate the idealized normal curve shown in Figure 5.3. Many of the statistical techniques described in the next chapter technically require nor-

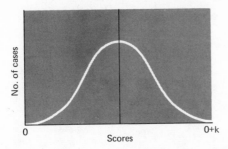

FIGURE 5.3. Idealized "normal distribution" of data.

mally distributed data. To the extent that they are not normally distributed, the results of statistical analysis are distorted.

(2) The second reason is to *simplify relationships* between two (or more) variables. For example, when raw scores on two measures are plotted against one another they sometimes prove to have a nonlinear relationship, as shown in the hypothetical example in Figure 5.4. But most correlation techniques make the mathematical assumption that the measures correlated have the simplest possible relationship, i.e., a linear one. If the measures in Figure 5.4. were correlated without transformation, the correlation coefficient obtained would understate their actual relationship.

(3) The third reason for transformation is to *stabilize variance,* which is desirable when using analysis-of-variance techniques (variance is defined in Section 6.2) and also for correlation and regression analysis. The problem was encountered in the "American Values" study, where the scores of early platforms on a particular value might range from .50 to .80, clustered closely

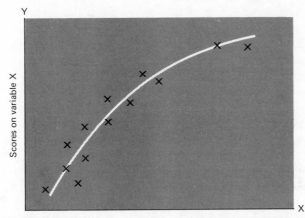

FIGURE 5.4. A hypothetical nonlinear relationship between two variables, after Blalock (1960, p. 313).

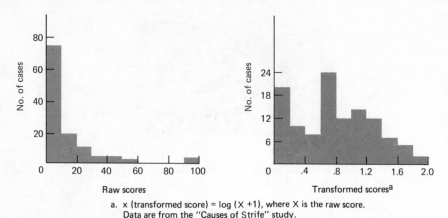

a. x (transformed score) = log (X +1), where X is the raw score.
Data are from the "Causes of Strife" study.

FIGURE 5.5. Actual distribution of scores, "turmoil" in 114 countries 1946–59, before and after logarithmic transformation.

around the average score, while the scores for the later platform would vary much more widely, say from .60 to 2.40.

Thus, in all three instances transformations are used to help meet the mathematical requirements of statistical techniques. The penalty for not making the transformations is reduced accuracy of results—usually but not necessarily a falsely low estimate of the strength of relationship between two measures. An important qualification is that such transformations are required only for some techniques. Generally, if the researcher intends to analyse his data using interval techniques, then an approximation of normality and linear relationships is needed. Normal distributions are not required by the "nonparametric" techniques used for analyzing most dichotomized, nominal, and ordinal data (see Chapter 6). On the other hand consideration should be given to stabilizing variance when analysis-of-variance techniques are being used. Another equally important qualification is that there often are theoretical and substantive reasons for knowing just what the shape of a relationship between two variables is. The preferred procedure, outlined in the next chapter, is to plot raw scores for two variables on a graph and examine how they are related to one another, or in some other way test whether they have a straight-line relationship or some curvilinear one. Linearity can later be imposed on them by data transformations, if necessary for graphic presentation or statistical analysis.

Macropolitical data are most often transformed to increase their normality. A very common kind of nonnormal distribution in political data is shown on the left side of Figure 5.5; the data are for extent of turmoil 1946–59, using data collected by Eckstein (1962). By far the most widely used transformation is logarithmic (to the base 10). A constant is added to the score for each case and the appropriate logarithm determined from a log table. The constant added is usually 1, and is needed because 0 scores cannot be logged (the log of 1 is 0). If there are no raw scores of 0, a constant need not be added. When a logarithmic transformation is applied to the raw scores in Figure 5.5, the distribution of logged scores is as shown on the right. The distribution is still skewed toward the lower end—there is no way to "transform" or spread out the 20 cases with raw scores of 0!—but it much more closely approximates the ideal normal curve than did the raw scores. The researcher can now be more confident in interpreting results of analysis, and in particular he no longer need worry that two extreme cases, which in the raw scores were in the 90–100 range, will distort the entire pattern.

There is great variation in the distribution of scores of macro-social, -economic, and -political data, as the reader can see for himself by looking through the distribution curves plotted for each variable in the *World Handbook of Political and Social Indicators* (Russett et al. 1964). Log transformations will not necessarily normalize them, though the compilers of the *World Handbook* did not use any other kind of transformation. In fact there are whole families of transformations, of which logging is one of the strongest. When raw scores are very highly skewed, as in Figure 5.5, strong transformations are in order. There are many milder ones, though, which ought to be considered when skewing is not so pronounced. The square root of raw scores can be taken, for example, which is a transformation that is considerably milder than logging. The "Causes of Strife" study made frequent use of geometric progressions, which were adjusted to suit the actual distributions of scores. Geometric progressions are members of what is called the "power family" of transformations. The logarithmic, square-root, and power transformations are all "one-bend" transformations: they attenuate scores only toward one end of the original range. There are also many two-bend transformations which attentuate both ends of the range. One, the *arcsine*, was used to stabilize variances in the "American Values" study. For a comprehensive review of kinds of transformations and the effects they have on data see Kruskal 1968.

A final comment about transformations and linear relationships: inspection of the distribution of scores on a measure usually will indicate if and how strong a transformation is needed. But whether or not a transformation is needed to increase the linearity of a relationship can be determined only by plotting the measures to be compared. The conventional procedure in macropolitical analysis has been to log any substantially skewed measure (but not to consider other possible transformations), and to ignore the possibilities of nonlinear relationships unless there were a priori reasons for expecting them. Neither of these two traditions is necessarily worth emulating; the researcher who ignores them might attain some additional precision at the cost of some additional work.

6

Methods of Data Analysis: Describing and comparing two variables

This and the next chapter are not a condensed text in statistics, nor are they a "cookbook," the faintly derogatory term applied to the indispensable texts and handbooks that provide detailed instructions about the use of particular techniques. *The central objective of these chapters is to explain the role of statistical methods in the research process.* This is attempted in two related ways. First, we provide a general guide to some basic graphical and statistical techniques, and second, we demonstrate their applications in the three studies.

The politimetrician who plans to use these techniques in his own work ought to consult some of the many texts which spell out their assumptions and derivations, provide computational equations, and offer many substantive applications. He may want to refer to advanced texts, especially in econometrics, for information on a number of newer and more complex techniques that are not discussed here. Reading in the methodological literature will be necessary to understand the intricacies of technical debates, only hinted at here, about the proper uses and interpretations of tests of significance, regression coefficients, and so forth. These two chapters thus offer only a general survey of the problems and procedures of data analysis in politimetrics.

One other point needs making here. We rarely set out our research plans without making preliminary decisions about how the data are to be analyzed. We have seen at several points that the mode of analysis is interdependent with a number of other aspects of research design. Some of these interdependencies will become evident in the discussion to follow.

6.1   The Nature of Statistics and Its Methods

Statistical methods are mathematical systems that exist independently of any applications, though many of them were developed to analyze data on concrete problems of agricultural and industrial production, census taking, education, and economic and psychological research. These chapters do not deal with the logical derivations of these methods. But the user should recognize their independent, analytic nature. Whether the relationships specified in an abstract equation hold true for the data he is studying depends on whether his data meet the underlying mathematical conditions of the system. If they do not, then the connection between the results of statistical analysis and the "real world" is problematical. Statistics as a discipline certainly has limitations. For example, there are problems of political data analysis for which existing methods are not wholly suitable. But most errors and follies of statistical analysis are the doing of those who use the methods, not of the methods themselves. They are powerful tools of description, theory testing, and induction; they can be applied to good and bad data with equal ease and no complaint.

Not all methods of analysis are equally relevant to macropolitical data. The most useful and widely used are the subjects of the following sections. Section 6.2 discusses *descriptive* techniques for analyzing and summarizing single measures. Graphic analysis is an especially important but somewhat neglected way of comparing measures; it is the subject of Section 6.3. Graphic analysis complements the techniques described in Section 6.4: *tests of significance,* which are made to determine whether measures have more than a random relationship with one another, and *measures of association,* which show how strongly or closely two measures are correlated. There are correlational methods for dealing with any number of measures. Section 6.4 deals with two-variable or *bivariate* comparisons. Extensions of bivariate analysis include time-series analysis, multivariate comparisons, and causal inference techniques, all of which are examined in Chapter 7.

6.2   Descriptive Analysis

The first step in almost any quantitative analysis is to examine and summarize the most important measures and indicators being studied. This is done independently of any comparisons among measures and is often a preliminary step to making transformations and constructing composite indicators.

Range, Mean, and Median

The simplest quantitative summary the researcher can make of any measure is to specify its range, mean, and median. Table 6.1 lists several measures of the extent of civil strife from the "Causes of Strife" study; we shall use these measures to illustrate various techniques in this chapter. The first measure is "man-days of strife per 100,000 population, logged." Its *range* is 0.0 to 5.11, i.e., the span from the minimum to the maximum scores. Its *mean* or average score of 2.475 is the total of all scores divided by the number of cases. Technically the average score is known as the *arithmetic mean,* and is an estimate needed for a number of analytic techniques. The *median* is an alternative to the mean; it designates the middle score of the distribution, the one which has the same number of cases above it as below it. The median of the "man-days" measure is not immediately apparent because the scores are not tabled in exact order. If they were listed in rank order, we would find that the median lies between the United Kingdom score of 2.426 and Australia's score of 2.643, in other words approximately 2.50. (Note that a useful convention when making tables is to list cases according to their rank on the most important measure in the table.)

Frequency Distributions

Frequency distributions are tabulations of the numbers of cases having each successive score, or group of scores, on a measure. Several examples were given in Chapter 5. In Table 5.1 (p. 104) the numbers of strife events having various categories of political motives were tabulated for all democracies, and for all authoritarian countries. These tabulations by category are frequency distributions; they are usually reported in proportions or percentages (a percentage is a proportion multiplied by 100), along with data on the total number of cases and, sometimes, the absolute numbers of cases in each category.

When the scores are measured on an interval scale, frequency distributions are constructed by grouping the scores in larger intervals of equal size. The frequency distribution of the "man-days" measure in Table 6.1 is shown in Table 6.2. This sort of information can also be presented graphically, for example in a bar graph of the kind illustrated in Figure 5.4 (p. 109). Frequency distributions have several functions. One is as a way of summarily reporting data. They provide a useful summary in research reports even if the individual scores are also listed. A second function is to estimate the distribution curve of the data, an item of information that is useful in deciding about transformations (see Section 5.2). A glance at Table 6.2 confirms that the "man-days" measure closely approximates a normal distribution: the middle intervals have the largest number of cases and the intervals toward either extreme have substantially fewer.

The *Lorenz curve* is a way of comparing two cumulative frequency

TABLE 6.1 *Measures of Civil Strife in 38 Democracies, 1961–65*

Country[a]	Man-days of strife per 100,000, logged[b]	Deaths per million, logged[b]	Total magnitude (summed standard scores)[c]
New Zealand	0.0	0.0	−2.544
Norway	0.0	0.0	−2.544
Netherlands	0.0	0.0	−2.544
Denmark	0.0	0.0	−2.544
Sweden	0.0	0.0	−2.544
Switzerland	0.041	0.0	−2.519
Jamaica	0.905	0.0	−1.993
Finland	1.440	0.0	−1.666
Costa Rica	1.456	0.0	−1.656
Puerto Rico	1.506	0.0	−1.625
Ireland	1.645	0.0	−1.540
Japan	2.221	0.0	−1.189
Mexico	1.706	0.359	−1.165
Malaya	2.297	0.078	−1.069
United Kingdom	2.426	0.034	−1.032
Uruguay	2.183	0.197	−1.027
Turkey	2.057	0.340	−0.969
Chile	2.345	0.190	−0.934
Australia	2.643	0.0	−0.931
Canada	2.831	0.033	−0.785
U.S.A.	2.829	0.154	−0.673
Morocco	2.185	0.609	−0.638
Austria	3.141	0.0	−0.627
Brazil[a]	3.238	0.077	−0.496
West Germany	3.473	0.0	−0.425
Israel	3.173	0.210	−0.410
Ceylon	3.655	0.057	−0.260
Greece[a]	3.573	0.131	−0.240
Italy	3.841	0.037	−0.165
India	2.960	0.622	−0.152
Libya[a]	3.602	0.131	+0.221
France	4.139	0.338	0.300
Philippines	3.571	0.866	0.450
Belgium	5.111	0.216	0.778
Singapore	4.165	1.322	1.242
Bolivia[a]	4.049	2.190	1.988
Venezuela	4.954	2.053	2.412
Colombia	4.691	2.902	3.050
Means	2.475	0.358	−0.696
Standard deviations	1.469	0.673	1.353

a Listed in increasing order of total magnitude scores. Judgments that these countries are "democratic," in the sense of having plural institutions and some freedom of political competition, are based on conditions in the early 1960s. Countries footnoted (a) were in 1971 largely or wholly authoritarian.

b Scores = $(1 + X)_{\log}$, where the constant 1 is added because 0 scores cannot be logged.

c Standard scores are explained in the accompanying text. These are calculated from the "man-days" and "deaths" scores for all 114 countries in the "Causes of Strife" study, not for the 38 democracies alone, both for reasons of convenience and so that each country would have a unique score, however countries were grouped for analysis.

TABLE 6.2   *Frequency Distribution of "Man-Days of Strife Per 100,000" in 38 democracies*

Man-days logged	Number of polities	Percent of polities	Cumulative percentage
0.00–0.99	7	18	18
1.00–1.99	5	13	31
2.00–2.99	11	29	60
3.00–3.99	9	24	84
4.00–4.99	5	13	97
5.00–5.99	1	3	100
	38	100	

distributions that is increasingly being used in political research to show how equally or unequally something is distributed: how equally legislative seats are apportioned by population, how equally land or wealth is distributed, and so forth. The Lorenz curve, other measures of inequality, and applications are presented in Alker (1965, chap. 3), Alker and Russett (1966), and Russett (1964).

Standard Deviations, Standard Scores

The *standard deviation* is a measure of how widely a set of scores are dispersed around their mean. Along with the mean, it is the most widely reported and useful summary measure for describing data. One substantive example should suggest why it is usually advisable to estimate dispersion when interpreting data. Suppose that we are evaluating the effects of the Cuban revolution on economic well-being, and find that Cubans' per capita income in 1958 was $302 compared with $280 in 1972 (the 1958 datum is correct, the 1972 datum is hypothetical). What we would also have to know before drawing any conclusions from this is whether there was any change in the proportion of people with very high and very low incomes, i.e., whether the dispersion around the mean was smaller, hence more egalitarian, in 1972 than in 1958.

The verbal definition of the standard deviation s is the *square root of the mean of the squared deviations from the mean*. The definitional equation is:

$$s = \sqrt{\frac{\Sigma (X - \overline{X})^2}{N}}$$

where X is the notation used for the scores being analyzed. It can be seen that the greater the average difference of the scores from the mean, the greater is s. If the square root is not taken, the statistic is symbolized s^2 and is called the *variance*.

	Man-days of strife per 100,000, logged (N = 114)	Deaths per million, logged (N = 114)
$\overline{X}$	2.837	0.864
s	1.638	1.062

The standard deviation is widely useful in describing and drawing conclusions from single measures. Along with the mean it is also used for some kinds of comparisons of variables. Finally, it provides the basis for computing *standard scores,* whose equation is:

$$Z = \frac{X - \overline{X}}{s}$$

Standard scores are frequently referred to as Z *scores.* When this formula is applied to a set of data, it transforms it into a distribution with a mean of 0 and each case's score expressed in its number of standard deviations above or below the mean. Standard scores have a number of uses, one of which we have already mentioned: combining different measures. This was done with the "man-days" and "deaths" measures of civil strife, for example, working with the accompanying table's values of X and s for all 114 countries (of which the 38 democracies are a subset). The data for Jamaica in Table 6.1 illustrate how this was done. Jamaica's "man-days" = 0.905. Using the above formula, Jamaica's standard score Z for man-days is

$$\frac{0.905 - 2.837}{1.638} = -1.179$$

"Deaths" in Jamaica from strife were zero. The standard score for deaths is similarly calculated:

$$\frac{0.000 - 0.864}{1.062} = -.817$$

A zero deaths score thus is slightly less than one standard deviation below the average. It is not farther below because the "deaths" distribution is so sharply skewed. Adding these two standard scores gives -1.993, the "total magnitude" score shown for Jamaica in Table 6.1. (The justifiability of combining measures of variables that are not directly additive is discussed in Section 5.2.)

The procedures sketched above are simple to use and provide ways to get considerable information from political data. If the data being studied are a sample, the interpretations of statistics like the mean and standard deviation are more complex. And note that these statistics usually are used for describing *cross-sectional* data. *Time-series* measures require description of their trends as well, using methods discussed in the first section of the next chapter.

6.3 Analyzing Relationships between Two Variables: Graphic Analysis

We are seldom satisfied with just describing measures. More often we want to know what relationship one variable has to another, and usually we have in mind some implicit or explicit notion about their casual connections. We can use three systematic techniques to study how one variable is related to another: *statistical tests of significance, measures of association,* and *graphic analysis.* I have listed them here in increasing order of how much information they give us about how data are related. Ironically, they have been used in political data analysis in reverse frequency to their information value. Tests of significance are most often used in politimetrics to determine whether two variables are or are not "significantly related." Clearly this is something we want to know about our data, but in most research designs this is only the beginning. We could take almost any large set of political indicators and find that some were "significantly related" to others, and many more which were not. The more interesting question usually is *how* strongly or closely any two variables are related. Measures of association, including the various correlation coefficients, help answer the question of whether a "significant" relationship is important in a substantive sense. A measure of association is still only one summary statistic, though, and if a relationship is not linear, or if its cases are oddly distributed, it is not an *accurate* statistic either. A graph or plot of the relationship between two measures is more informative than a correlation coefficient alone. From it we can usually see whether a relationship is approximately linear, and whether cases tend to cluster in one or another part of the plot. Most usefully of all, we can see where each particular case is in relation to others, and can pinpoint the "deviant" or "outlier" cases, those which deviate most from the relationship being studied. An examination of deviant cases is instructive about the adequacy of our measures, the consistency of our cases, and other variables that ought to be taken into account in analysis. Measures of association should not be substituted for graphic analysis; the two kinds of analysis are complementary.

We will examine some principles of graphic analysis in this section and illustrate them with some of the "Causes of Strife" data. In the next section we survey some of the more common tests of association and significance. We shall see there that graphic analysis often clarifies the interpretation of statistical tests, while correlation and regression analysis help make explicit the results of graphic analysis.

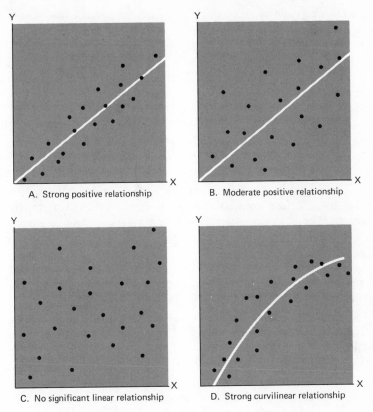

FIGURE 6.1. Hypothetical graphed relationships

Principles of Graphic Analysis

In graphic analysis two measures are first plotted against one another on graph paper. The units of one measure are marked off along the base or X axis, and the units of the second are marked off on the vertical or Y axis. Then each case is located on the graph at its coordinates—the intersection of lines drawn at right angles from the case's respective scores on the two axes. Four scattergrams that might result from plotting are shown in Figure 6.1. The distributions are hypothetical, so no units of measurement are shown along either axis. The lines drawn through the coordinates are lines of "best fit," or "least squares," which pass through the intersection of the means of the two sets of scores and thereby summarize the relationship. How best-fit lines are calculated and interpreted is explained below.

Scattergram (a) in Figure 6.1 shows a strong positive relationship: the higher the "X" score the higher the "Y" score, without much deviation.

Relationships as close as this are rare in social research.[1] Plot (b) is more representative of what the researcher can hope to find in political data. The coordinates have a clear trend but there is a good deal of variation around the best-fit line. Plot (c) is an example of what we hope *not* to find, but very often do: there is no apparent relation between increasing scores on X and an increase or decrease in scores on Y. By a stretch of visual imagination we might detect a slight trend from lower left to upper right. Such weak relationships will often occur by chance. Tests of significance and association must be applied to them to determine whether they signify anything more than a random relationship. But it is not likely that a researcher would impute much substantive importance to a pattern like that shown in Figure 6.1(c). The last scattergram, (d), shows a relationship that would almost never be detected in a correlational analysis: a curve, not a straight line, provides the best fit. Conventional correlational statistics assume a monotonic, linear relationship between variables. Curvilinear relationships such as this are not identifiable unless the researcher looks for them, using graphic or other techniques.

Before going on to more technical issues, a few points should be made about the mechanics of graphing data. One is how to choose which measure to place on which axis. It is both customary and useful to plot the dependent variable, called Y, from the X or horizontal axis. This is described as "plotting Y on X," and the investigator often thinks of it in terms of increases in scores along the X axis "causing" proportional changes in the Y scores on the vertical axis. If the researcher has no causal notions in mind then it matters little which measure is plotted against which. But the mathematical equation for the best-fit line differs according to whether Y is plotted on X or vice versa.

A second mechanical question is what scales to use along the two axes. It is important for visual inspection and presentation that the scores along one axis not be unduly compressed or stretched out in comparison with the other. Such distortions often mislead, in much the same way that a graph which does not show the zero or base point misleads. A rule of thumb for plotting data is that the units of measure on the axes should have approximately the same ratio to one another as their standard deviations (s). This was done in preparing Figure 6.2. The s of "deaths from strife" is about 0.7, that of "man-days" is about 1.5. Their ratio is approximately 1:2, so in Figure 6.2 each unit on the "deaths" axis is equal to two units on the "man-

---

[1] We might equally well find *negative* relationships among variables, in which every increase in X is associated with a corresponding decrease in Y. The slope of the best-fit line in negative relationships is from upper left to lower right. The researcher may find it convenient to plot all significant relationships with a "positive" slope. If so, a negative plot can be transformed into a positive one by reversing the measures on one axis. If the X scores range from 0 to 100, for example, the scores on the X axis can be arranged from 100 to 0. This is only a matter of graphic convenience and does not change the computed slope or the interpretation of the results.

days" axis. The researcher who follows this rule of thumb will be able to see the relationship with a minimum of distortion.

The last mechanical question is one of time and efficiency. Graphing can be very time-consuming, especially if we are working with many measures or cases. A number of package computer programs include plotting routines, which the user is well-advised to use for any relationship of possible interest in his analysis. Otherwise we can simplify our task somewhat by plotting only the most important or summary measures being studied.

Best-Fit Lines in Graphic Analysis

A more technical aspect of graphic analysis is how we determine the best-fit line and define it in algebraic terms. If two measures have a perfect, straight-line relationship, the line can be drawn by inspection. The algebraic equation for any such line is given in these general terms: $Y = a + b(X)$. We can determine the Y score of any case in a perfect linear relationship from its X score by multiplying X by the constant b and adding the constant a. When the relationship is not perfect—and it almost never is, except in hypothetical illustrations—the best-fit line is the one which fits the Y scores with the greatest average accuracy. The algebraic equation for such a line is called a *linear regression* equation. Verbally, it is defined as the equation which minimizes the squared differences between the *predicted* values of Y, symbolized Y' or $\hat{Y}$, and the *observed* values of Y. The equation for any straight-line relationship can be determined by solving the following equation for the constants a and b:

$$a = \bar{Y} - b\bar{X}$$

$$b = \frac{N \sum XY - (\sum X)(\sum Y)}{N \sum X^2 - (\sum X)^2}$$

where N is the number of cases and the symbol Σ means "sum of," $\Sigma\, X$ is the sum of all the X scores, $\Sigma\, XY$ is the sum of the product of each case's X and Y scores, and so forth. The a and b estimates are then inserted in the general equation, $Y' = a + b(X)$.

An example using real data illustrates some of these principles. Figure 6.2 shows a plot of "deaths from strife" (Y) on "man-days of strife" (X) for the 38 democracies. The equations given above for calculating a and b in the regression equation can be used to fit a straight line to these data and any others, whatever the actual shape of the relationship. The equation for the best-fit line in Figure 6.2 is $Y' = -.26 + .25X$. This indicates that the best estimate of the Y (deaths) score of a country can be determined by multiplying its X (man-days) score by .25 and subtracting .26 from the result. Such "predicted" values of Y all will fall exactly on the line itself. Several general properties of this and other regression equations are worth noting. The best-fit line always passes through the intersection of the means

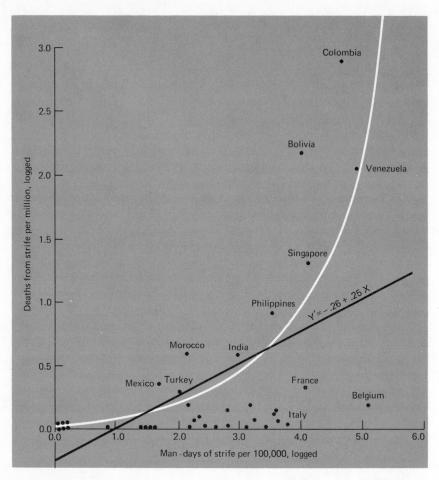

FIGURE 6.2. Man-days of strife, graphed against deaths from strife, 1961–65, in 38 democracies.

of the X and Y scores. The value of a is the point at which the regression line crosses the 0 axis on Y, $-.26$ in the figure. The value of b is known as the *slope* of the regression line. It is positive or negative depending on the slope, and indicates the amount by which the estimated score for Y changes for each unit change in X. Comparison of slopes from one set of data to another provides the basis for various kinds of substantive interpretations. One last, terminological note: a and b are the symbols conventionally used in equations based on data from samples. Constants in equations for data representing complete populations or universes are represented by the Greek letters α and β.[2]

---

[2] Somewhat confusingly, the letter ß (beta) is also used to symbolize standard weights in multiple regression equations; see Section 7.2.

One reason for examining the relationship between man-days and deaths from strife is to determine whether there is a consistent relationship between increasing participation in peaceful protest (a major component of man-days in the democracies) and the escalation of protest into violence, as reflected in deaths. The regression equation suggests a distinct relationship of this sort. Once a low threshold is reached, each 1.0 unit increase in man-days is likely to be associated with an increase of 0.25 units of "deaths." This "best-fit" line is represented by the solid line in Figure 6.2. But another interpretation of the data is equally plausible. It is that a *parabolic* relationship holds between deaths and man-days, represented by the curved, dotted line. There are statistical procedures, not reviewed here, that can be used to determine whether a parabolic or linear equation best fits such data. Note that if the parabolic interpretation is correct in this instance, there is no threshold effect.

The data plotted in Figure 6.2 also illustrate an important point about data transformations. Both the deaths and man-day figures are logged, which is a strong transformation (see Section 5.2). It is often difficult to interpret the substantive meaning of relationships, like Figure 6.2, between transformed variables. But when both measures are expressed in logarithmic terms, the regression equation has a direct and useful interpretation. The *b* weight represents the *proportional or percentage change in Y that results from a proportional change in X*. If we accept the linear regression equation for Figure 6.2, this "proportionality" interpretation means that each 1% increase in man-days of strife "causes" an increase of 0.25% in deaths.

The linear regression equation identifies a threshold of man-days below which deaths are unlikely to occur, as we noted above. This is graphically represented by the fact that the best-fit line crosses the X axis before Y, "deaths," reaches 0. We can determine the threshold by setting $Y' = 0$ and solving for X in the regression equation: the threshold is $X = 1.04$. Since this is a logged score we can convert it to a raw score using a log table, subtract the constant 1, and determine that the threshold is approximately 10 man-days of strife per 100,000. Putting this and the preceding information together, the data suggest that among the democratic nations, a 100% increase in man-days of strife, say from 100 to 200 per million people per five years, would on the average be accompanied by a 25% increase in deaths per million.

Analysis of Residuals

Before we rush out to report such a "scientific finding," though, we should consider two other interpretations of the data plot. We can see that there is an enormous spread of cases around the best-fit line, especially in the upper ranges. The "parabolic curve" interpretation is attractive, but both measures have already been logged. Since that is a very strong transformation, it counsels caution about further transformations. Another approach

is to *analyze the residuals*—which are the differences between the actual
Y scores ("deaths") and the Y' scores predicted by the equation. We should
be especially concerned with the cases that are farthest from the regression
line. Although only some of the cases are named on the figure, a pattern
is immediately apparent: all the countries with significantly more deaths
than we would predict from their man-days scores are non-European nations. Some of them, including Bolivia and Morocco, have only dubious
standing as democracies. By contrast, the nations with substantially less-than-
predicted deaths are prosperous European democracies.

What we now propose to do is to study more systematically whether
and how the European versus non-European distinction affects the man-
days deaths relationship. There are a number of ways this might be done.
One is to calculate the residual scores for each case and to plot them against
or correlate them with whatever measures we think might help explain them.
A second approach to the question is to divide the cases according to some
criterion, in this instance according to whether they are European or non-
European, and calculate separate regression lines. A third approach, beyond
the scope of this example, would be to do a *multiple regression* analysis,
including a third variable as a control (see Section 7.2). You should keep
in mind that the following application is a special case of procedures which
are applicable to analyzing residuals in almost any kind of interval-like
data.

The residuals for each case are listed in Table 6.3. Residuals are
arithmetically determined by using the regression equation to calculate the
predicted value of deaths for each man-days score. This estimated (Y')
value is then subtracted from the actual value for Y. Residuals can also be
estimated directly from the scattergram, if the cases have been precisely
plotted and the regression line accurately drawn. In graphic analysis the
residual score is the number of Y scale units that each case is above or below
the regression line (at right angles to the X axis, not to the regression line).
Cases above the line are *positive residuals,* having more Y than predicted.
Cases below the line are *negative residuals,* with less-than-predicted Y. When
we examine the residuals in Table 6.3, we see that one of our original specu-
lations is confirmed: except for the bracketed zero-strife countries, almost
all the positive and low negative residuals are non-European countries. The
meaning is clear enough. A given quantum of strife in man-days is likely to
be much more deadly in non-European than European democracies. The
statistical test of this is to divide them on some reasonable grounds and
calculate their regression lines separately. This is done is Figure 6.3. The
"European" group of 19 democracies includes the Western European countries plus Israel, Australia, Canada, New Zealand, and the United States,
denoted on the scattergram by crosses. The "non-European" group includes
all the others. The results are two strikingly different regression lines, each of
which provides a good visual fit to almost all cases in the subgroups. More-

TABLE 6.3   *Residuals in "Deaths from Strife" as Predicted from "Man-Days of Strife"*

Polity[a]	"Deaths" Residuals (actual minus predicted values)[b]	Polity[a]	"Deaths" Residuals (actual minus predicted values)[b]
Belgium	−.80	Costa Rica	−.10
Italy	−.68	Finland	−.10
W. Germany	−.62	Uruguay	−.09
Ceylon	−.59	Jamaica[c]	+.03
Austria	−.53	Turkey	.09
Greece	−.50	India	.14
Brazil	−.47	Mexico	.19
France	−.43	Philippines	.24
Canada	−.42	Switzerland[c]	.25
Libya	−.41	New Zealand[c]	.26
Australia	−.40	Norway[c]	.26
Israel	−.32	Netherlands[c]	.26
United Kingdom	−.32	Denmark[c]	.26
Japan	−.30	Sweden[c]	.26
U.S.A.	−.30	Morocco	.32
Malaya	−.23	Singapore	.54
Ireland	−.15	Venezuela	1.07
Chile	−.14	Bolivia	1.44
Puerto Rico	−.12	Colombia	1.99

[a] Listed in order of increasing residuals.
[b] Actual values (scores) are listed in Table 6.2; the predicted values were computed from the regression equation in Figure 6.2, $Y' = -.26 + .25X$. A negative residual indicates that the polity had fewer deaths from strife than predicted on the basis of its man-days of strife. A positive residual indicates that it had more than predicted.
[c] These countries experienced little or no strife and no deaths, hence their positive residuals are only an artifact of the analysis.

over the regression equations suggest a major change in the conclusions we arrived at on the basis of the combined grouping. Each 100% increase in man-days of strife in the European democracies is likely to lead to an increase in deaths of less than 4%, compared with an average 60% increase in deaths in the non-European democracies. *Why* this should be so is not something to be considered further here, but it is open to many kinds of empirical and theoretical inquiry.

6.4   Analyzing Relationships between Two Variables: Tests of Association and Significance

I have described and illustrated graphic analysis in considerable detail because statistics texts usually give it little attention. Statistical measures of association and significance tests are more numerous, more complex, and

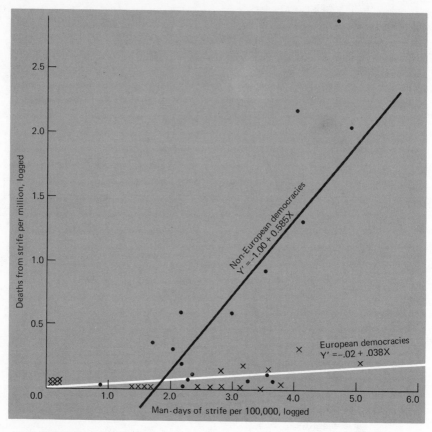

FIGURE 6.3. Deadly strife in European and non-European democracies

presented in more detail in the texts, so what follows is a brief and partial survey. The key to this survey is Table 6.4 (pp. 130–31), which lists most of the statistical tests in general use for examining relationships between two variables.

Tests of Association

Tests of association have been devised for most quantitative comparisons; they show the strength or closeness of relationship between two measures or indicators. Most of these tests are constructed so that if variable Y can be estimated exactly from X, the absolute value of the test statistic is 1.00; whereas if there is no relationship between the two, the test statistic is 0.00. The tests of association for ordinal and interval measures vary from -1.00 to $+1.00$. That is, they show both how strong a relation is and whether it is positive (each increase in X is associated with an increase in

Y) or negative (each increase in X is associated with a decrease in Y). There are tests of association which do not vary between 0.0 and 1.0, but because of this they are not easy to interpret.

Tests of Significance

Tests of *significance* are designed to show how probable, or improbable, some statistical result is. The rationale for tests of significance is easy enough to understand from the following illustration. Many of us have had elderly relatives who claimed that when their joints ached, we were in for a major change in the weather within the next day or so. Now we know that aging joints frequently ache, and the weather often changes, so that we could expect quite by chance that the two would occasionally be connected. Our skeptical question is, "What proportion of correct predictions do we require before accepting that Uncle Simon's left knee really responds to changes in barometric pressure?" This skeptical question is a *null hypothesis:* it states that there is no relationship. If we organize an informal experiment and find that Uncle Simon is right in 9 out of 10 cases, our conclusion is not likely to be in doubt; but if he is right only 4 out of 10 we will probably be as perplexed as before. Is it coincidence, or an imperfect barometer? Significance tests will show what number and proportion of correct to incorrect predictions are needed for us to come to a conclusion at a given level of confidence. Uncle Simon, on the other hand, may claim that his knee is a *perfect* predictor of weather changes. This presents us with another kind of null hypothesis: that there is *no significant difference* between aches and rains. Here again, significance tests help us decide how many correct predictions are needed to accept or reject this null hypothesis at a given level of confidence.

The example can be generalized. Assume that we have measured two properties of a set of cases and want to determine whether or not they are similar. The two extreme possibilities are that they are identical, or that they are entirely independent. These possibilities occupy the ends of the following continuum. Significance tests provide estimates of the *probable accuracy* of either of the null hypotheses, approaching but never reaching absolute certainty. The probabilities vary according to the observed closeness of the relationship between X and Y, and the number of observations for each. Significance tests do not, however, provide much information about

FIGURE 6.4. Degree of Similarity or Association Between X and Y

the area of uncertainty between the extremes; they do not indicate the *degree* of similarity or association.

The most common use of significance tests in politimetrics is to test the *null hypothesis* that measures of two variables are unrelated. When an investigator reports that his results are significant "at the .05 level," he is saying that he rejects the null hypothesis because the likelihood of its occurring by chance is less than 5%. Scholarly skepticism generally precludes politimetricians from rejecting the "no relationship" hypothesis unless the probability of error is .05 or less ("error" in this instance being to accept Uncle Simon's knee as a barometer when the connection is only coincidental). Significance levels of .10 are sometimes reported diffidently in "suggestive" support of an argument. Probabilities as low as .01, .001, and beyond are pointed to with increasing certainty and pride. At the other end of the continuum, however, there has been little use of significance tests in politimetrics to test null hypotheses of "no difference" between two measures or indicators. The substantive reasons for making such tests are relatively few. They might, though, shed some additional light on questions about whether such closely correlated measures of "development" as literacy, mass communications, urbanization, and industrial productivity ought to be conceptually distinguished.

Significance testing is not restricted to relationships between measures. Pairs of statistics like means, standard deviations, and some correlation coefficients can be compared to test null hypotheses that they are either identical or unrelated. Here are four examples:

1. We might want to know whether large cities in non-Western regions have more strife events than Western cities. We can calculate the mean of strife events for each set of cities and apply a "difference of means" test to evaluate the null hypothesis that they are the same. In this example we already know the *degree* of difference between the two sets of cities; the significance test helps us decide how consequential the difference is.

2. In the "Causes of Strife" study we found that "historical levels of strife" correlated .64 with 1961–65 strife in highly developed nations, but only .37 in the least-developed countries. Does this reflect a "real" difference between these groups of countries, or could we expect the correlations to be this different by chance? A significance test can be used to test the null hypothesis that they are the same.

3. Also in the "Causes of Strife" study, we found that the historical *success* of strife in the most-developed countries correlated .54 with strife in 1961–65, compared with $r = .64$ for historical *levels* of strife. For this single set of cases, does this signify that levels of past strife are truly more important than its success as a source of contemporary strife? A significance test will help us estimate the probability that the difference could arise by chance.

4. Assume that we have plotted a relationship between two measures which looks curvilinear rather than linear. We can test it for nonlinearity by computing both a *correlation ratio,* which does not assume linearity (described

under "analysis of variance," below), and a Pearson r (described below), which does assume linearity. The difference between the two correlations can then be tested for the null hypothesis that they are not significantly different. If they prove to be different we face another question, not *how much* different, but, "What is the shape of the best-fit curve?"

These examples suggest the kinds of problems and questions to which significance testing can be applied. There are many other applications as well, such as testing the normality of data distributions, identifying the "band of confidence" about a regression line, and estimating the desired size of samples when all cases in a universe cannot be studied. There remain two major limitations of significance testing in politimetrics. (1) The first is technical: data in politimetrics seldom fully satisfy the requirements of significance tests. Such tests usually are appropriate only when applied to information derived from random samples, and many tests further require that the measured properties of those samples be normally distributed. Since these requirements are seldom met by macropolitical data, the interpretation of significance levels is problematic. (2) The more important limitation of significance tests is that they are not as important for the kinds of research that interest us as we are usually led to believe by the texts or the published literature. Tufte puts the case this way:

> Probability levels and test statistics tell us very little about the strength and nothing about the substantive significance of a relationship. The important question is "Does the result show a relationship which is of substantive interest because of its nature and magnitude." Significance tests are silent on this matter (Tufte 1969, p. 644; interior quote from Kish 1959, p. 336).

Our summary judgment, then, is that significance tests are secondary in importance to tests of association for answering most of the questions of contemporary political comparisons. The politimetrician who intends to use significance tests will want to refer to some of the many textbook discussions, for example Blalock 1960, chap. 9; Mosteller, Rourke, and Thomas 1961; Palumbo 1969, chaps. 4 and 5; and especially Morrison and Henkel 1970.

The Variety of Statistical Tests

Most of the variety in statistical tests, apparent in Table 6.4, is due to the fact that the different levels of measurement reviewed on pages 59–63 have different mathematical properties, hence require different analytic techniques. The most precise measurement makes use of interval or ratio scales, to which the most powerful statistical techniques can be applied. Scores assigned by ranking clearly are less precise, hence ought to be analyzed by tests that assume only that scores are ordered, not that they represent proportional differences among cases. Sets of categories, or nominal scales, are most easily treated with the "weakest" techniques, those which require and use little information from the data. Researchers often use weaker techniques than are justified by their data, sometimes from caution and sometimes for

TABLE 6.4 *Some Statistical Tests of Association and Tests of Significance for Two-Variable relationships*[a]

Types of comparisons to be made	Tests of association	Tests of significance[b]	Notes on usage
Measures dichotomized in 2 × 2 tables	*Phi (ϕ) Contingency coefficient (C) Lambda beta (λ_b) Kendall's Q Tau beta	*Chi² (χ^2) Fisher's exact test Binominal test (Runs test) (Difference of means test)	Usually applied to nominal data but applicable to all others. Easy to use. ϕ and C are derived from χ^2. For dichotomous measures ϕ is equivalent in interpretation to the Pearson r, below. χ^2 is used when the expected frequency in each cell > 5. Otherwise use Fisher's exact test.
Measures organized by category in tables larger than 2 × 2	*Lambda beta (λ_b) (Contingency coefficient, C) (Tau beta)	*Chi² (χ^2)	Designed for nominal data but applicable to all others. C and tau beta are difficult to interpret in tables larger than 2 × 2
Dichotomous measure compared with an interval measure	Point-biserial correlation coefficient (r_{pb})	t test	r_{pb} is comparable in calculation and interpretation to the Pearson r, below.
Categorized measure compared with an interval measure	Coefficient of determination (ω^2) Unbiased correlation ratio (ϵ^2 or CR^2) Interclass correlation coefficient (r_i)	F test, based on analysis of explained vs. unexplained variance	Ordinarily used in comparing a nominal scale having more than two categories to an interval measure. The textbook label is *analysis of variance*. The coefficient of determination is comparable in interpretation to the Pearson r, below. The other two tests of association have variable lower limits, hence are difficult to interpret.

Ordinal with ordinal measure	Spearman's r_s Kendall's tau (τ) Kolmogorov-Smirnov Wald-Wolfowitz Mann-Whitney	For ranked data. Easily computed, sometimes applied to interval data. r_s is used if tied ranks are few. Otherwise use tau. Smirnov test is indicated when ties are numerous. Otherwise use W-W or M-W. Of these M-W is most sensitive to differences in means, W-W to differences in distribution.
Interval with interval measure	*Pearson or product-moment r F test Fisher's Z Critical value of r	r is the most powerful and widely used measure of relationship, sometimes applied to ranked data as well as interval data. Computation is difficult. Fisher's Z is computed from the value of r and the N; F from the r only. They are equally appropriate for sample data. Critical values of r can be determined for a particular N and used in evaluating correlation matrices.

convenience. The point to be kept in mind is that when this is done, the weaker techniques use only part of the information contained in the data.

We also sometimes find it necessary to compare data representing different levels of measurement. We can almost always do so by using "weaker" techniques, but in many situations there are special techniques for such comparisons that do not sacrifice information from the more precisely measured variable. With these generalizations in mind we shall now illustrate a few of the most-used techniques.

Tests of Significance and Association for Contingency Tables

Contingency tables are constructed by cross-classifying two measures. Usually they are applied to nominal (categorized) data, but sometimes we want to use them to make a quick comparison of two indicators for which we have ordinal or interval data. Assume that we want to determine whether deaths from strife are significantly greater in the non-European than in the European democracies. The European/non-European distinction is a dichotomy; deaths from strife per million can be converted in a dichotomy by dividing the cases into those with deaths above and below the median (midpoint) of scores shown in Table 6.1. The resultant tabulation of cases (countries) in a 2×2 contingency table is shown in Table 6.5.

The differences in "deaths" between the two groups of democracies appear substantial. The number of countries in the cell marked (a) is the number of European democracies with more than the median number of deaths from strife; in cell (c) are European democracies with less than the median number; and so forth. To determine whether the distribution is greater than what might be expected by chance, we can calculate a *chi-square test of significance* (χ^2) using the following definitional equation.

TABLE 6.5 *Contingency Table for a Dichotomized Measure of deaths from Strife Compared with the European/Non-European*

Deaths from strife per million, logged	Type of Democracy		Total
	European	Non-European	
Above median	(a) 5	(b) 14	19
Below median	(c) 14	(d) 5	19
Total	19	19	38

a Numbers of countries are shown in each cell. The data for deaths are from Table 6.1. The "European" group of democracies includes those of Western Europe plus Israel, Australia, Canada, New Zealand, and the United States.

Such tests can be applied to contingency tables of any size, 2×2, 2×3, 3×3, or larger.

$$\chi^2 = \Sigma \frac{(f_0 - f_e)^2}{f_e}$$

where f_0 refers to the observed frequency in each cell and f_e refers to the expected frequency. The *expected frequency*—the number that would be expected by chance—can be obtained by multiplying the *marginal totals* corresponding to each cell and dividing by N.[3] "Marginal totals" are the totals of cases in all cells of a row, and all cells of a column. For cell (a) in Table 6.5, for example, the row total is (a) + (b) = 19 and the column total is (a) + (c) = 19. The value of f_e for cell (a) is

$$\frac{(a + b)(a + c)}{N} = \frac{(19)(19)}{38} = 9.5$$

Detailed examples of computations for obtaining chi-squares are given in statistics texts. There is one restriction on the use of chi-square: the researcher should have a relatively large number of cases, otherwise the probability assumptions on which the test is based are not satisfied. The criterion usually used is that the *expected* frequency (number of cases) in each cell be greater than 5. If it is 5 or less there are corrections that can be made or, better, a significance test called "Fisher's exact test" can be used.

The chi-square value for the data in Table 6.5 is 8.52. The statistical significance of this value can be determined from a table of the chi-square distribution. To use the table we need to know the *degrees of freedom* (df) afforded by the table as well, which for chi-square tests is equal to the number of rows minus one, multiplied by the number of columns minus one.[4] In this instance $df = (2 - 1)(2 - 1) = 1$. For one degree of freedom, the table indicates that a chi-square of at least 3.841 is needed to meet the .05 level of significance, and 6.635 for the .01 level. Our obtained value of 8.52 thus has less than a .01 probability of occuring by chance—if our cases had been selected at random, which they were not.

Measures of association for contingency tables usually are more in-

3 Expected frequencies do not necessarily have to be computed from the marginals. The researcher may have theoretical grounds for some nonrandom distribution of cases, and calculate "expected frequencies" on those grounds. The chi-square test then becomes a test of how well or badly the actual distribution of cases meets the theoretical prediction. I am endebted to J. Zvi Namenwirth for bringing this to my attention.

4 "Degrees of freedom" is an important concept in tests of significance, and in statistical theory generally. Their number is defined by Blalock as "equal to the number of quantities which are unknown minus the number of independent equations linking these unknowns" (1960, p. 156). For discussions see this source, *passim,* and Buchanan 1969.

teresting than significance tests, because they tell us how accurately we can predict how a case will be categorized on one variable from the way it is categorized on the other. If in Table 6.5, for example, all European democracies were below the median and all non-European ones above, we would have perfect predictability: by knowing whether a country was European or non-European, we could always specify whether strife deaths would be low or high. One measure of predictability that is based on chi-square is *phi*, represented by the Greek letter ϕ. It is defined as the square root of χ^2/N. For Table 6.5

$$\phi = \sqrt{\frac{8.52}{38}} = .50.$$

For a 2×2 table the interpretation of ϕ is simple: if we know whether a country is European or non-European, we can predict whether deaths from strife will be high or low with an accuracy of 50% better than chance. For a 2×2 table, ϕ is mathematically equivalent to the Pearson r (see below) and can be compared directly with r. But ϕ cannot be easily interpreted when applied to tables larger than 2×2.

Lambda b, symbolized λ_b, is a measure of association based on the chi-square which has two advantages over ϕ: it can be computed directly and easily from the contingency table values without making the more laborious calculations necessary for chi-square; and it is applicable to tables larger than 2×2. Formulas for λ_b, examples using tables larger than 2×2, and other measures of association for contingency tables can be found in Goodman and Kruskal 1954, and Palumbo 1969, pp. 160–63.

Contingency tables are easy to set up, and test statistics are easily calculated for them. For an earlier generation of social scientists they provided the only technically acceptable means for statistical analysis of categorized data. But it is now generally accepted that each nominal category can be treated as a dichotomized or "dummy" variable and can be subject to the most powerful statistical techniques. An example using categories of civil strife events was given on page 61.

Tests of Association and Significance for Ordinal Measures

Ordinal measures are those on which cases are assigned scores according to their rank. Tests for them are useful because easily computed. On the other hand, if the investigator knows enough about his cases to rank them on a variable, he often knows enough to place them approximately on an interval or ratio scale, thus gaining a good deal in precision and statistical power. Consequently the tests for comparing ordinal measures are most often suitable for the researcher who is either impatient on practical grounds or conservative about technical matters. There are two common *tests of association* for ordinal measures and three related *tests of significance* (listed and briefly annotated in Table 6.4). They are described in most statistics texts.

Tests of Association and Significance for Interval Measures

The Pearson or product-moment correlation coefficient, r, is the appropriate and recommended test of association for comparing two variables that are measured on interval scales. Texts sometimes show other measures of association for interval measures, but r is universally and almost exclusively used throughout the social sciences. It is most easily understood by reference to the scattergrams with which we worked earlier in this chapter: *r is a measure of how closely the regression line fits the points on a scattergram.* The greater the squared deviations of cases from the regression line, the closer r is to zero. It is called a *goodness-of-fit* measure and varies from $+1.00$ for a perfect positive and linear relationship through 0.00 for no relationship to -1.00 for a perfect negative, linear relationship. The computational equation most often used for determining r for any two measures, X and Y, is

$$r_{xy} = \frac{N(\Sigma\, XY) - (\Sigma\, X)(\Sigma\, Y)}{\sqrt{N \Sigma\, X^2 - (\Sigma\, X)^2}\, \sqrt{N \Sigma\, Y^2 - (\Sigma\, Y)^2}}$$

Note that all the sums required by the equation are the ones required for determining a and b in regression equations.

One of the problems of graphic analysis that we considered was the nature of the relationship between "man-days" and "deaths" in strife in the 38 democracies. Remember that we made decisions about how well the regression lines fitted by looking at how far particular cases deviated from the lines. The r's provide a precise statistical summary of these deviations. For all 38 democracies the r for man-days of strife versus deaths from strife, plotted in Figure 6.2, is 0.55. When the polities were divided into two groups of 19 each, the resultant r's were 0.64 for the European democracies and 0.79 for the non-European democracies. The increase in the correlations for the recategorized groups confirms the desirability of treating them separately.

INTERPRETING THE PEARSON r It can be shown—and is, in statistics texts—that r has a simple interpretation: it is the square root of the amount of variation in Y that is "explained by" or attributable to variation in X. Thus the square of the correlation coefficient r^2 is called the *coefficient of determination*. For our initial comparison of "man-days" and "deaths," $r^2 = .550^2 = .3025$: we can say that 30.25% of the variation in "deaths" is accounted for by the variation in "man-days," while $1 - .3025$ or 69.75% is unexplained. When the European democracies are separately analyzed, the explained variation is $.64^2 = 41\%$. For the non-European democracies the estimate is $79^2 = 62\%$. These estimates of explained variation make it evident that the magnitude of r must be fairly large before we have a substantial degree of "explanation." A correlation of .316 is required to account for 10% of the variation of Y about X, or of X about Y. A correlation of .707 is required to explain 50% of the variation.

"Explanation" in the sense the word is used here has this specific, technical meaning: it is the proportion of variation in a set of known scores on variable Y that we can estimate correctly from a set of known scores on variable X. Whether this is explanation in the sense that "X *causes* 62% of Y" the correlation coefficient alone cannot tell us. We could say with equal accuracy from the statistical results that Y "explains" 62% of the variation in X. For this reason the use of "explanation" in this context seems undesirable: it confuses a statistical relationship of unspecified directionality with theoretical statements of causality. We *can* make some causal inferences from patterns of association among time-lagged data, and from the intercorrelations of three or more measures. Some ways of doing so are described in Section 7.3. We shall see there that theory, in combination with the results of statistical analysis, can help us make informed judgments about causation. But the analytic results themselves are not a substitute for judgment.

GRAPHIC AND CORRELATION ANALYSIS   The investigator also must keep in mind that correlation analysis is not a substitute for graphic analysis. While r is a useful summary of the closeness with which a regression line fits plotted data, r is also quite sensitive to extreme cases. A few extreme values or coordinates, depending on how they cluster, may either exaggerate or reduce r by a considerable degree. Figure 6.5 shows two hypothetical distributions of cases for which r would be a misleading measure. In (a) the cluster of three cases at the upper left will cause r to be substantially lower than it would be if based on the remaining cases alone. The dashed line is an approximation of the best-fit line with the three deviant cases included; the solid line suggests how it might otherwise appear. A distribution of cases as

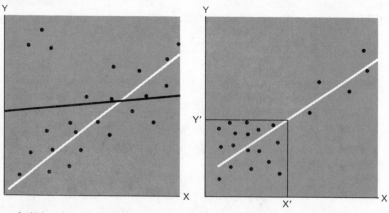

A. Value of r minimized by outlyers   B. Value of r enhanced by outlyers

FIGURE 6.5. Hypothetical relationships for which r is an inadequate summary.

in (b) is considerably more common than (a) in real political data. The cases within the box drawn from x' and y' at the lower left show little apparent relationship between X and Y; the linearity among the five outlying cases is great enough to give quite a high value for r. We showed in Section 6.3 that a straight line can be an inadequate summary of a curvilinear relationship. This is equally true of the r which summarizes that relationship. In fact the r is more likely to mislead the researcher: pronounced curvilinearity is usually apparent on a graph, but it is never apparent from an r alone.

What to do about relationships like those in Figure 6.5 is a substantive question for which there is no one technical answer. A pattern such as Figure 6.5(a) strongly suggests that something quite different is going on in the outlying cases than in the others. If the investigator has some notion why they are or should be different they could be dropped from the analysis. A pattern such as Figure 6.5(b) might be coincidental, especially if only one or two cases anchor the extreme of the best-fit line. If the distribution of one (or both) of the measures is strongly skewed, the (b) pattern is quite likely to occur. So we can partly insure ourselves against it by transforming the measures toward normality before the analysis. Or we might delete one or two extreme cases, especially if we think that they are poorly measured or clearly different from the others (on some grounds other than their extreme scores!). On the other hand, the pattern shown in (b) may reflect a real and important *threshold effect* in the relationship between the two variables. Until X reaches a value of x' it has little effect on the magnitude of Y; beyond x' it has a pronounced effect. One or two outlying cases do not provide enough evidence to argue for such an effect, but if 10–20% of the cases follow the same outlying pattern, a threshold effect is likely. However, outliers in macropolitical comparisons are more likely the result of skewed data distributions than of threshold effects. For a useful analysis of the effects of various kinds of skewness on correlation coefficients, and how to take skewness and outliers into account, see Carroll 1961.

SIGNIFICANCE TESTS FOR r   We suggested on pages 128–29 a number of situations in which we might want to test the statistical significance of r, or of differences between r's. There are two tests for the significance of a single r: Fisher's Z and the F test. Values of Z and F can both be computed from the obtained value of r using simple formulas; the probability level of the Z or F value is then determined by reference to tables of Fisher's Z or F, found in the appendices of statistics texts. Differences between r's can be tested for significance by extensions of the same tests, and are described in the texts. A straightforward presentation, with examples relevant to problems in politimetrics, is given in Blalock 1960, chap. 18.

Significance tests for r's are also used in politimetrics to evaluate *correlation matrices*, the r's obtained when a large number of measures are correlated with one another. Even if the cross-correlated measures are for a closed population rather than a sample, we can use significance tests to help decide which relationships have enough substantive importance to justify further consideration. The critical value of r for any given number of cases is the r required to meet a particular level of significance, say .05 or .01. Many texts provide equations for determining critical values of r for any number of cases (see Palumbo 1969, p. 199).

Cross-Level Comparisons

We have reviewed some basic techniques for comparing two sets of categorized data and two measures using interval scales. These methods are suitable for many but not all the statistical comparisons we might want to make between two variables. On some occasions we want to make *cross-level comparisons*: comparisons of variables represented by different levels of measurement. There are several widely used techniques for comparing interval measures with categorized data, two of which are mentioned below. There is also a technique for comparing ordinal measures with categorized data.

POINT-BISERIAL CORRELATIONS   The simplest kind of nominal scale is a dichotomy, like the "European versus non-European democracies" distinction. The strength of association between any such dichotomy and an interval measure can be determined using the *point-biserial correlation coefficient,* symbolized r_{pb}. One way to compute r_{pb} is to give each case a 0 or 1 score on the dichotomous variable (for example, European = 0, non-European = 1) and to use the equation for the product-moment r. This is the procedure followed when "dummy variables" are incorporated in complex, computer-performed analyses. A method that is simpler, especially if computations are to be done manually, uses the following equation:

$$r_{pb} = \frac{\overline{Y}_1 - \overline{Y}_2}{s_Y} \sqrt{\frac{N_1 N_2}{N(N-1)}}$$

where $\overline{Y}_1$ and $\overline{Y}_2$ are the means of the intervally measured scores for each category of cases, N_1 and N_2 are the numbers of cases in each category, and s_Y is the standard deviation of the intervally measured scores.

We can illustrate r_{pb} by comparing the data in Table 6.1 on "man-days of strife" as the interval measure with the European versus non-European dichotomy. We have already seen that "deaths" are proportionally much greater in the non-European democracies. Now we are asking how much of the difference in "man-days" among the democracies is attributable to whether they are European or non-European. The data needed for the computation are as follows:

Average man-days for non-European democracies, $\overline{Y}_1, = 2.83$
Average man-days for European democracies, $\overline{Y}_2 = 2.13$

Standard deviation, man-days, all democracies, s_Y, $= 1.469$
Non-European democracies, N_1, $= 19$
European democracies, N_2, $= 19$

$$r_{pb} = \frac{2.83 - 2.13}{1.469} \sqrt{\frac{19 \cdot 19}{38(37)}} = .21$$

The r_{pb} estimate of .21 is interpreted in the same way as a product-moment correlation coefficient. The square of .21 $=$ .04, the proportion of variation in "man-days" that is dependent upon the European/non-European distinction. Whether a democracy is European or not evidently makes very little difference in its man-days of strife. The statistical significance of r_{pb} also can be determined.

ANALYSIS OF VARIANCE   We may still be convinced that there is a connection between the nature of democratic regimes and the extent of their domestic conflict as reflected in the "man-days" measure, a connection that the dichotomous European/non-European distinction only weakly represents. Another possible basis for distinguishing among them is how deeply rooted their democratic traditions are. We could reasonably expect that effective, peaceful methods of conflict resolution were best-established in old democracies like Sweden and the United Kingdom, less deeply rooted in democracies of intermediate age, and least adequate in countries whose first or most recent attempt at creating popular institutions of government occured within the last generation. *Analysis of variance* is the traditional method for answering this kind of question. The cases measured on an interval scale are classified and compared across three or more categories of a nominal scale. The test of significance used in analysis of variance is the F test. Three measures of association can be applied to analysis-of-variance data. The most useful of them is the *coefficient of determination,* which has an upper limit of 1.0 and a lower limit of approximately 0.0. The other two measures are the *correlation ratio* and the *interclass correlation coefficient.* Both have upper limits of 1.00 but no fixed lower limits, which makes them difficult to interpret. The reader will find procedures and examples for analysis of variance in most texts, for example, Blalock 1960, chaps. 16 and 20, and Palumbo 1969, chap. 11.

The use of most cross-level statistical techniques seems to be declining in most of the social sciences, and the decline is likely to continue. The same appears true of techniques for ordinal and nominal comparisons. There are several reasons for this, both practical and technical. *Practically,* the popularity of these techniques was based partly on the ease with which their test statistics could be calculated. The rapid expansion of high-speed computer facilities has eliminated much of this advantage, except in the dwindling number of colleges where such facilities are not yet available. *Technically,* there is a growing tendency to use interval- and ratio-order techniques for the analysis of all social data. We have discussed and recommended two legitimate procedures by which this is done. The categories of a nominal scale can be transformed into dummy or dichotomous variables which are suitable for analysis by the most powerful techniques. Ordinal data can be transformed into interval-like data by rating cases on judgmental scales that have equal-appearing intervals. Thus both practical and technical factors make it less necessary for the researcher to settle for analytic procedures like rank-order correlation and analysis of variance.

7

Methods of Data Analysis: Time series, multivariate, and causal analysis

Most of the methods surveyed in this chapter are derivations or interpretations of those in Chapter 6. Since the methods discussed here are designed for more complex problems, they are sometimes more difficult to comprehend, and usually more difficult to apply to a set of data. Few computational equations are given here. We are mainly interested in how these methods are applied to real data and what interpretations can be made of the results. Methods surveyed in this chapter include those most used in recent work in politimetrics. But the researcher should recognize that there are additional and alternative methods, some of which are almost certainly better for some of our theoretical and data problems than those in widest use. This is especially true of multivariate and time-series methods developed in econometrics. Politimetricians have begun to use some of these methods, but there are as yet no texts or readers in advanced politimetrics where they are presented and applied to macropolitical comparisons. The lack cannot be remedied in this introductory text.

7.1 Time-Series Analysis

Most studies using macropolitical data are static: variables are measured at one point in time for a number of cases. This kind of research is called *cross-sectional,* to distinguish it from *longitudinal* studies in which variables are studied across time in one or a few settings. The two approaches are complementary. Comprehensive theory about political phenomena will have to take into account both static properties and dynamic relationships, and should be tested empirically using both cross-sectional and longitudinal data. Political scientists' predilection for cross-sectional research design in most macropolitical studies is a function more of the lack of time-series data for most political data than of a professional commitment to static analysis.

The techniques we have surveyed thus far were illustrated with cross-sectional data, and were mostly designed for static analysis. But the analysis of time-series data need be no more difficult than analysis of cross-sectional data, and most of the techniques used in static analysis are applicable or adaptable to time-series data. There are also a number of complex and powerful techniques, devised mostly by econometricians, for treating time-series data which have the depth and precision of economic data. We can expect these techniques to be increasingly used in politimetrics. In the sections that follow we review some simple applications of now-familiar graphic and correlational techniques to time-series analysis. More technical introductions to time-series analysis will be found in Johnson (1963), Christ (1966), and especially Hannan (1970).

The Description of Time-Series Data

Time-series data are sometimes gathered with descriptive purposes in mind—for example, to establish the direction and rate of change in a variable over time or to identify its variations. Long-term trends are described as *secular* trends; distinctions are made among types of short-term variations in trends: for example, *seasonal, cyclical,* and *irregular* variations. Seasonal variations are not of much substantive interest in politimetrics. Cyclical variations are of great potential interest, but not enough time-series analysis has been done in politimetrics even to warrant a prejudgment about how often and in what phenomena cycles are likely to be found. Singer and Small (1970) have found rather clear 20-year cycles in the *amount* of war underway in the international system, but not in its onset. Sorokin (1937) found evidence for much longer-term cycles in social change and conflict across a 2,400-year span. Important as cycles may be, in macropolitical comparisons we are most likely to be interested in *long-term trends, irregular variations* around long-term trends, and in the causes, or correlates, of those trends and the variations around them.

Whether or not time-series data have a trend is not always obvious. Urban population figures will certainly have a trend; levels of civil conflict in a country may not. There are procedures for determining whether such data have systematic trends. One is *serial correlation,* used to determine whether and to what degree each successive score in a time-series depends on the preceding score. Serial correlation only helps identify straight-line trends, though not cyclical ones. Other procedures can be used to identify the presence of cycles.

If trends exist in our data, the first step is to describe them. Graphic plotting is the indispensable point of departure. Alliance data from the "Alliances and War" study are plotted in Figure 7.1; the curves represent the percentages of all nations which participated in any kind of alliance by year from 1920 to 1939. A trend line can be fitted to the data by any of several techniques. The simplest is the *semiaverages trend line,* which is determined by dividing a time period in half, averaging the Y scores for each half, locating the coordinates of these averages at the midpoint of each half, and then drawing a trend line through the two coordinates. This procedure is used only if a rough estimate of the trend is needed.

The most precise *linear* trend estimate is a least-squares regression line, which is calculated by the equation given in Section 6.3's discussion of graphic analysis. Remember that the regression line has the general equation

$$Y' = a + b(X)$$

In graphic analysis of time-series data the data are always plotted over time, and the X axis is labeled t—the month, year, decade, or whatever time unit is used. Y is the measure which varies over time. The regression equation for the "alliances" data for this 20-year period is shown in Figure 7.1(a). Note that 1900 was subtracted from each t score to simplify computation.

The limitation of linear trend lines is that time-series can seldom be described adequately by a linear equation or regression line. This is evident from the "alliance" data. The linear equation is substantively impossible: the a weight is -76, indicating that in 1900 we would expect -76% of nations to be involved in alliances! The plot of the data in the figure shows that they lie above the regression line at the beginning and end of the pre-World War II era but fall below it in the intervening years. The apparent trend line approximates a distended "S," a trend common in time plots of variables which have a natural upper limit. We would likely obtain such curves if we plotted proportional urbanization or literacy over time in the histories of the developed nations, for example. Curves with this shape are called *sine curves. Exponential* trend lines are often observed in variables that have no upper limit, such as population and economic growth, which tend to increase at a constant rate. There are mathematical techniques for describing these and many other kinds of trends in nonlinear equations. The *moving average* is one simpler kind of description. It has the advantage of smoothing out the more abrupt short-term trends without imposing arbitrary assumptions about linearity or a particular nonlinearity on the data. A three-year moving average of the "alliance" data is plotted in Figure 7.1(b). The coordinate for each year is the average of "alliance" scores for that year and the preceding and following years. The moving averages most often used are for three or five periods of observation. The larger the number of observations averaged, the less pronounced will be the fluctuations.

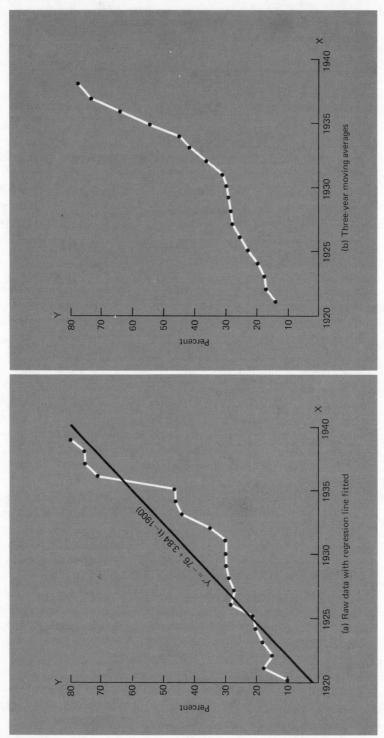

FIGURE 7.1. Percentage of nations in the international system involved in any alliances, 1920–39 (from Singer and Small 1966b, p. 13).

Analyzing Relations in Time-Series Data

SOME GENERAL CONSIDERATIONS   The researcher almost always wants to determine and describe the trends in his time-series data. What he does with those trends, though, depends on the theoretical questions he is asking. Here are three questions that are often studied with time-series data.

1. *What causes the trends?* One basic question is what the causes, or correlates, of a long-term trend are. One simple approach to answering this question is to correlate time-series data for each of the several variables under study. Such data are usually *lagged*: a time difference is introduced between the two measures being correlated. This is illustrated by the "Alliances and War" study, in which several different lags were used. Measures of alliance aggregation for year X were correlated with the "war" measures for years $a - 3$, $a - 1$, $a + 1$, $a + 3$, and so forth. The general pattern of correlation results was that alliance aggregation had a delayed effect on extent of war, but that extent of war did not predict to alliance aggregation. Such procedures are sometimes criticized because the data for each successive time-period is partly dependent on the previous period's score. In the "alliance" data, for example, each year's "alliance" score depends partly on the score for the preceding year. Technically this dependence violates the requirement of correlation procedures that observations must be independent of one another. Substantively, it may mean that a correlation between two time-series measures is "spurious," the result of some common underlying process or "cause." The technical and theoretical ways of dealing with this kind of problem are largely beyond the scope of our discussion here.

2. *Why do trends change?* Trends often change over time, and researchers are often interested in the dynamics of those changes. What outside conditions or events caused the trend change? One promising approach to this kind of question is called "quasi-experimental analysis," in which trends are analyzed before and after some abrupt external change to determine whether it significantly affects the trend. The procedure could be used, for example, to determine what effect the 1917 Russian Revolution had on Russian economic growth. The technique is described in Campbell (1963); an application to the process of European political integration is Caporaso and Pelowski (1971).

3. *What causes variations around trends?* This is probably the most common question asked about time-series data. Some examples from the "American Values" study are given in the following section. The general approach to studying such variations is to *detrend* the time-series data: the data to be analyzed and related to other measures are the variations around the trend. These variations are equivalent to the residuals around a regression line, discussed in Chapter 6; they are the extent to which each observation is above or below the trend or best-fit line. Detrending has the advantage

of resolving the problem of dependence among time-series data, mentioned under question 1 above. Often, though, it is the trend itself which is of interest, in which case detrending is out of the question.

A CASE STUDY IN TIME-SERIES ANALYSIS   Namenwirth's analysis of references to wealth in political party platforms provides a number of examples of time-series analysis (Namenwirth 1968). The data he used were proportional frequency counts of words dealing with "wealth-other" in the Democratic and Republican platforms for each election between 1844 and 1964. The "wealth-other" category includes a great variety of words such as "affluence," "currency," "livestock," and "unemployment" which signify specific material concerns. Here we will refer to it by the more descriptive term "material well-being." The raw data are plotted by 20-year moving averages in Figure 7.2. Note that the 20-year moving averages represent five elections each, since in this study elections rather than years mark the periods of observation.

A long-term increase in concern with material well-being is evident in the platforms of both parties. When linear regressions are calculated (not

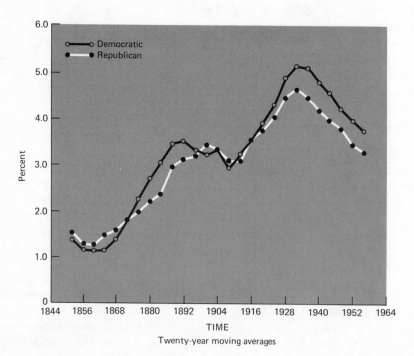

FIGURE 7.2. Relative concern of Democratic and Rupublican Party platforms with material well-being, 1844–1964 (percentages in Figures 7.2, 7.3, and 7.4 represent the proportion of all words in each platform categorized as "wealth-other" in the "American Values" study).

shown here), it appears that from about 1860 on the Democratic Party's concern with these material concerns began to exceed those of the Republican Party, and continued to do so at an increasing rate down to the 1960s. But linear regressions do not accurately represent the two sets of data. It is evident from Figure 7.2 that the upward trend in concern with material well-being was not continuous. Instead there were two peaks, each coinciding roughly with periods of economic dislocation and each followed by a decline. The first peak occurred late in the nineteenth century, with the Republican Party lagging some years behind the Democratic Party in reaching the peak. The second coincided with the depression of the 1930s, Democratic concern being absolutely greater then and later. After that depression the relative concern with this category of values steadily declined in the platforms of both parties. The 20-year averages can be compared by correlating them: r is .98, very close to identity despite the small but consistent differences apparent from the graph.

Once the long-term trends are established, a primary interest is in determining what *social trends* correspond to them. Figure 7.3 shows graph-

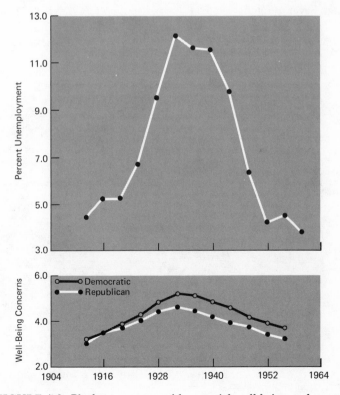

FIGURE 7.3. Platform concern with material well-being and percent unemployment, 1912–56, using 20-year moving averages

ically an apparent correspondence between percentage unemployment and party concerns with material well-being between 1912 and 1956. The unemployment data are 20-year moving averages, the first representing the period 1901–20, the second 1905–24, and so on; national unemployment data were not available before 1900. When the two sets of well-being measures are correlated with unemployment, the r's are quite high: .94 for the Democratic platforms and .91 for the Republican. Other economic indicators also were studied, but without significant results. The business failure rate, for example, correlated .08 with the material well-being concerns of the Democratic Party and .33 with those of the Republican Party, neither of them statistically significant for $N = 12$. We might reasonably conclude that over the long run both parties' platforms reflected serious malaise in the economy, in particular that aspect of economic malaise, unemployment, which had the greatest popular impact. The relative degree of stress on economic issues was greater in the Democratic than Republican platforms, however.

The next stage in the analysis was to detrend these data and to examine the correlates of short-term variations in party concern with material well-being. Several methods could have been used. One is to determine residuals from the linear regression equations and compare them with election-to-election measures of conditions that might cause a temporary

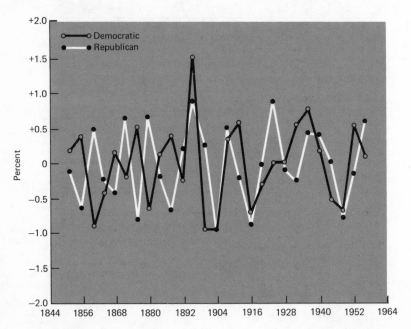

FIGURE 7.4. Material well-being residuals from moving averages, 1844–1964

increase or decline in concern with material issues. But we have already seen that the long-term trends in the material well-being measures were not linear. Another and better measure of short-term fluctuations can be devised from the moving averages. In this case, residual scores were calculated by subtracting the "material well-being" score for each platform from the moving, five-election average for that year. These residuals, one per platform per party, are graphed in Figure 7.4.

The most interesting feature of the short-term fluctuations is that in the early period, up to about 1892, at each election the two parties tend to move in opposite directions. When the Republicans placed special emphasis on material issues (above the moving average), the Democratic Party was quite likely to do the opposite. Subsequent to that time they tend more and more to resemble one another in their deviations from the average. Namenwirth's interpretation is that until the 1890s, "the Democratic and Republican parties depended on reacting to each other in their competition for the electorate." They did so partly for lack of information about the value concerns of the electorate, and partly because of the polarization caused by the intense political and regional conflicts of the second half of the nineteenth century. "Once these overbearing domestic issues had been settled...the campaign-to-campaign responses became more dependent on common external factors" (Namenwirth 1968, p. 131).

7.2 Analyzing Relationships among Three or More Variables

When we analyze macropolitical data there are three situations in which we may need to relate three or more measures:

1. We may suspect, or hypothesize, that a bivariate correlation is affected by a third variable, one which either minimizes or exaggerates the association between the two measures we are studying. In this circumstance we will want to introduce a measure of the third, *control* variable to see what effect it has on the initial relationship.
2. We may want to test a theoretical notion that our dependent variable has several independent causes, which together account for it better than any single causal variable. To test this kind of argument we need to determine how much variation in a measure of the dependent variable is accounted for by several different measures of the independent variables acting together.
3. We may have a large number of measures of one or several different variables whose common dimensions of variation we want to identify.

Five techniques of multivariate analysis are applicable to these problems. *Two-way analysis of variance* is a means of dealing with the first problem, and sometimes with the second: it enables us to compare interval data that are cross-classified according to two different sets of nominal categories. It is not further discussed here; for references see the discussion of simple analysis of variance in Chapter 6 (p. 139). If we are working with interval or dichotomous measures, or some combination of the two, we can deal with the first and second kinds of problems with three techniques more powerful than analysis of variance: *partial correlation, multiple correlation,* and *multiple regression.* We can crack the third problem by *factor analysis.* These multivariate techniques are understandably more complex than bivariate techniques, so the brief descriptions below focus on their applications and interpretations, not on their computation or derivation.

Multiple and Partial Correlation

Partial correlation is one of the multivariate techniques. When we are examining a relation between X and Y, we may suspect that a third variable, Z, is acting as a contaminating influence. In this situation we will want to *control* for the effects of Z, or in other words to eliminate its influence from the relationship that really interests us. A *partial correlation coefficient,* symbolized $r_{xy.z}$ or $r_{12.3}$, summarizes the relationship between X and Y with the effects of Z controlled. The effects of any number of extraneous variables may be controlled, though we seldom have occasion to control for more than two or three.

Multiple correlation is a related technique. We may, as before, want to "explain" Y but regard both X and Z as independent and equally interesting causes of Y. In this case we want to determine what proportion of the variation in Y is accounted for by X and Z acting together. The measure which summarizes this relationship is called the *multiple correlation coefficient,* symbolized R. The square of R is analogous to r^2: it is called the *coefficient of multiple determination* and identifies the "explained" proportion of variation in Y. Any number of independent variables can be included in multiple correlation, although there are both common-sense and statistical limitations to the number that can be used in any particular instance.

Multiple regression is a way of summarizing the results of multiple correlation. For any given R^2 we can determine a multiple regression equation which specifies what proportion of each independent measure is needed to obtain the best estimate of the dependent variable.

THE MULTIPLE REGRESSION MODEL   In Section 6.3 we explained simple regression analysis in graphic terms, as the equation for the best-fit line for data on a scattergram. The product-moment correlation coefficient r is a measure of how well the line fits the data. Partial and multiple correlation, and multiple regression, can all be understood by reference to this basic model. Recall that when we "predict" variable Y from variable X, the predicted Y' scores for each case are to varying degrees different from the actual Y scores; the differences are called *residuals.* Graphically, residuals are represented by the vertical distance between the coordinate for each case and the best-fit or regression line for the whole set of cases. Figure 7.5 shows a hypothetical scattergram with the residuals symbolically represented by

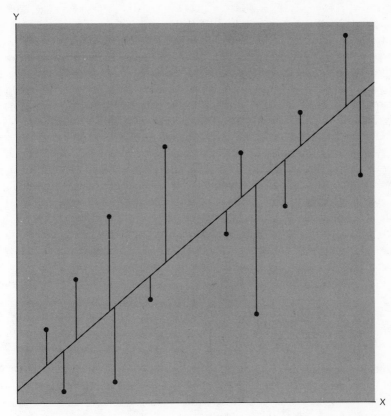

FIGURE 7.5. Hypothetical scattergram with residuals represented graphically.

lines drawn vertically from the best-fit line to the case coordinates. The numerical value of each such residual can be computed from the equation for the regression line; we demonstrated this in Table 6.3, which listed the residuals in "deaths from strife" in 38 democracies that were unexplained by "man-days."

What is done in multiple correlation, in effect, is first to correlate X with Y; next to determine the residuals of Y regressed on X; and then to correlate Z with these residuals. This process can be repeated for as many independent variables as we want to add: the residuals are determined after each step and correlated with the next measure. There are computational short-cuts by which R and R^2 can be determined from a matrix of r's among all the measures being used.

Partial correlation also can be explained in terms of the analysis of residuals. Assume that Z is the variable whose effects we want to control or eliminate. First, then, we correlate Z with the dependent variable Y. We want to ignore whatever variance in Y is explained at this stage, because it is associated with the irrelevant Z. The Y residuals are what we are really interested in explaining. So we correlate the Y residuals with X, which is the independent variable whose effects we want to test. *This* correlation, of X with the Y residuals, is a partial r. We could control for the effects of several independent variables in a similar way: all the "control" variables would be entered first, and the final Y residuals calculated and correlated with X. The only relationship to interest us would be r $_{xy.abc...}$, or in other words the correlation between X and the final set of residuals for Y.

Whenever multiple correlation is used with more than three variables, we can calculate a partial r for each independent variable. These partial r's represent the variation "explained" by that particular measure when the effects of all the others are held constant. If we used four independent variables, numbered (2) through (5), to predict to dependent variable (1), then the partial r for variable (2) correlated with the residuals of (1) is r $_{12.345}$; the partial r for variable (3) correlated with the residuals of (1) is r $_{13.245}$; and so forth. Now we know from examining simple two-variable relationships that each r is a summary of a regression equation of the form $Y' = a + bX$, with b a constant weight. A *multiple* regression equation shows the analogous weight for each partial r in a multiple correlation analysis, in this general form:

$$Y' = a + b_1(X_1) + b_2(X_2) + \cdots + b_n(X_n)$$

In other words there is one constant a for the equation and a b weight for each independent variable. The equation can be used like a simple regression equation, to make a best-fit prediction for Y for each case: its score on each independent variable is obtained by multiplying by the appropriate b weight, adding the constant, and summing. Perhaps needless to say, it is difficult to represent a multiple regression equation graphically because plotting its points could require as many dimensions as there are independent variables.

AN ILLUSTRATION OF MULTIPLE REGRESSION   This abstract explanation may be clearer if we use an example from the "Causes of Strife" study. The three multivariate techniques can be used to explore the relations between total magnitude of strife in the 38 democracies and three summary indicators of our independent variables, "relative deprivation" (called "discontent" below), "justifications," and "social balance." We first require a correlation matrix of the four measures, given in Table 7.1. One of the theoretical arguments was that "social balance" substantially influences the effects of "discontent" on strife. In statistical terms, this implies that if we correlate "discontent" with strife and control for the effects of "social balance," the partial r for discontent versus strife should be considerably less than it was initially.

There is a simple computational equation for determining a partial r between any two variables with a control for a third:

$$r_{13.2} = \frac{r_{13} - r_{12}r_{32}}{\sqrt{1 - r_{12}^2}\sqrt{1 - r_{32}^2}}$$

TABLE 7.1   *Correlation Matrix of Summary Measures in the "Causes of Strife" study for 38 democracies*[a]

	Discontent	Justifica-tions	Social balance	Total strife
Discontent	1.00			
Justifications	.46	1.00		
Social balance	−.65	−.66	1.00	
Total strife	.54	.65	−.63	1.00

[a] Correlation coefficients are rounded to the nearest two digits to emphasize their lack of precision. The three-digit estimates are used in the accompanying illustration of the computation of partial *r*'s.

Applying this equation to the example, we have the following:

$$r_{ds \cdot b} = \frac{.539 - (-.654)(-.625)}{\sqrt{1 - -.654^2} \sqrt{1 - -.625^2}}$$

$$= \frac{.130}{.590} = .22$$

In the example "discontent" is symbolized d, strife is s and "balance" is b. When we compute partials manually, the substantive meaning of our computations is more easily followed if we use meaningful symbols rather than numbers to represent the variables.

The initial r between "discontent" and strife was .54; when we control for the effects of "balance" it declines to .22. For both these r's we can determine a coefficient of determination by squaring them. In this comparison we find that "discontent" initially accounted for 29% of the variation in strife. With "balance" controlled, however, the proportion of strife independently explained by "discontent" is only 5%.

Before interpreting this decline we might also want to see what happens when "balance" and strife are correlated with a control for "discontent." In this comparison we find a partial $r_{bs \cdot d} = -.43$, compared with the initial r of −.63 between "balance" and strife alone. Here the proportion of variance "explained" declines from 39% without the control to 18% with "discontent" controlled. These results are easily interpreted in light of the theoretical argument. Most of the effects of "discontent" on the extent of strife in democracies are mediated by the social balance between regimes and dissidents. On the other hand popular discontent has a moderate effect on strife independent of the effects of social balance. In Section 7.3 we will mention some of the various "causal" interpretations of such patterns among partial r's.

Now we can demonstrate the results of using all three independent measures to predict variations in magnitudes of strife. We obtain the following regression equation, beneath which the partial r's for each independent variable are shown:

$$Total\ strife = -.574 + .0029\ (dis.) + .2238\ (just.) - .0204\ (balance)$$
$$(.22) \qquad\qquad (.40) \qquad\qquad (-.20)$$

The R for this regression equation is .716, giving a coefficient of multiple determination (R^2) of .51. The researcher must be prudent in the number of independent variables added to such equations, however, because as their number approaches the number of cases, he capitalizes on chance variations that inflate the value of R.

THE RELATIVE IMPORTANCE OF INDEPENDENT VARIABLES   The regression equation obtained above can be used as a predictive equation by applying it to the country scores for discontent, justifications, and balance. The best estimate of any democracy's total strife can be gotten by multiplying its "discontent" score by .0029, its "justifications" score by .2238, and its "balance" score by $-.0204$; summing these three; and subtracting the constant, $-.574$. The predicted scores thus obtained will by definition correlate about .72 with the true scores.

A basic theoretical question about a multiple regression equation is the relative importance of its independent variables. "Importance" can mean different things from different perspectives. A group seeking to change the magnitude of strife in a system might regard "balance" as most important because it seems more easily manipulated than the psychological or psychocultural variables in the equation. If our concern is accurate prediction rather than manipulation, we probably will be most interested in *how much variance* in strife is explained by each. The partial r's provide this information: they represent the amount of variation in strife that each independent measure explains when the other independent variables are controlled. We can see from the partials listed below the equation that "justification" is the most important in this sense; "discontent" and "balance" are considerably weaker.

A third way of judging the relative importance is to ask *how much change* each of them produces in the dependent variable. This can be thought of as their relative effects on the slope of the regression line, something that cannot be directly determined from either the partial r's or the b weights in the regression equations. The measure of relative degree of change is called a *beta weight,* and is derived from the b weights by standardizing them. Recall that the measures used in the multiple correlation analysis represent much different scales of measurement. "Discontent" is measured on a 0 to 400+ scale; "justifications" is a sum of standard scores and ranges from -5.4 to $+3.6$; and so forth. Beta weights permit a direct, standard comparison of how much effect each has on the dependent variable. Using beta weights, the above equation is

$$Total\ strife = -.574 + .207\ (dis.) + .402\ (just.) - .226\ (balance)$$

These weights cannot be applied directly to the raw data to predict strife scores; they could be used if the raw scores were also standardized. It will be noted that in the strife analysis the beta weights correspond quite closely to the partial r's. This is not always the case. Blalock distinguishes between partials and betas as follows: "The partial correlation is a measure of the *amount of variation explained* by one independent variable after the others have explained all they could. The beta weights...indicate *how much change* in the dependent variable is produced by a standardized change in one of the independent variables when the others are controlled" (1960, p. 345).

Methodologists have given much attention in recent years to the uses and misuses of b weights, beta weights, and partial r's, depending on the kind of problem that concerns the investigator. Blalock (1967) argues, for example, that r's and beta weights ought to be used when we are interested in describing relationships in closed populations; they tell us which variables are most closely related to which others, and how, *in that population*. But if we are interested in comparing populations, or stating general laws, it is preferable to work with the unstandardized b coefficients. The reader of this book needs a good deal more information than can be presented here about the multiple regression model, and the debate over its applications to particular problems, if he is to resolve all of his own theoretical and analytic problems. Blalock's works (1960, 1967) and also Blalock and Blalock (1968) should help.

MULTICOLLINEARITY   This jawbreaking word refers to a special problem of multiple correlation and regression analysis, one that makes it difficult or impossible to make causal interpretations of regression equations. The crux of the multicollinearity problem is that if any of the independent variables are highly correlated, their b and beta weights in the regression equation are unreliable. Technically, the greater their correlation with one another, the greater the standard errors of their regression coefficient. (The technical rationale and examples are given in the literature: for example, Blalock 1963, and Forbes and Tufte 1968.) The consequence is that their separate effects on the dependent variable cannot be untangled with any certainty. So it cannot be said that one is more important than another— which also makes it impossible to unambiguously test causal models, of the kinds described in the last section of this chapter. As a general rule, the greater the empirical or theoretical implications the researcher expects to draw from small differences in b or beta weights, the less multicollinearity should be accepted.

SIGNIFICANCE TESTS   Finally we should mention that standard tests can be used to evaluate the significance of the multiple R and partial r's, and of b and beta weights. R and the partial r are evaluated with the F test, which takes into account the number of cases included and the proportion of variation explained (see Blalock 1960, pp. 354–57). For b and beta weights the t test of significance can be used. Technically the tests require the familiar assumptions of random sampling, normality, and several others. Practically, they often are invaluable in answering such questions as which independent variables, and how many of them, should enter a regression equation; and whether differences between b or beta weights are great enough to warrant conclusions about their substantive differences.

Factor Analysis

THE NATURE OF FACTOR ANALYSIS   What factor analysis does is not difficult to grasp intuitively. In the words of the technique's most active proponent in politimetrics, Rudolph Rummel, "it takes thousands and potentially millions of measurements and qualitative observations and resolves them into distinct patterns of occurrence" (1967, p. 445). Said differently, it searches systematically through any large number of measures (for countries, cities, parties, years, or any other unit of analysis) to find their common dimensions of variation. The input is a correlation matrix, containing the r's between each measure and every other one in the analysis. Interval and dichotomous measures are appropriately included: ranked data is sometimes also included, though without full methodological justification. Different kinds of patterns can be sought in these data, depending on the researcher's interest. He may want to determine which measured characteristics vary together. This is R factor analysis, and is most commonly used in political analysis. Or he may want to know which cases cluster together, by virtue of having similar scores on the measures used; this is Q factor analysis. There are other kinds of factor analysis especially suited to identifying patterns of changes over time and similar time periods. The complexities of the technique preclude any attempt to explain it here; it has a vocabulary and contingent methods distinct from those of other kinds of bivariate and multivariate analysis. A good, relatively nontechnical introduction is Rummel 1967; more technical surveys are found in most statistics texts, a comprehensive one being Palumbo 1969, chap. 13. The definitive reference in politimetrics is Rummel 1970.

What factor analysis can do is best illustrated by an example from the "American Values" study. In this study 69 categories of values were defined and their frequencies in each of 24 platforms counted. Most of these 69 measures of value concerns varied substantially among platforms. One of the researchers' questions was this: Are there some sets of values that vary together, that are commonly stressed in some platforms but little mentioned in others? This is the kind of question R factor analysis is designed to answer. All 69 measures of value frequency were correlated, with $N = 24$, and the 69×69 correlation matrix which resulted was factor analyzed, using various rotations. (There is no single factor "solution" to be found for a given set of data: different solutions are tried using different rotations. Those which make the most theoretical sense, or which satisfy some a priori technical criteria, are used.)

TABLE 7.2   *The "Modern Times" Factor in 69 Measures of Value Concerns in American Party Platforms*[a]

Value Measure Positively Related to the Factor		Value Measures Negatively Related to the Factor	
Measures	*Loading*[b]	*Measures*	*Loading*[b]
Scope indicator	.92	Respect-indulgence	−.65
Wealth-other	.90	Power-participant	−.56
Wealth	.90	Others	−.53
Skill	.86	Rectitude-scope indicator	−.47
Skill-other	.85	Undefined	−.44
Transaction-indulgence	.83	Rectitude	−.40
Base indicator	.79	Power-authoritative	
Wealth-transaction	.78	participant	−.39
Selves	.77	Well-being–indulgence	−.35
Nations	.77		
Power-scope indicator	.75		
Well-being–somatic	.72		
Affection	.72		
Wealth-participant	.69		
Power-doctrine	.67		
Transaction	.64		
Power-indulgence	.62		
Well-being–participant	.60		
Well-being	.58		
Republican	.54		
Power-doctrine	.51		
Supranational institutions	.48		
Well-being–deprivation	.37		

[a] From Namenwirth and Lasswell 1970. The measures used are the percentage frequency with which words of each value category appeared in each platform.
[b] Loadings are approximately equivalent to a correlation between a measure and the underlying factor.

The researchers' preferred factor result identified six major factors in the 69 value measures. These factors were interpreted as common dimensions or themes of value concerns. Some results are illustrated in Table 7.2, which lists the value measures that were most closely related to the strongest factor. Such factors do not necessarily have any "real" existence in the data; they take their meaning from the measures that are most closely associated with them. The "loadings" shown in Table 7.2 signify how closely each measure listed is related to the dimension. Loadings are interpreted like correlation coefficients: the square of any particular loading indicates the proportion of variation in the measure that is accounted for by the factor.

INTERPRETING FACTOR ANALYTIC RESULTS   Factor analytic results always pose problems of interpretation. A fundamental source of dispute is whether the factors are merely useful artifacts of the analysis, or whether they represent latent but real phenomena. The "realist" position has been predominant in politimetrics. One of the problems of interpretation is apparent from the list of measures associated with the factor in Table 7.2. It is by no means apparent what underlying dimension is represented. Examination of the words coded in each value category suggested a simple interpretation, though: most of the categories positively related to the factor are concerned with material well-being and transactions, while the strongly negative categories indicate mostly values of respect and morality. The authors interpret the dimension as one which signifies the values and value transactions of an industrial age as opposed to the dominant values of a preindustrial age. When they examined particular platforms that scored high or low on this factor, they found this quite evident. Wealth, well-being, and related values were strongly represented in the recent platforms, much less in the nineteenth century ones; the nonmaterial, "moral" considerations were much the stronger in the nineteenth-century platforms.

The "modern times" factor, as the investigators labeled it, accounted for some 23% of the variation in the 69 measures. It is not surprising that such a strong modernity factor would be found when political statements are compared across a century. The second-strongest factor distinguished between platforms that were primarily *contemplative* and those, often of the same era, that had a strong *action orientation*. The third-strongest factor, with about a tenth of the variance, clearly demarcated a cluster of *conservative* themes at one pole from a cluster of *liberal* themes at the other.

CONSTRUCTING SUMMARY INDICATORS WITH FACTOR ANALYSIS   One common application of factor analysis is to use its findings to construct *factor scores* for each case for each major dimension. The loadings provide the basis for factor scores. In the "American Values" study, for example, a "modern times" score was calculated for each party platform using the loadings shown in Table 7.2. This was done as follows: a platform's score on each of the "modern times" value measures was multiplied by the loading shown, and these scores were then summed to a single "modern times" score. This was repeated for each platform and for each major dimension. The effect was to reduce 69 scores for each platform to a much more manageable —and easily interpreted—set of six factor scores. Factor scores can be used in any kind of further statistical analysis. The technique is particularly useful when the researcher has constructed a number of indicators for a few conceptual variables, and wants to combine the indicators in some statistically justifiable fashion. Constructing factor scores is, in effect, the one quantitative technique that enables us to add (the common properties of) eggs, apples, and tennis balls without violating mathematical proprieties. Whether the canons of good sense are observed is a different matter which, as always, no statistical test alone can illuminate. (A useful discussion of some of these issues in factor analysis is Haas 1970.)

SOME OTHER MULTIVARIATE TECHNIQUES   The techniques we have just reviewed for comparing three or more variables are those that have been most widely used in politimetrics. This is not to say that they are universally understood or employed by politimetricians. They are applicable to a variety of studies for which only the weaker, or simpler, techniques have been used. On the other side of the technological divide are methods of multivariate analysis that are understood and used by only a few politimetricians, even though they are appropriate to many theoretical questions and analytic problems of macropolitical comparison. They will be more widely used as our familiarity with them increases. Some are mentioned here.

The basic multiple regression technique is designed to answer questions about the *one-way, additive, linear* effects of a set of independent variables on a *single* dependent variable. The conditions emphasized in the preceding sentence are not always approximated. When they are not, there are a variety of alternatives.

1. *Independent variables are not linearly related to the dependent variable.* In Chapter 5 we considered one solution to this problem: measures of one or both variables can be transformed. But this may raise contingent problems of substantive interpretation. An alternative is to estimate the nonlinear equation that best describes the relationship between the independent and dependent variable, and to incorporate it into the multiple regression equation. For a similar approach see Blalock 1960 (pp. 351–54).

2. *There are a number of (measures of) dependent variables.* One solution is to factor analyze the dependent-variable measures, and to use factor scores as the summary measure of the dependent variable. If there are several strong factors, separate regression analyses can be made for each. An alternative is *canonical correlation*. Its basic procedure is to identify the linear combination of independent, X variables, and the linear combination of dependent, Y variables, that have the highest correlation with one another. The procedure is repeated for other, maximally different (orthogonal) sets of linear combinations. The technique was developed by Hotelling (1936). Applications in political analysis have been few, despite its relevance to a number of research problems. It can help resolve the indeterminacy that results from multicollinearity, for example. One reason for its lack of use may be that its results are more difficult to interpret than those of conventional multiple regression.

3. *The relationship between independent and dependent variables is not one-way, or recursive.* The problem here is that one or more independent variables are not wholly "independent" of the dependent variable: the latter has some kind of feedback or reciprocal effect on the former. The "Causes of Strife" study provides an example. One component of the independent "social balance" variable is the regime's coercive control, which hypothetically influences the extent, or lack, of strife. But the extent of strife has a plausible reciprocal effect on coercive control: the greater the strife, the more likely the regime is to increase its coercive control by expanding military and police forces, soliciting external support, etc. The multiple

regression equation ignores any such feedback. As a result we cannot certainly determine how much of the variance in strife depends on previous coercive control, and how much coercive control depends on previous strife.

One approach to this problem is to compare time-series information on strife and coercive control in one or several countries, using the time-series techniques described in Section 7.1. But we will not be able to generalize these results beyond the few countries studied. Theoretically what we want to test is the nature of the relationship in a large cross-section of cases. An alternative is the cross-lagged panel correlation technique, discussed in Section 7.3, below. The technique does not avoid problems of serial correlation, however.

A third, powerful alternative has been developed by econometricians, the *two-stage least-squares method*. The basic procedure is, first, to set aside the final dependent variable—"magnitude of strife" in the above example. The wholly independent variables are then used in a regression equation to predict the reciprocally influenced variable, here "regime coercive control." This is the "first stage." Then predicted, Y' scores for this "dependent" variable are calculated, and substituted for the original data. Finally, the revised set of independent variables is used to predict to the final dependent variable. This is the "second stage" of the process. In effect, what we have done is to eliminate from the "regime coercive control" variable all possible influence that might be due to concurrent civil strife. The procedure can be applied to several independent variables which we think are influenced by feedback from the dependent variable that most interests us. There is also a "three-stage least-squares method." Technical discussions of these multi-stage methods will be found in econometrics texts, e.g., Christ 1966 (pp. 432–53). Their relevance to politimetrics will be more fully appreciated by examining their application to specific problems; one recent example is Averch and Koehler 1970.

The reader's attention should also be called to a related issue in econometric-type analysis, that of "identification." It makes little sense to apply a technique like that of two-stage least-squares to a set of measures without some clearly formulated a priori assumptions about which variables affect which others in which ways. Multivariate techniques are generally used in econometric analyses, and in a growing number of politimetric studies, to test such fully stated "models" of relationships among variables. A "model" is a theory about how variables are interrelated; often, competing models are tested. It is often found that two different models, or theories, provide equally good explanations for the observed patterns in the data. Such models are said to be *unidentified*. The objective of the researcher is to propose an *identifiable* or *identified* model of relationships among variables, one which is exclusively consistent with the data. As Christ puts it, "the ideal situation is one in which the model is just restrictive enough so that exactly one hypothesis is consistent with both data and model" (1966, p.

300). The issue of "identification" raises a whole set of questions about theory and empirical verification, some of which we have discussed in this book in different terms. The reader may well profit from reading the econometricians' discussions of identification problems; one is to be found in Christ 1966 (chap. 8). But their full implications for politimetrics are likely to be apparent only to politimetricians who have learned to think like econometricians, or alternatively to econometricians who have applied their approaches to the problems of macropolitical comparison.

7.3 Making Inferences about Causation

Philosophers of science abstractly debate whether cause and effect are ever determinable in nature or in human affairs. Mathematical statisticians point out that statistical techniques only describe relationships, they do not explain them. Yet we repeatedly act as though there were cause-and-effect relationships in political events, and when we evaluate and theorize about political phenomena we almost always assume that they fit in some web of causal interactions. We organize a delegation to visit a congressman ("cause") in the hope that we will change his position on a legislative issue ("effect"). We generalize about the sources of international tensions in terms of ideological, economic, and other differences among nations. And by a natural extension of this causal mode of thought, we look for patterns in quantitative data that support or disconfirm explanations posed in cause-and-effect terms.

No statistical techniques enable us to say that X causes Y with the same certainty that we can describe how X and Y covary. What have developed in quantitative analysis are conventions, built on plausible assumptions, by which we claim that certain kinds of statistical results are more or less consistent with causal theories. We cannot statistically demonstrate the accuracy of a particular causal theory; we *can* use these conventions to determine whether such a theory is consistent with the patterns in our data, and hence to weed out inaccurate theories. Two kinds of conventions in causal interpretation are reviewed below. The first assumes that cause and effect are time-dependent: if X regularly precedes Y, it is a likely cause of it. The second infers causal sequences from patterns in correlation and regression coefficients among static measures.

Time-lags and Causation

It is reasonable to suppose that if condition X regularly precedes Y, it is probably a cause of Y. Various phrases are used to describe such relationships. X may be said to be a "precondition of" Y, or a "preceding" or "predisposing" factor. Such language is on the one hand a response to the philosophic and extreme empiricist criticisms of causal theorizing, and on the other a reflection of genuine scientific caution. Only the latter need concern us here. One of the grounds for caution is that some preceding condition A may be causing both X and Y.

A second ground for caution when inferring causation from time-dependence is that, although X may have a definite, time-lagged correlation with Y, the mechanisms by which they are or could be connected are obscure. Consider the finding of several early U.S. voting studies that, in various regions of the country, periods of less-than-average rainfall usually preceded elections in which the "outs" replaced the "ins" in the state capitol and in congress. There is a plausible explanation, to be sure: low rainfall causes poor crops causes rural discontent causes a not-wholly-rational impulse to "turn out the rascals" who have not taken remedial action. But without concrete evidence to show that some such causal sequence is involved, the investigator is understandably reluctant to report baldly that "low rainfall causes voting swings in the Great Plains states."

A third, pervasive problem in making causal inferences from time-lagged data is that time-lagged correlations, like cross-sectional ones, seldom approach 1.00. Questions of possibly random relationships, measurement error, and the near certainty that all important political phenomena have multiple causes may make us hesitant to say that X causes Y on the basis of a time-lagged correlation coefficient of, say, $r = .45$. The probabilistic nature of statistical results does not fit well with the deterministic nature of much of our causal thinking. Even with such problems in mind, though, the researcher ought not to be discouraged from using time-lagged comparisons to test causal arguments. He should keep in mind that adequacy of causal arguments using statistical results depends on the kinds of theory and substantive knowledge he brings to the problem.

TIME-LAG COMPARISONS USING TIME-SERIES DATA   The basic procedure in time-lag analysis is to compare measure X at time a with measure Y at time $a + 1$. There are three variations of the procedure. One is to use dynamic or time-series data for X and Y, as was done in the "Alliances and War" study. Alliance aggregation in the international system was measured for each successive year a from 1815 to 1939, and was correlated with measures of the onset of war beginning in year $a + 1$. The researchers had no a priori grounds for thinking that one year rather than two or three was the best period of observation. Consequently they tested the nine different combinations of observation periods shown in the accompanying table. The upper right comparison in the table, for example, is between the five-year average alliance measure and a one-year measure of war. The middle, 3/3 comparison proved to be "best," because it represented the time-span comparison at which the r's approached their stable maximum. For example, the one-year "alliance" measure was weakly correlated with the three-year "onset of war" measure; the three-year "alliance" measure was much more

Alliance Measures Represented Average of	year (a)	years (a − 3) to (a)	years (a − 5) to (a)
year (a + 1)	1/1	3/1	5/1
years (a + 1) to (a + 3)	1/3	3/3	5/3
years (a + 1) to (a + 5)	1/5	3/5	5/5

strongly so; the five-year "alliance" measure was just slightly more strongly correlated with "war." You should note that the time periods were immediately adjacent in all the comparisons: they were not "lagged" in the sense that some fixed time interval was used to separate the measures. Just as the investigators had no a priori reason for thinking that one year was the best unit of observation, they offer no reason for thinking that the effects of alliance aggregation should be felt beginning the following year, rather than beginning two or three years later. The nature of the increasing correlations, just described, does, however, provide empirical justification for their procedures.

Time-series data ordinarily should be correlated using several different lags in the direction of the predicted relationship, *and one or two lags in the opposite direction as well.* The latter is called *time-leading* comparison and provides a partial test of whether a supposedly prior, "causal" variable is in turn influenced by the supposedly dependent variable. In the "Alliances and War" study this was done by correlating "onset of war" scores for year(s) a with "alliance aggregation" scores for year $a + 1$. (Many defensive alliances are in fact spurred by war, but the researchers were uninterested in such alliances. They had dealt with their potentially confounding effects by excluding war-formed alliances from their data.) The time-leading correlations showed that there were no substantial effects of this sort in the remaining alliance and war data.

TIME-LAG COMPARISONS USING CROSS-SECTIONAL MEASURES   The second variation on time-lag analysis is to make a static comparison of X measured across a number of cases at time 1 with Y similarly measured across a number of cases at time 2. More convincing evidence can be gotten by measuring X across all cases at time 1 and again at time 2, then comparing X_1 and X_2 separately against Y measured at time 2. (Of course, Y could also be measured at time 3.) We might obtain any of three patterns of significant correlations:

X_1 more closely related to Y_2 than X_2
X_2 more closely related to Y_2 than X_1
X_1 and X_2 equally related to Y_2

The first result offers the strongest evidence for a time-dependent causal relationship between X and Y. The second result does not necessarily invalidate a causal argument, but it suggests that if there is, the best that can be inferred, to save a causal argument, is that X_2 has an all-but-simultaneous effect on Y. From the correlation results alone, we could just as easily conclude that Y causes X. The third result is consistent with a long-term causal effect of X on Y, but is not convincing without further information on how both X and Y vary over time.

One twice-measured X was incorporated in the "Causes of Strife" study. A "discontent" measure, the short-term decline in value of foreign trade, was determined for 1957–60 and again for 1960–63. The r's for these two measures with total strife 1961–65 are shown in Table 7.3 for each of three groups of countries, distinguised by level of economic development, and for all countries combined. The r's between trade decline and strife are all relatively weak, but without exception the earlier time-lagged measure of trade decline is more closely correlated with strife than the simultaneous measure. The hypothesis that short-term trade declines have a causal effect across time on magnitudes of strife is supported. It is not *confirmed;* no statistical test could confirm this or any other causal argument. The hypothesis would be more strongly supported if the same kind of pattern were found across time in one or several countries.

This example also demonstrates the usefulness of dividing a larger universe of cases into several more homogeneous ones. The advantages are both technical and theoretical. Technically, if we had only the single pair of r's for 114 cases, in what is a closed population, we would have no basis for estimating the effects of chance on what is at best a weak relationship. Moreover, the difference between the two r's is too small to reject the null hypothesis of "no difference" by using a conventional significance test: the difference might well be the result of distributional irregularities too subtle to be seen on a scattergram. By partitioning the cases, however, we can make

TABLE 7.3   *Correlations Between Decline in Foreign Trade 1957–60 and 1960–63, and Magnitude of Civil Strife 1961–65, in Three Groups of Countries*

	Correlation between Strife		
Group of Countries	*1957–60 trade decline*	*1960–63 trade decline*	1957–60 with 1960–63 trade decline
Most developed (N = 37)	.285	.272	.533
Less developed (N = 39)	.226	.198	−.158
Least developed (N = 38)	.200	.101	.251
All countries (N = 114)	.198	.145	.192

three pairs of comparisons, all of which are of comparable strength and in the same direction. Theoretically, we now have much more confidence that the results reflect a real, dynamic relationship between the variables. If X has a time-lagged effect on Y of similar magnitudes in three different populations, our confidence in the *generality* of the causal relation is also strengthened.

CROSS-LAGGED COMPARISONS USING CROSS-SECTIONAL MEASURES An extension of the one-way time-lagged comparisons just discussed is a two-way comparison. X and Y are each measured at times 1 and 2, and all possible XY comparisons are made. They are essentially the same as the time-lead/time-lag comparisons mentioned in connection with the "Alliances and War" study, above. X_1 is compared with Y_1, X_1 with Y_2, X_2 with Y_2, and X_2 with Y_1. The method is called the "cross-lagged panel technique." The general argument is that if X is a cause of Y, then the following pattern of correlation coefficients should hold:

1. X_1 correlates most strongly with Y_2
2. X_1 correlates moderately with Y_1
3. X_2 correlates moderately with Y_2
4. X_2 correlates weakly with Y_1

The rationale is simply that if X causes Y, and the two are temporally separate, then X now should have some distinct effect on Y later, but that Y now will have little effect on X later. The correlations of interest in determining the direction of causality are those labeled (1) and (4), above. Immediacy of effect is reflected in (2) and (3). If they approach (1) in strength, the implication is that X is a short-term cause of Y; if (2) and (3) are no or little stronger than (4), the inference is that X is a long-term cause of Y.

None of the three studies uses the cross-lagged technique, and it has only begun to be widely used in politimetrics. Publication of extensive time-series data in the second edition of the *World Handbook of Political and Social Indicators* will probably increase its fashionability. It does pose a number of problems that may lead the unwary researcher to dubious applications. Its technical problems relate to measurement error and the trendiness of data, among others. There are also theoretical questions concerning the kinds of a priori causal assumptions that must be made when interpreting results. The basic reference is Campbell 1963. Subsequent discussions include Pelz and Andrews 1964; Rozelle and Campbell 1969; and Duncan 1969.

Partial Correlation Coefficients and Causal Inference

Earlier in this chapter we examined the relationships among "discontent," "social balance," and strife in the 38 democracies. One of the findings was that "discontent" alone correlated .54 with strife, but that when the effects of "balance" were controlled, the partial $r_{ds.b}$ was a much weaker .22. By contrast, when "balance" and strife were correlated, a control for "discontent" had less effect on the strength of relationship. An elaborate theory of causal inference has been based on the "case of the disappearing partial." The crux of the argument is that if X and Y are significantly correlated, and no antecedent "control" variable Z reduces r_{xyz} near to 0.00, then the relationship between X and Y can be considered a causal one. This does not enable us to say whether X causes Y or vice versa; we must specify on some other grounds, theoretical or empirical, which variable is the dependent one. Clearly, too, we can never test all the Z variables that might be responsible for a correlation between X and Y, but if we can take account of the likely ones, and the XY relation still holds up, we are justified in making the causal inference. (A good brief summary of the logic and application of causal inference theory is Alker 1965, chap. 6, on which the following discussion draws heavily; a thorough and straightforward presentation is Blalock 1964a.)

Both the theory and practice of causal inference analysis are a good deal more complicated than this would suggest; only a few complications can be considered here. Let us consider all the possible relationships that might hold among X, Y, and Z, provided we assume that Y is a dependent variable which influences either X or Z. There are eight possibilities, diagrammed and labeled in Figure 7.6. If we are prepared to make one additional assumption, then analysis of the simple and partial correlation coefficients among measures of the three variables will enable us to infer which type of causal relationship holds among them. The additional assumption is that no external variable is a major cause of any two of the three variables in the system; if there is such an external variable, a measure of it should be included in the system.[1]

To summarize, we begin with these assumptions. (1) X and Y are significantly correlated, and so are Z and Y. (2) Y is the effect, not a cause of either X or Z. (3) There is no major variable outside the system that affects any two of these three variables. Given these assumptions, the r's among the three measures enable us to eliminate many of the causal patterns shown in Figure 7.6. The properties of simple and partial r's associated with each type of causal pattern are shown in the accompanying table. It should be noted that the "pattern of r's" and the associated partial r's shown for the second and third case are mathematically equivalent. Moreover, when "real" data are used, it is not required that the partial r's sum exactly to 0, or that the product of the simple r's precisely equal the third. We regard a particular type of causal pattern to be supported if the appropriate partial r is not significantly different from 0, or if the product of the two simple

---

[1] Mathematically, the requirement is that the residual error terms of the variables in the system must be uncorrelated. Blalock provides a good explanation of why this assumption is required (1964a, pp. 44–50).

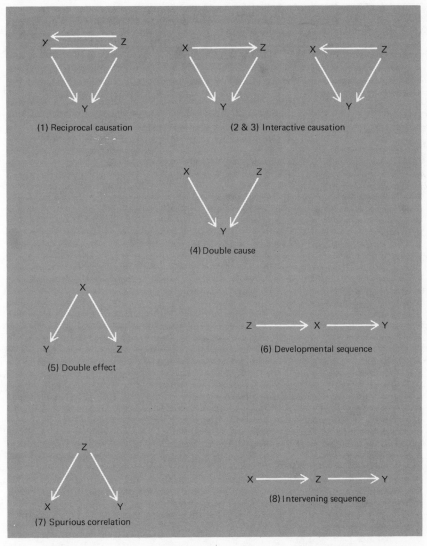

FIGURE 7.6. Three-variable causal relationships among two independent variables and a dependent one (after Alker 1965, chap. 6).

r's is approximately equal to the predicted value. It would be useful if we had equally simple means of distinguishing between (5) and (6), and between (7) and (8). But the theoretical argument should help us make these distinctions (also see Blalock 1964b).

Before we apply these principles to an example, it should be made as clear as possible that such applications are tentative because the accuracy of the assumptions is almost always in doubt. The only possible exception

Pattern of r's	Equivalent partial r's	Type of causal relationship
$r_{xz} = 0$	(no distinguishing partial r)	(4) double cause
$r_{zy} = r_{zx} \cdot r_{yx}$	$r_{zy \cdot x} = 0$	(5) double effect *or* (6) developmental sequence
$r_{xy} = r_{xz} \cdot r_{yz}$	$r_{xy \cdot z} = 0$	(7) spurious correlation *or* (8) intervening sequence
None of the above	No 0 partials	(1, 2, 3) reciprocal or interactive causation

would be if we had a set of measures which almost wholly accounted for *Y*, a watertight theoretical argument to explain why they did so, and a demonstration that our data had minimal error.

We can return briefly to the "Causes of Strife" study to show how we can test for different causal interdependencies among "discontent," "balance," and strife. For the purpose of this example, strife, the dependent variable, is *y*, discontent is *x*, and balance is *z*:

Possibility	Predictions	Results	Decision
1. Discontent and balance are independent causes of strife.	$r_{xy} = 0$	$-.65$	Discontent and balance are not independent causes.
2. Discontent separately causes both balance and strife; *or* balance causes strife via effects of discontent.	$r_{zy} = r_{zx} \cdot r_{yx}$ <hr> $r_{zy \cdot x} = 0$	$-.63 = -.35$ <hr> $-.43$	No support whatsoever for these contentions.
3. Balance separately causes both discontent and strife; *or* discontent causes strife via effects of balance.	$r_{xy} = r_{xz} \cdot r_{yz}$ <hr> $r_{xy \cdot z} = 0$	$.54 = .41$ <hr> $.22$	One of these contentions is plausible, though not wholly accurate.

We shall consider the two remaining contentions, those which are very approximately supported by the data, more closely. The "spurious correlation" interpretation is that discontent has no causal effect on strife: its correlation with strife is the result of the fact that variations in social balance cause variations in both discontent and strife. The "intervening sequence" argument, which is equally consistent with the data, is that discontent is correlated with strife because it acts upon or through the effects of social balance. We cannot distinguish between these alternatives solely through analysis of partials: we must make some prior theoretical assumptions. The theoretical argument in this instance makes the "spurious correlation" explanation highly unlikely. We postulated, consistent with most theories and case studies, that discontent is a fundamental cause of strife. Moreover, our theoretical argument is precisely the "intervening sequence" one: we hypothesized that the effects of discontent on strife are mediated by social balance. The causal inference results thus tend to support the theoretical argument. Equally important, they make it possible for us to reject the plausible competing models.

Theories or systems of variables seldom include only two independent variables. Models which include larger numbers of variables can be evaluated by causal inference techniques that are straightforward extensions of those for the three-variable case, though with the limitation that the simplifying assumptions become less and less realistic. For some straightforward illustrations, see Blalock 1964a (pp. 71–76).

Causal inference techniques can be applied to the data in any matrix of product-moment correlations, and can be an instructive exercise. A great many cautions and reservations must be kept in mind when evaluating the results, though. To review some of them, the assumptions of uncorrelated error terms and lack of "feedback" effects of the dependent variable on independent variables may very well be unrealistic. Multicollinearity—high r's among several independent variables—has distorting effects on causal inference, just as it does in multiple regression analysis. Some correlation coefficients may be poor estimates of relationships that are nonlinear or badly skewed. From here we can move back to questions of error in measurement, the validity of indicators, and the adequacy with which problems have been formulated. Such cautions are only a degree greater for causal inference analysis than they are for most other kinds of quantitative analysis. In recent years it has become fashionable to promote and use causal inference techniques in quantitative politics; some misuses, and critical reactions to them, are to be expected before the techniques become fully established.

Other Causal Techniques

There are at least two other mathematically related techniques that can also be used to evaluate causal models. Neither has yet been much used in politimetrics, but growing attention to them can be expected. *Dependence analysis* is a straightforward elaboration of partial correlation analysis which makes use of algebraic equations to describe causal networks (see Boudon 1965, 1968). *Path analysis* is a technique for expressing relationships among variables in a causal network in terms of "path coefficients" that are analogous to the beta weights in linear regression equations. The principal difference in usage between the Blalock-type partial r approach to causal modeling and path analysis is this: partial r's are used to test among competing causal models, while path analysis is used to assess the relative importance of various relationships in a given model. (See Duncan 1966; Boudon 1968, in Blalock and Blalock 1968).

We seem justified in concluding that politimetricians do not want for ways of studying cause-and-effect questions with quantitative data.

8

The Three
Studies:
Analysis and
interpretation

In previous chapters we used the three studies to provide examples of analytic methods. In doing so we surveyed many of their procedures and quantitative results, and offered interpretations of some of their findings. In this chapter we shall summarize and interpret some principal results of each study. These summaries resemble the concluding section of the papers and journal articles in which researchers report and interpret the results of empirical research. We shall begin the chapter by outlining the ideal research report, and suggesting why it includes what it does.

8.1 The Research Report

Empirical studies in political science are reported in various formats: as typescripts, mimeographed papers, journal articles and research notes, monographs, and sometimes as books. Whatever their format, the majority of research reports follow a conventional four-part outline that parallels the idealized schema of the research process which we sketched in Figure 1.1.

The first part of the ideal research report is a *statement of the problem*. In it the author reviews the theoretical or substantive issue being studied, and proposes whatever definitions, conceptual distinctions, and hypotheses he intends to use in the report. Researchers are seldom pioneers in the study of a particular question, so the "statement of the problem" ordinarily includes a commentary in which the writer shows how his research is intended to build upon or qualify others' work. In some instances this review is general and critical; in others it concentrates on a single hypothesis or set of earlier findings.

The research report deals in its second part with *operational procedures*. The universe of analysis is identified and justified, operational measurement of the variables is described, and procedures used in data collection and processing are summarized. The procedural sections of research reports vary principally in the detail with which procedures are described. If procedures are innovative, they will be explained and justified. The increasing use of narrative historical materials in politimetrics, for example, is still unfamiliar to some readers and controversial for others. The sources used and the operational procedures applied to them will, or certainly should be, fully and carefully described. But if cases, sources, and procedures are familiar ones, the writer usually will summarize them in a brief and technical way which communicates clearly enough to experienced researchers but often mystifies students. If there is any doubt about the extent of prospective readers' familiarity with procedures, they should be described in some detail—more so than is often now the case.

The third segment of the research report describes *data analysis and results*. If the basic data are of intrinsic general interest to other researchers, they may be reported for each case. More often they are summarily described, for example in a histogram accompanied by means and standard deviations. Relatively little raw data are included in most published reports because tabular material is expensive to print and consumes scarce space that editors prefer to reserve for textual summaries. Analytic techniques are seldom described in detail either, for the same reasons that operational details are not often reported. The professional reader is expected to know generally, if not specifically, what is meant when he reads that the researcher made a "two-way analysis of variance" or a "Q factor analysis with both oblique and orthogonal rotations." The analytic or "results" section of the typical report consists largely of scattergrams, graphs, and tables which report summary results, accompanied by a narrative commentary on them. Not all analytic results are so summarized—only those the researcher thinks are basic to the analysis and most interesting substantively.

The *results* of quantitative analysis do not "speak for themselves." In the last section of the typical research report the writer provides an "interpretation" or "discussion" of the results. If hypotheses were proposed at the outset, they must be evaluated in light of the results. If descriptive or relational questions were raised, they are now answered as best as they can be. Quantitative research always produces *some* result, even if it is the negative one that a question cannot be answered, or that a hypothesis must be discarded. Whatever the results, they have some substantive implications, and some implications for further empirical research. To spell these implications out precisely, with reference to their empirical bases, is the objective of the whole research enterprise.

This idealized outline of the research report is a general model, not a detailed prescription. All these four topics ought to be covered in any research report in politimetrics, whether a student paper or professional monograph. Whether they are done in precisely this sequence, using just these four divisions, depends on the logic and emphasis of the particular research project. We should also mention that this model resembles the basic communications model used in the empirical reports of all the empirical sciences, physical, biological, and social. The particular style of the research report in politimetrics probably has been most influenced by the styles prevailing in social psychology and sociology.

By far the most important point to be made is that the typical research report is not a straightforward chronicle of the research process. It reflects the *reconstructed logic* of research, not the actual process. Moreover, any attempt to describe the process in its true sequence and details is very likely to mystify and antagonize the professional reader. After all, the purpose of scientific communication is to report ideas and evidence with succinctness and precision. Readers do not often want to follow the writer down every operational dead end or through the results of every preliminary analytic step. Nor do they want to read through the long list of nonanswers to uninteresting questions that almost every quantitative study spawns in large numbers. The research report will often indicate what the actual sequence of research was. It also should mention major dead ends and fruitless analyses, so that other researchers will know what alternatives were tried and what to avoid in their own work. But these concerns ought to be subordinated to the writer's primary objective, which is to present a coherent, one-track argument and analysis. The only significant exceptions are "case histories" of research projects, which students sometimes write to demonstrate their research skills to teachers, and which professional scholars infrequently write for the instruction and amusement of their colleagues.

This helps introduce our final appraisal of the three studies. We examined in previous chapters the questions they were designed to answer, some of their operational procedures, and their analytic techniques. What follows is a survey of their principal results and the interpretations placed on them. Somewhat greater attention is given to the "Causes of Strife" study because its results, for the democracies, have not been previously published.

8.2 American Values

Some principal findings of Namenwirth and Lasswell's 1970 study, "The Changing Language of American Values," are reviewed here. Most results of Namenwirth's 1968 study of "wealth concerns" (surveyed in Section 7.3) are generally consistent with the 1970 study results.

The basic data of the "American Values" study are straightforward and were simply obtained. Their analysis was complex and the interpretation of the results is subtle and detailed. Some of the interpretations coincide with conventional wisdom about differences between the parties, but nonetheless add considerable richness and detail to our understanding of what those differences are and how they have been expressed.

Differential Value Concerns

The "American Values" study bases most of its conclusions on the relative frequency with which different categories of value words are used in the Democratic and Republican party platforms of 1844–64 and 1944–64. Two-way analysis of variance was used to compare the differences between parties, and between eras, in each of 69 categories and subcategories of words. Relatively strong differences occurred in 32 of the 69 cross-time comparisons but in only a few of the Democratic-Republican comparisons. Some of these comparisons are shown in Table 8.1, along with the associated values of ω^2 (omega), which is equivalent to a squared correlation coefficient (see Section 6.4). The contents of each value category are seldom self-evident, so representative words counted in each are indicated in parentheses after the category label. The value subcategories are also shown for each significant comparison. Consider the first subcategory, "doctrine": the 16 platforms of 1844–64 had an average of 0.22% of their words so categorized, compared with an average of 0.46% of words in the 16 platforms for 1944–64. (The average *number* of words in all platforms was 4,414, so an average-length 1844–64 platform would have 11 doctrinal words in contrast with 23 in a comparable 1944–64 platform.)

This skeleton outline of results is dust-dry and not very informative. We could have no better illustration of the fallacy that results "speak for themselves." To give meaning to these statistical abstractions we need a detailed appraisal of the specific materials that went into each comparison, the patterns among similar comparisons, and the shifting tides of party politics and national life that generated these symbolic changes. Namenwirth and Lasswell's monograph devoted to this kind of careful appraisal cannot be easily summarized. Rather than attempt a summary, we shall consider only their discussions of changes in "power" and "rectitude and respect" concerns, part of which are reprinted below.

DIFFERENTIAL POWER CONCERNS   There was no change between the two periods in overall concern with *power,* but there was change in a number of its subcategories. *Doctrine* was the only substantive subcategory that changed; the others shown in Table 8.1 refer to value transformations.

> The subcategory *doctrine* contains the names of political ideologies such as socialism, conservatism, etc. Since present-day English vocabulary has many more words to describe ideological distinctions than mid-nineteenth century vocabulary, the increasing concern with *doctrine* might be explained as merely a reflection of the change in political language. Yet, such an explanation misses the crucial point: the change in language itself is an expression of changing concerns. Clearly *doctrine* and *doctrinal* distinctions

TABLE 8.1 *Substantial Changes over Time and between Parties in Value Categories*[a]

Value Category and Subcategories	Average % Frequency by Era			Average % Frequency by Party		
	1844-64	1944-64	ω²	Democratic	Republican	ω²
Power, total	no difference					
Doctrine[b] (Socialism, conservatism, etc.)	.22	.46	.27	(.39)	(.29)	(.09)
Nations (names of nations, institutions)	.08	.38	.53	(.27)	(.20)	(.07)
Indulgence (to enrich, protect, contribute, etc.)	.42	1.18	.48	no difference		
Scope indicator (leadership, policy, recommendation, etc.)	.44	.66	.30	no difference		
Republicans	.10	.30	.21	no difference		
Democrats	no difference			.52	.06	.61
Authoritative participant (reference to leaders)	1.88	1.40	.18	no difference		
Participant (references to followers, citizens, etc.)	1.45	.92	.18	no difference		
Deprivation (to deny, to deprive, to punish, etc.)	.39	.57	.17	.54	.42	(.10)
Supranational institutions (United Nations)	.00	.04	.16	no difference		
Wealth, total	1.62	4.26	.72	no difference		
Wealth, other[b] (affluence, property, employment, etc.)	1.34	3.51	.76	no difference		
Wealth, transaction (to buy, spend, borrow, trade, etc.)	.10	.34	.47	no difference		
Wealth, participants (employer, farmer, worker, etc.)	.19	.40	.26	no difference		
Skill, total (efficient, machinery, work, etc.)	.42	1.14	.64	no difference		
Well-being, total (illness, relief, social security, etc.)	.88	1.35	.33	no difference		
Rectitude, total	2.50	1.97	.22	no difference		
Scope indicator (duty, faith, to pray, etc.)	1.18	.55	.38	no difference		
Respect, total	1.00	.64	.18	no difference		
Indulgence (to honor, to approve, to apologize, etc.)	.30	.09	.31	(.13)	(.26)	(.09)
Affection, total	1.68	3.08	.49	no difference		
Enlightenment, total or any	no difference			no difference		

[a]Subcategories with substantial differences over time or between parties, ω² greater than .15, from Namenwirth and Lasswell 1970. Differences shown in parentheses were statistically significant for the cross-party comparison at the .05 level or beyond, but have ω² values less than .15. The words listed in parentheses after each subcategory are examples or descriptions of the words counted in that subcategory. Note that ω² values were calculated from transformed scores, as explained on page 109.

[b]References to a substantive value; all other subcategories refer to transformations of these values.

have greater saliency today than in an earlier age. Also, our conclusion is a relative one. The concern with *doctrine* in the early period was smaller, not absent.

The value transformation subcategories *nations* and *supranational institutions* are self-explanatory. They contain the names of the nations and institutions of the world. The increase in concern with these two categories reflects both the changing position of the United States in the international order and the changing saliency of the international order and its actors for American domestic politics.

The subcategories *power-indulgence* and *deprivation* are equally unambiguous. *Power-indulgence* is largely a category of verbs describing the transference of *power* from an actor to a *power* subject; examples are: to contribute, to enrich, to gratify, and to protect. *Power-deprivation* describes the reverse process as indicated by the examples: to deny, to deprive, to punish, and to frustrate. The present-day political language contains many more references to *power-indulgence* than past platforms. Oddly enough, the same is true, although to a lesser degree, for *power-deprivation*.

This growing attention within party platforms to *power-indulgence* reflects the welfare state's concern with the *powers* by political intervention, by civil rights, and by welfare legislation. This value category suggests that at present the federal government wants to *protect* its citizens, to *contribute* to the social process, and to *enrich* the life of the nation; and it wants to do so to a greater extent than in years long past. . . .

The decreasing concern with *participants,* both leaders (*authoritative-participants*) and followers, indicates that at present a party in its campaign platform directs itself to society at large rather than to individuals. This diminishing attention toward the distinguished, such as the president and his cabinet and senators, may well indicate a denial of status differentiation in favor of the image of a citizenry untouched by the strifes and conflicts of interest, status, and national origins.

The increasing reference toward *power-scope indicator* identifies the programmatic nature of more recent political language. This category contains words such as leadership, policy, recommendation, and others which indicate a concern with means and instruments to attain *power objectives.* . . .

Finally, the increasing concern with the concept *Republican* implies that the Republican party has become of greater importance to both the Republican and the Democratic parties, probably as an actor as well as a subject of power politics. . . .

[The comparison in Table 8.2] shows that on the average, all Democratic party platforms look like *late* party platforms (both Democratic and Republican) while, on the other hand, the average Republican party platform resembles the *early* party platforms of both parties. We are tempted to conclude that Republican platforms are still part of an earlier elitist tradition of political organization, whereas Democratic platforms have the earmarks of a mass movement.

Before we overemphasize the differences between the Republican and Democratic parties, it should be noted that these differences are hardly constant over time. In fact, they are largely concentrated in the early period and have virtually disappeared in recent times. . . . In their justification of past practices and demands for the future (*doctrine*), in their concern with inequality (*power-deprivation*), and in their attention to international politics (*nations*), the two parties have become very much alike. Although both parties have increased their concerns, the Republican platform has done so to

TABLE 8.2   *Average Value Concerns in Three Power Subcategories*

Subcategories	Average % Frequency			
	Democratic	*Republican*	*1844–64*	*1944–64*
Deprivation	.54	.42	.39	.57
Doctrine	.39	.29	.22	.46
Nations	.27	.20	.08	.38

a far greater extent. From these interactive findings we infer that the Republican party has trailed the Democratic in its conversion from elitist to mass political organization as revealed by changing concerns with these *power* categories.

Summarizing our findings, the changes from the early to the late period indicate an increasing concern with procedures and means of power politics rather than with its ends. As a matter of fact, the increasing concern with *doctrine* reinforces this interpretation for, although *power-doctrine* suggests attention towards objectives, the use of ideological terms most often merely labels policies rather than describes specific preferences and values. This increasing programmatic concern with *power* procedures rather than objectives, which we shall meet time and again in our subsequent analysis, seems a revealing aspect of contemporary political language as well as action. The conversion of Republican and Democratic value preferences underscores this very point (Namenwirth and Lasswell 1970, pp. 19–21).

RECTITUDE AND RESPECT CONCERNS   References to both *rectitude* and *respect* declined between the earlier platforms and the later ones. *Rectitude* refers to the moral values such as virtue and goodness. The decline was principally in its *scope indicator,* including such words as creed, duty, faith, virtue, to bless, to pray, to promise. Declining concern with *respect* was manifest primarily in fewer references to verbs describing the process by which *respect* is given, for example, to apologize, to approve, to congratulate, to honor.

Speculating on the wider implications of these findings, they reveal a decreasing deference to the power of the supranatural and social orders: the gods and the masters. This interpretation stresses the diminishing importance of status differences in moral and social judgment and the general decrease of hierarchical structures in the processes of evaluation. At present, matters are considered to be different rather than better or worse.

The decreasing concern with *rectitude* and *respect* values, in general, can be given two opposing interpretations. First, the stress on these values in the early party platforms reflects some basic qualities of mid-nineteenth century American society, as exemplified in the dichotomous theory of Gemeinschaft versus Gesellschaft. . . . In this view, pre-industrial American society consists of a conglomeration of small communities where people order their relationships on the basis of well-articulated and commonly shared notions of *respect* and *rectitude.* Present-day industrial American society, on the other hand, orders its relationships on the basis of hedonistic and instrumental considerations which are shaped and shared by the anonymous processes of the economic market and of national political mechanisms. This explanation interprets, if not explains, in striking fashion the increasing concern with *wealth, skill,* and *power* values and the decreasing concern with *rectitude* and *respect* values; yet we are not convinced.

The second explanation is as follows: As indicated before, we believe that party platforms do not merely reflect operating values but rather value problems. In our times, *wealth* and *skill* are of great concern to party platforms because it is in these areas that the political process meets its most serious problems. Accordingly, the early party platforms show concern with *rectitude* and *respect* values because of the widespread corruption of appointed and elected political officials. The authors of the early party platforms wanted to convince the electorate of the elevated nature of the party's principles in order to overcome the well-founded skepticism about the character of the office seekers. This is not to say that corruption does or does not exist to a similar degree today as it did in the past. Today corruption is of less importance than mismanagement, given the increasing share of the national product spent by the government.

Republican party platforms, on the average, have remained more concerned with *respect-indulgence* [see Table 8.1] than the Democratic platforms have. The Republican platforms resemble the average early platforms (both Democratic and Republican), while the opposite is true for the Democratic platforms.... Thus we again find that the Republican party uses more conservative language (Namenwirth and Lasswell 1970, pp. 29–31).

OTHER CHANGES IN VALUE CONCERNS   We can mention Namenwirth and Lasswell's interpretations of several other substantial changes in value concerns. The greatest changes occur not in the "power" or "rectitude/respect" categories, but in increased references to the related values of "wealth," "skill," and "well-being." The differences have occurred across time, not between parties, and are easy to explain: "In general, our party platforms have become more and more oriented toward the nation's economic processes, roles, and institutions, revealing the increasing involvement of the government with the creation and distribution of wealth" (1970, p. 27). The growing concern with "well-being" indicates that economic involvement is partly directed toward promoting the well-being of individual citizens, not merely with increasing total national wealth: there are increasing references to aspects of material well-being ("wealth") such as medicine and relief, and also to psychic well-being, as indicated by such words as amusement, satisfaction, and disappointment.

Dimensions of Value Concerns

The authors acknowledge that the interpretations they propose for the changes in value concerns "were often unrelated and the choice or explanations were both ad hoc and ex post facto" (1970, p. 38). Ex post facto (after-the-fact) explanation is inevitable in empirical studies which begin without specific hypotheses in mind. Moreover, a good deal of after-the-fact explanation goes into quantitative studies designed to test specific hypotheses, because the researcher almost never gets results which exactly fit his theoretical predictions. When his results differ, he should and will try to explain why, and not merely conclude that his hypotheses are inaccurate. After-the-fact explanation does not necessarily have to be ad hoc, though. The ideal object in explaining a set of findings is the same as the ideal object of social theory: to provide a general, parsimonious, internally consistent explanation of observed patterns.

In the "American Values" study, we saw that similar explanations were advanced for diverse results. The increase in many categories of "power" was explained in terms of a more general increase in party concern with the procedures and means of power rather than its end. Another general pattern of change underlies many specific increases in references to "wealth," "well-being," and "skill." There is no scientific expectation that we rely only on reason and insight in the search for general explanations of a set of findings. In this study the authors resorted to factor analysis to answer two such general questions:

1. What general pattern emerges in our findings; in more precise terms, what distinct content *themes* (rather than individual categories) can be discerned in our party platforms?
2. How do these themes change over time and differ between the parties (1970, p. 38)?

We reviewed in Section 7.2 the factor analytic procedures the authors used. The 69 value categories were correlated for all 24 platforms ($N = 24$), and six relatively strong dimensions or factors were found. The strongest factor was labeled "modern times," because it showed that "wealth," "skill," and "well-being" themes all tended to be stressed in the same set of platforms, while emphasis on "rectitude" and "respect" tended to be low in these platforms but high in the others. The other factors were also labeled, according to the kinds of value categories most closely associated with each of them. Then six factor scores were calculated for each party platform, as measures of the prevalence of each factor in each document. For example, on the "modern times" factor a recent Republican platform would have a high positive score, while a nineteenth century Whig platform would have a high negative score. An examination of platforms with very high and low scores on each factor helped clarify factor interpretations. We summarize below the characteristics of four important factors, relying on Namenwirth and Lasswell's interpretations.

MODERN TIMES   Four rather different value themes are stressed in platforms with high "modern times" scores. These include (1) a concern with wealth and skill values; (2) the use of programmatic language, that is, language which stresses the desirability of social change and growth without identifying specific ends; (3) an emphasis on physical well-being; and (4) a concern with nations and supranational institutions. At the other, "pre-modern" pole are platforms with few references to these concerns but many to respect, holders of power, and rectitude. The Whig platform of 1848 exemplifies the pre-modern end of the dimension. It dwells largely on the integrity and patriotic virtues of its presidential candidate, Zachary Taylor. The platform with the highest "modern times" factor score is the Democratic one of 1952. Its central theme is a concern for the future, indicated, for example, by the frequent use of such words as plans, programs, future, and progress.

There were no significant differences between the parties on "modern times," but a very strong variation over time. The ω^2 value for the difference between the early and late platforms is .86. Moreover, none of the early platforms had as high a score on "modern times" as any of the later platforms; the time difference is not only statistical but absolute.

The central question in interpreting this factor is whether it is a "real" one or not. In other words, do the changes over time in these rather different kinds of value concerns represent a polarized system of beliefs, those of modern, industrial society versus those of pre-industrial society? Or were there several different changes in American value concerns, between the mid-nineteenth and mid-twentieth century, which are partly or largely independent of one another, but which cluster together "spuriously" because of their common variation with time? Namenwirth and Lasswell tested these possibilities in several ways, for example by controlling the "time" variable in a factor analysis. They conclude that the second of the two possible explanations is the correct one, and elaborate that conclusion as follows (1970, pp. 41–45):

1. Early platforms elaborate on different values and value transformations than late platforms.
2. There is no latent and ideological value theme (or dimension) which changes from early to late platforms and which explains the changing prevalence of particular value concerns.
3. The casually unrelated change in each of the pertinent value categories must therefore be attributed to another kind of change, and most likely to changes in social structure.
4. A plausible explanation is that pre-industrial and industrial societies are confronted with qualitatively different kinds of social and political problems, which lead to differential value articulations over time in American party platforms.

CONTEMPLATION VERSUS ACTION   The second strongest factor distinguished between platforms that stressed *conciliatory contemplation* and others stressing *divisive action*. Two important differences were found. First, the parties reversed their orientation between the two periods. The early Democratic platforms are strongly action-oriented and show a great concern with the uses of power. The Republicans give much more emphasis to understanding and conciliation. In the recent period the Democratic platforms are consistently more contemplative than the Republican, but the difference is not nearly so great as it was before the Civil War. The second difference is that before the Civil War the parties polarized on this dimension: when one party took a contemplative position the other took an activist one. In the modern era, though, their positions are approximately the same in any given election. The interpretation is that in the mid-twentieth century the parties had become more sensitive to external conditions and public opinion than to each other: both respond in the same way, though in different degrees, to changing conditions and opinion.

CONSERVATISM VERSUS LIBERALISM   Another factor distinguished between conservative and liberal themes. Toward one pole were platforms with frequent references to values suggesting "conservative morality." These included the Democratic platform of 1860 and the Whig's of 1852, both of which were centrally concerned with the constitutional issue of state's rights. Toward the other pole were platforms that emphasized individual happiness and rights, such as the Democratic platform of 1864. The greatest polarization of platforms in a single campaign year on the conservatism-liberalism dimension occurs in 1964, the year in which the conservatism of Senator Goldwater contended with the liberalism of President Johnson's "great society."

AUTHORITARIANISM VERSUS ENGLIGHTENMENT   This polarity resembles the conservative-liberal one at its conservative extreme. But whereas the former factor incorporates positive aspects of conservatism, such as constitutional obligations, the "authoritarian" pole includes frequent reference to negative qualities such as deprivation, contraction, and restriction. Also associated with the "authoritarian" pole are value categories of religious morality and reference to Republicanism. These "authoritarian" references are in contrast to an opposing set of platform themes emphasizing the *enlightenment* values of learning and understanding. Interestingly, the most "authoritarian" document is the Republican platform of 1860, with its vehement denunciations of slavery and accusations that its Democratic opponents are guilty of corruption and treason. The authors interpret it as a nineteenth-century manifestation of authoritarianism on the left. The "enlightenment" polarity is strongest in the Democratic platform of 1964, which stresses the danger of political extremism and advocates understanding and knowledge as a means to overcome national divisiveness and world problems. By contrast, the Republican platform of the same year was the third most "authoritarian" of all platforms of either era, as well as being the most "conservative" of the recent era.

Namenwirth and Lasswell conclude "that authoritarianism is not just a different form of conservatism. It is an altogether different dimension or quality of political thought which may be directed to conservative or liberal causes" (1970 p. 57).

Conclusions and Interpretations

Content differences between the Republican and Democratic platforms are few, but show a consistent pattern: the parties differ in their concern with means and procedures of value transformations, but not with regard to substantive goals. Where significant differences exist, Republican platforms seem more like early ones, Democratic platforms like recent ones. This conservative flavor of Republican platforms is evident in the Republican stress on status differentials, in contrast with the greater inclusiveness of the Democratic platforms.

Interactive comparisons across time show that most differences between the parties have strikingly diminished. They have converged especially in regard to their relative emphasis on status differences and social inequalities. No longer do they formulate their value positions largely by reference to one another; instead they have become much more responsive to aggregate value preferences. Two explanations are suggested for the change:

> First...the platform committees are far better informed about the aggregate state or value preferences in American society. Secondly, regional and class disputes in American society have greatly diminished; consequently, aggregate value preferences do not merely represent some statistical average but an existential reality of its own. Responsiveness to public opinion therefore limits [party] value choice (1970, p. 60).

The greatest differences are those that distinguish the platforms of the early period from the recent one.

> Recent platforms show a far greater concern with the problems and values of the economy, the technology, the health and education of the citizenry, and the international order. In addition, they reveal a diminishing concern with status differences and the religious or secular rationales of social inequality. Finally, in arguing their respective cases, contemporary platforms tend to stress programmatic arguments by articulating procedures rather than polemic ends. In this manner, they often operate as if the political ends are given in an obvious consensus while the contending parties merely dispute the best or most efficient means to attain those values (1970, p. 60).

One unexamined question has been shadowing us: How valid is it to infer value differences and changes from content analysis? Superficially, the party platforms contain many things: they make promises for the future, explain past successes and failures, criticize the opposition, and provide supposedly objective descriptions of the state of the nation. These themes probably reflect, or at least are consistent with, the value orientations of the party leaders. Even if we assume that platform writers are wholly cynical, they could not contradict going common sense about what the party does and represents. Moreover, they must tailor their document to what they know of the values of its potential audience. These are plausible arguments, not proof. We can also consider the results of the value analysis. They are internally consistent, and are congruent with much of what we know of American political history. This too is evidence, not proof. In fact there is no *proof* that party platforms, or any other document or statement, reflects accurately the states of mind of the communicators or the audience. The best we can do is seek converging evidence to help verify or reinterpret the results of content analysis. Ultimately the validity of content analysis, and all social indicators, rests on assumptions that are plausible, and testable, but never definitively proven.

8.3 Causes of Strife

This study evaluates the relative importance of three proposed causes of civil strife in 38 democracies: discontent arising from relative deprivation; psychocultural orientations toward governments and violence; and the balance of support between dissidents and government. We saw in previous chapters how some of these variables were measured, and showed some results of their analysis. The principal findings are reviewed and interpreted here as they would be in a professional research paper. A similar analysis of the causes of strife in 21 nations of the Western Community has been published (Gurr 1970b).

Magnitudes of Strife

First we shall briefly review the measures of the dependent variable, the magnitude of civil strife 1961–65.

1. *Total strife* is the sum of standard scores of (1) man-days of participation in strife per 100,000 population, and (2) deaths from strife per million population. The component indicators were separately analyzed and compared in Chapter 6. The standard scores on these indicators are based on data for 114 polities, not just the 38 democracies.

2. *Turmoil* and *rebellion* are components of total strife. Turmoil includes riots, clashes, demonstrations, and political strikes. Rebellion includes plots, coups, terrorism, and guerrilla and civil wars. Each is measured like total strife, by summing standard scores of man-days and deaths for each of the two types of events.

3. *Nonviolent* and *violent* strife are categories that cut across the turmoil-rebellion distinction. Nonviolent strife includes all events which resulted in neither casualties nor damage: demonstrations and political strikes are usually peaceful forms of turmoil; plots are nonviolent or pre-violent conspiracies. The measure for nonviolent strife is the man-days standard score for such events. Violent strife is measured like total strife, by summing standard scores of man-days and deaths for all violent events.

Since our measure of total strife is based on quite different kinds of actions, one of our first analytic questions is whether democracies with one

TABLE 8.3   *Correlations among Strife Measures for 38 Democracies, 1961–65*

	Nonviolent	Turmoil	Violent	Rebellion	Total strife
Turmoil	.71	1.00			
Violent	.37	.80	1.00		
Rebellion	.11	.38	.77	1.00	
Total strife	.53	.84	.97	.75	1.00

type of strife are also likely to have other types. The correlation matrix in Table 8.3 helps answer this question. The four component types are listed in order of increasing relative violence. Looking down the column of r's for "nonviolent" strife, we see that it is rather strongly related to turmoil, $r = .71$, but not to violent strife or rebellion: democracies with high levels of nonviolent strife are only slightly more likely than others to have high levels of violent strife or rebellion. On the other hand there is no evidence that peaceful protest is a *substitute* for the more violent forms of strife. If it were, we would expect a negative correlation between nonviolent strife and some of the measures of the more violent kinds. Generally, the *occurrence* of different forms of strife tends to coincide, even if their magnitudes are not always closely related. One comparison supports this conclusion: of the 33 democracies with any strife at all between 1961 and 1965, 28 had two or more of the four kinds in our cross-cutting distinctions and 19 had three or more.

Our final question is whether the r's among the forms of strife are strong enough to warrant using total magnitude of strife as a summary dependent variable. A glance at the bottom row of Table 8.3 indicates that total magnitude of strife correlates very closely with the measures of turmoil and violent strife, and hence is a good summary measure of them. It is less adequate as a summary of rebellion, and least adequate for nonviolent strife. This suggests that we test our causal hypotheses using three indicators of the dependent variable: magnitudes of nonviolent strife, rebellion, and total strife.

Discontent as a Cause of Strife

To what extent do variations in discontent among the citizens of democracies determine national differences in strife? The correlation results for our separate and combined measures of deprivation (= inferred discontent) are shown in Table 8.4. The r between "all deprivation" and total strife is a moderately strong .54, which signifies that 29% of the variation in strife can be attributed to variations in discontent ($.54^2 = .29$, expressed here in percentage terms). But we also see that the more violent forms of strife are much more influenced by deprivation than is nonviolent strife.

TABLE 8.4 *Percentages of Different Forms of Strife Explained by Different Kinds of Deprivation*[a]

Deprivation	Type of Strife		
	Nonviolent	*Total*	*Rebellion*
Short-term economic	−1%	12%	26%
Short-term political	5	13	21
Persisting	2	22	17
All deprivation (sum of above three measures)	2	29	40

[a] Squared r's × 100.

The separate deprivation measures are not even significantly related to nonviolent strife; but together they explain 40% of the variation in rebellion. This deprivation/rebellion relationship is graphed in Figure 8.1. The only substantially deviant cases are Colombia and Venezuela. An exponential

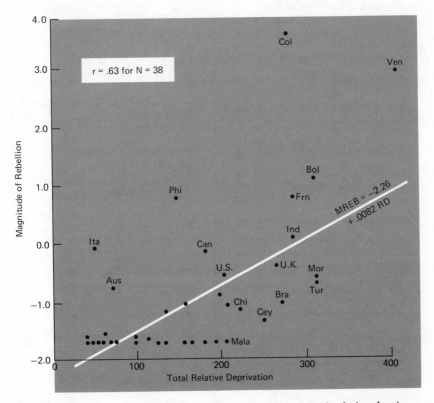

FIGURE 8.1. Magnitude of rebellion 1961–65 and total relative deprivation.

curve might fit the data plot slightly better: the magnitude of rebellion tends to increase only gradually until very high levels of deprivation are reached. Either best-fit line would leave three substantially deviant cases above and to the left, i.e., countries with substantially greater rebellion than would be predicted from their deprivation scores. They are the Philippines, Italy, and Austria, each of which has experienced terrorism by tiny, dissident minorities whose intense discontent probably is not well-represented in our summary measures of deprivation.

Cultural Justifications and Low Legitimacy as Causes of Strife

How important are the cultural experience of violence, and the legitimacy of the political system, as causes of contemporary strife in the democracies? Our summary measure of these "justifications for strife" is more closely related to strife magnitudes than either deprivation or social balance: it explains about 42% of the differences in strife (Table 8.5). The relationship is shown graphically in Figure 8.2. The fit is remarkably good, with five exceptions: the five countries with the highest magnitudes of strife are substantially off the best-fit line. Strife in most of these countries was also poorly predicted by deprivation.

The different facets of "justifications" have different effects on strife, as we see from the percentages of explained variance in Table 8.5. A lack of political legitimacy tends to increase nonviolent strife in democracies, but has no consistent, independent effect on the extent of rebellion. The extent and success of past strife have the opposite effects: they tend to increase the more violent forms of rebellion but have little effect on nonviolent strife.

We can combine these results for "justifications" with our analysis of "deprivation." Nonviolent strife in the democracies seems to be more a consequence of how citizens feel about the legitimacy of their governments than of intense grievances. The most serious forms of strife, on the other hand, appear to be direct responses to intense frustrations which are not much affected by political loyalties. Traditions of violence have their greatest

TABLE 8.5 *Percentages of Different Forms of Strife Explained by Different Aspects of Justifications*[a]

Indicators of Justifications	Type of Strife		
	Nonviolent	*Total*	*Rebellion*
Illegitimacy	36%	28%	4%
Extent of strife 1946–59	7	28	31
Success of past internal wars and turmoil	12	31	24
All justifications (sum of above 3 measures)	22	42	27

[a] Squared *r*'s × 100.

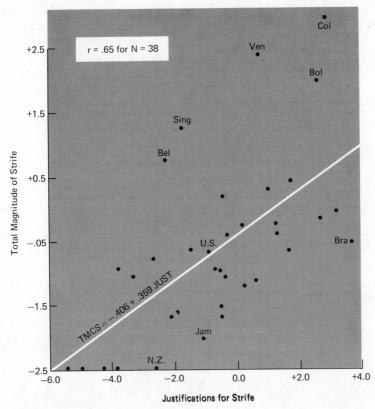

FIGURE 8.2. Total magnitude of strife 1961–65 and all justifications for strife.

impact on strife of moderate to high intensity. The following verbal "equations" are consistent with the quantitative results:

$$\frac{\text{governmental}}{\text{illegitimacy}} = \frac{\text{nonviolent}}{\text{protest}}$$

$$\frac{\text{violent}}{\text{traditions}} + \frac{\text{governmental}}{\text{illegitimacy}} = \frac{\text{violent}}{\text{turmoil}}$$

$$\frac{\text{intense}}{\text{deprivations}} + \frac{\text{violent}}{\text{traditions}} = \text{rebellion}$$

$$\frac{\text{intense}}{\text{deprivations}} + \frac{\text{violent}}{\text{traditions}} + \frac{\text{governmental}}{\text{illegitimacy}} = \frac{\text{multiform protest}}{\text{and violence}}$$

The Balance of Institutional Support and Coercion as Causes of Strife

In our theoretical model the most immediate of the causes of strife is the balance of institutional support and coercive control between governments and dissidents. In effect, "balance" is intended as a measure of how much freedom people who are motivated to strife have to act on that motivation. The relationship is plotted in Figure 8.3. It is moderately strong: about 39% of the variation in strife is explained by "balance." The three most deviant cases are the familiar ones of Colombia, Venezuela, and Singapore, all of which had substantially more strife than we would expect on the basis of their "balance" scores. Since all three have also been among the extreme positive residuals in both previous comparisons, some special explanations may be in order. In Venezuela, much of the strife of the first half of the 1960s was due to a concerted effort by the extreme left to topple the Betancourt regime, an effort in which Cuba was implicated. This strategic kind of motivation for strife may be poorly measured by our indicators. In Colombia the larger part of the violence of the early 1960s was the subsiding wave of *la Violencia*, a bloody rural war between supporters of the Conservative and Liberal parties that began in 1948. By the early 1960s it was confined largely to one province and resembled little more than violent banditry, though it had some Communist support. The social conditions that spawned *la Violencia* were those of the late 1940s and the early

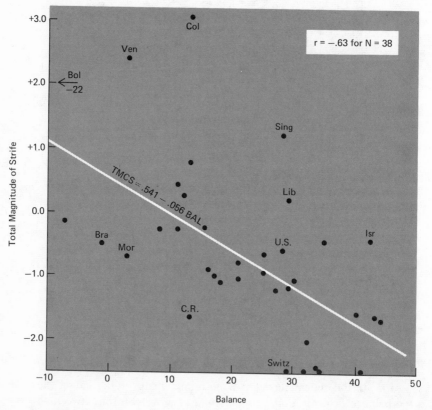

FIGURE 8.3. Total magnitude of strife 1961–65 and coercive/institutional balance

TABLE 8.6 *Percentages of Different Forms of Strife Explained by Different Aspects of Coercive and Institutional Balance*[a]

Balance Indicators	Type of Strife		
	Nonviolent	*Total*	*Rebellion*
Dissident institutional support	33%	24%	11%
Regime institutional support[b]	21	27	13
Dissident coercive control	8	32	38
Regime coercive control[b]	1	10	29
Balance (arithmetic combination of above)[c]	17	39	33
Balance (multiple correlation of above)[c]	36	42	46

a Squared *r*'s and *R*'s × 100.

b These relationships are negative, i.e., the greater are regime institutional support and coercive control the less is strife.

c The first of the "balance" figures was obtained by subtracting the sum of the two "dissident" scores from the sum of the two "regime" scores and computing bivariate *r*'s. The second set was obtained by entering the four measures separately in multiple correlation analyses, yielding multiple *R*'s.

1950s more than those of the 1960s. In the case of Singapore, most of the strife in that island city-state was nonviolent protest, which is easily organized in an urban setting and not so disruptive as the high strife score might suggest. This kind of case-specific explanation for deviant cases may be plausible, but of course it is not definitive. There may be some important additional variable(s) that accounts for the unexplained variance of these and some other cases as well.

The "balance" indicator is a composite of separate measures of the institutional and coercive capabilities of regimes and dissidents. These are separately compared with the several strife measures in Table 8.6. We should look at the last row of percentages first. They show the results of using *multiple correlation* (see Section 7.2) to relate the four separate "balance" indicators to strife. There is not much difference among the forms: rebellion is best explained (46%) and nonviolent strife is least well explained (36%). The next-to-last line shows the results obtained when we added the balance indicators, then correlated the sum with the strife measures. The levels of explanation are lower, which suggests that in this comparison our addition of independent indicators is a poor substitute for multiple correlation.[1] But this is a technical issue. Let us consider the substantive implications of the Table 8.6 results.

1 The reason for the decline in variance explained is that some of the separate "balance" indicators are only weakly correlated with some strife measures. It is generally true that when we combine several indicators of an independent variable, one of which is considerably weaker than the other(s) as a predictor of a dependent variable, the effect is the same as adding error to the better indicator: the correlation between independent and dependent variables declines.

Institutional support signifies the extent to which regimes, and dissidents, have secure organizational bases for action. The empirical components of *regime* institutional support include the government's economic resources, the coherence of its political support, and the loyalty of the organized labor movement. *Dissident* institutional support is indexed by the extent of dissident control of labor organizations, extent of Communist parties, and the ecological concentration of dissidents (see pp. 30–31). Table 8.6 shows that these regime and dissident institutional factors have similar effects: they substantially affect nonviolent and total strife but have little impact on the extent of rebellion. They have opposing effects on each particular form of strife, of course: a high degree of dissident institutional support means high levels of nonviolent strife and turmoil, whereas high regime support minimizes both. Of the two, dissident institutional support is the more important. It explains more variance in both nonviolent strife and total strife than any other single "balance" measure..

Coercive control contrasts the objective coercive capacity of the regime to dissidents' potential for coercion. We see in Table 8.6 that the coercive control measures have effects opposite to those of institutional support: they affect rebellion, and to a lesser extent total strife, but do not increase or decrease nonviolent strife. Dissident coercive control is more important: it is the strongest facilitator of rebellion and the second strongest facilitator of total strife. The coercive control exercised by governments tends to minimize rebellion, but has no substantial effect on other facets of strife.

One substantive implication of this pattern of results is that, in democratic societies, an intensification of regime coercive capacity seems the social policy least likely to reduce the less violent forms of strife. If any general regime policy might be effective in reducing turmoil, it is to increase the scope and activities of institutions supporting the government—but see the next section for a major qualification. A reduction in the capacities of dissidents to use force substantially decreases the likely extent of rebellion; it decreases the extent of turmoil somewhat less. It is unlikely to have any effect on nonviolent protest. From the point of view of dissidents, the prospects of rebellion or revolution are enhanced if they can increase their coercive capacities. Their chances of using peaceful means of protest and political pressure probably are enhanced most by organizational efforts. Similar results in a study of the causes of strife in the 21 nations of the Western Community led us to a similar conclusion. Our qualification of that conclusion is equally applicable here: "The evidence is cross-sectional, not based on the experience of particular groups and governments across time; it says nothing about the effects of various kinds or intensities of strife, nor about the effects of specific kinds of tactics. The analysis of these questions requires more detailed studies and measures" (Gurr 1970b, p. 141).

The Extent of Explanation

Taking all three levels of explanation into account, we can use multiple correlation and regression to estimate which are most important and how much of the differences in strife among the democratic nations they account for. In the correlation analyses we have examined thus far we used all 10 summary measures: three of deprivation, three of justifications, and four of balance. But we have only 38 country cases, and the more independent variables used in multiple correlation, relative to the number of cases, the greater the artificial inflation of R^2. (Even if relationships were entirely random, we would be able to "explain" one case with one variable.) Our compromise solution was to use seven measures of the independent variables in the final multiple regressions. We combined the two short-term deprivation measures because earlier analyses (Table 8.4) showed them to have similar effects for different forms of strife. The measures of *extent* and *success* of past strife were also additively combined, on the same grounds (Table 8.5). We eliminated the "balance" indicator that had the lowest r with each successive dependent variable studied.

The seven independent variables account for 55 to 68% of the variance of the different forms of strife, as shown in Table 8.7. Rebellion and violent strife are least well explained: $R^2 = .56$ and .55, respectively. The variation in turmoil—the most common form of strife in the democracies—is best explained: $R^2 = .68$. The regression equation for each form of strife gives beta weights; these indicate the relative impact of each independent variable on strife magnitudes when the effects of the others are controlled. Also shown in parentheses below each beta weight are, first, the bivariate r between the measure and strife; and, second, the partial r, which shows what proportion of variance in strife is explained by each measure when the others are controlled. Note that the explained variances for rebellion and nonviolent strife are not much greater than some of the R^2's obtained using indicators of only one level of explanation (see Tables 8.5 and 8.6). Substantively, what this means is that democracies whose social balance favors rebellion also tend to have high discontent and strong justifications for strife.

Before we examine some implications of the multiple regression analysis, it is helpful to review the uses, and limitations, of the technique for this kind of research problem.

ADEQUACY OF PREDICTION   The technique is ideally suited for estimating the extent to which a set of independent variables accounts for the variance of a dependent variable. In this particular application it gives us a numerical estimate (R^2) of how well this is done. From this we can infer how well, or badly, we have succeeded in (1) theoretically identifying the significant causal conditions of strife, and (2) operationalizing them. Of course it does not tell us what parts of the unexplained variance are

TABLE 8.7 Results of Multiple Regression and Correlation Analysis of the Causes of Strife in Democracies 1961-65

Type of Strife	Constant	Relative Deprivation[b]	Justifications[c]	Balance[d]	Explained Variation (R² × 100)
		Independent Variables and Standard Weights[a]			
Nonviolent =	−1.30	− 0.14S* (10, −16) − 0.15P* (12, −17)	+ 0.52L (60, 57) − 0.03T* (37, 03)	+ 0.48DI (57, 39) − 0.02RI* (−46, −01) + 0.08DC* (28, 06)	58%
Turmoil =	−3.20	− 0.06S* (28, −07) + 0.15* (42, 20)	+ 0.40L (56, 52) − 0.05T* (49, −05)	+ 0.57DI (71, 50) + 0.07RI* (−57, 07) + 0.13DC* (53, 11)	68%
Total strife =	−3.75	+ 0.18S* (44, 20) + 0.18P* (47, 21)	+ 0.32L (53, 41) + 0.19A* (57, 21)	0.39DI (58, 34) + 0.17RI* (−52, 16) + 0.02DC* (56, 02)	60%
Violent =	−3.69	+ 0.19S* (46, 20) + 0.21P (49, 23)	+ 0.22L (43, 28) + 0.22A (56, 23)	+ 0.35DI (55, 29) + 0.20RI (−48, 17) + 0.09DC* (59, 06)	55%
Rebellion =	−1.64	+ 0.33S (59, 34) + 0.05P* (41, 05)	+ 0.01L* (21, 01) + 0.32A (55, 32)	+ 0.18RI* (−36, 19) + 0.18DC* (61, 16) − 0.23RC (−54, −28)	56%

* These weights are significant at less than .10 using the one-tailed t test.

[a] The initial correlation coefficients and partial coefficients are shown in parentheses below each equation, with decimals omitted.

[b] S = short-term deprivation; P = persisting deprivation.

[c] L = illegitimacy; T = historical justifications for turmoil; A = historical justifications for internal war and turmoil.

[d] DI = dissident institutional support; RI = regime institutional support; DC = dissident coercive control; RC = regime coercive control.

due to incompleteness of the theoretical system, and which to bad measurement. The regression equation is also a tool that could be used for predictive purposes. If the causal conditions of strife in the democracies are stable over time, then current measures of the independent variables would enable us to predict magnitudes of strife in the near future with approximately the accuracy signified by the R^2 estimates.[2]

EVALUATING CAUSAL POTENCY   The beta weights permit us to say which of the independent variables have the most immediate impact on the dependent variable. Similarly, the partial r's enable us to say which independent variables account for the greatest amount of variance in the dependent variable. (Whether there are more important determinants outside our system of variables is another question; this can only be inferred from the size of the unexplained variance.) But the betas and r's do not ordinarily enable us to estimate the *independent* importance of each variable. It is important to understand this distinction. *If* our independent variables are not significantly correlated, then the beta weights and partial r's tell us how much each independently affects the dependent variable. However, if the independent variables are correlated, as they are in the strife data, we can only tell which independent variable(s) is potent enough to control the effects of the others.

EVALUATING CAUSAL INTERACTIONS   The multiple regression technique can be used to test directly a causal model which holds that the independent variables are uncorrelated with one another, and hence have additive effects on the dependent variable. They can also be used to test causal models which identify one particular intervening variable. Look at the regression equation for "nonviolent strife" in Table 8.8. The two highest beta weights, and highest partial r's, are for "illegitimacy" (L) and "dissident institutional control"(DI). These two variables control the effects of all others, a pattern which is consistent with a model which stipulates a causal sequence in which they are the *most immediate* causes of strife. But this tells us nothing about the interactions among the independent variables that *precede* L and DI in the causal chain. In general, we can usually draw limited inferences about causal sequences from multiple regression results—by examining the pattern of beta weights and partial r's—but we cannot test the adequacy of the more complex kinds of causal models.

2 The component measures of the independent variables represent various time periods, but the only serious qualification to the over-time predictive capability of the model is that a few of these measures are synchronous with those for strife. Short-term political deprivation and four of the 21 components of the "social balance" indicator make significant use of information from the early 1960s, some of which was influenced by the occurrence of strife that we purport to explain. It seems likely that if synchronous measurement for these indicators was replaced with time-lagged measurement, the levels of prediction would not decrease substantially.

COMPARING CAUSAL PATTERNS   The foregoing comments apply to multiple regression equations taken separately. *Comparison* of regression equations also gives us a very important diagnostic technique. We may compare equations for *several different subsets* of cases to test whether similar or different processes are at work in them. Or we may compare equations for *different facets of a dependent variable,* as in Table 8.7, to assess similarities and differences in their causes. We might also compare equations for *different measures of variables* related to the same dependent variable to see whether they have the same causal efficacy. All of this can be done whether or not we have a particular causal model in mind about interactions among the variables. The pattern of beta weights and partial r's in successive equations provides many clues by which we can test a priori causal assumptions, identify and revise partly formulated models, and, in the absence of prior theory, infer causal interrelationships.

A detailed comparison of causal patterns in the "Causes of Strife" study is beyond the scope of this book. What we do in the next section is to summarize the major implications of the correlation and regression analyses. The reader who studies the regression equations in Table 8.7 will understand some of the technical grounds for our conclusions.

Conclusion

We can begin a summary of major findings by reviewing the status of the basic hypotheses of the "Causes of Strife" study, given in Section 2.2.

1. *The greater the intensity and scope of discontent, the greater the magnitude of strife.* In the democracies this hypothesis is strongly supported for the more violent forms of strife, rebellion most of all. For the less violent forms of strife, though, it is not supported. The regression equation for nonviolent strife, for example, shows both deprivation measures to be *negatively* related to strife. This seems to suggest that the lower is deprivation, the greater is the extent of peaceful protest. But this is most unlikely. The alternative explanation is that the more discontented people are, the less likely they are to resort to nonviolent protest and the more likely they are to rebel. Our results reflect the greater prevalence of nonviolent strife in democracies with *relatively* low social discontent.

2. *The greater the justifications for strife, the greater the magnitude of strife.* This hypothesis is also supported, on the basis of indicators of governmental legitimacy and cultural traditions of violence. Legitimacy tends to inhibit the less violent forms of strife but not the more violent ones. Violent traditions cause an intensification of strife's more violent forms.

3. *The greater the institutional and coercive capacities of dissidents relative to the regime, the greater the magnitude of strife.* This hypothesis has qualified support. As dissidents' institutional support increases, the less violent forms of strife in democracies also increase, irrespective of governmental capacities. Coercive capacities of dissidents tend to facilitate strife;

regime coercive capacities tend to minimize only its most violent forms. The one surprising result is the effect of *regime institutional control* (RI). In the bivariate comparisons (Table 8.6), it was, as predicted, a negative correlate of strife. But when other variables were controlled in the regression equations (Table 8.7), in four of five comparisons RI is a *positive* cause of strife. Other things being equal, democracies with relatively strong and pervasive institutions have slightly more strife, especially violent strife. Our results are only suggestive. One interpretation is that they reflect a sort of institutional paralysis in some democracies which intensifies opposition.

4. One other aspect of the causal argument is that *discontent and justifications are indirect causes of strife whose effects are mediated by social balance.* This is not supported by the results presented here. We could support this conclusion only if the beta weights and partial r's for discontent and justifications in the regression equations declined to or near zero. The conclusion is that the three variables have interacting effects on strife which are only partly controlled by social balance. The interactions remain to be specified and tested, a task which is beyond the scope of this book.

5. Finally, the theory is said to be complete, i.e., *it identifies all the significant social causes of the several forms of strife.* The test of this ambitious assumption is how well the several independent variables account for variation in strife. On the average 60% of the variation is explained— not enough to justify the assumption. Part of the unexplained variance is the result of inadequate and erroneous measurement. The measures of justifications and discontent seem especially inadequate. Imperfect measurement is not enough to explain the unexplained variance, though. Some other, unmeasured variables that distinguish among the democracies are significant causes of strife. These may include a simple property like the new/old democracies distinction, or a complex one like the extent of class cleavages, or a series of "special explanations" for each deviant country. Most likely it is some combination of these kinds of variables.

The results of the study have definite substantive implications for particular countries. They can be used, for example, to identify the *strife potential* of a particular democracy or group of democracies. Two of the three independent variables represent relatively enduring conditions: justifications for violence and the social balance. They indicate a country's cultural and structural potential for strife. In Figure 8.4 the 38 democracies are cross-categorized according to these two variables, using dichotomous distinctions. The cross-classification distinguishes four groups of countries. The 15 in the top quadrant (I) are structurally and culturally most prone to strife; the 11 in the bottom (IV) are least so. The smaller numbers of democracies in quadrants (II) and (III) have opposing cultural and structural potentials for strife, low on one and high on the other.

Social discontent is more susceptible to short-term variation than are

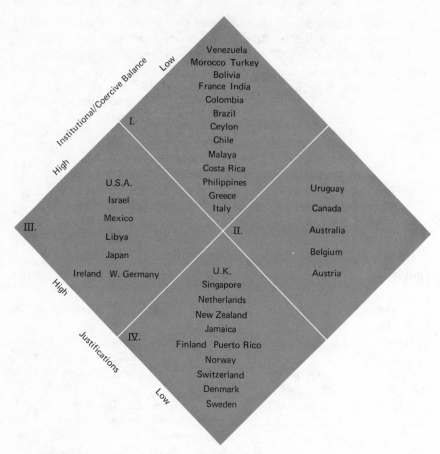

FIGURE 8.4. Strife potentials among democratic nations. (Nations are ranked in each diamond in decreasing levels of measured deprivation. Nations shown on the same line within a diamond have equal or nearly equal deprivation scores. Overall potential for strife decreases from top to bottom of the larger diamond.)

"justifications" and "balance." Within each group of countries in Figure 8.4 we would expect magnitudes of strife to vary according to the intensity of discontent, and have listed the countries in decreasing order of their deprivation scores in the early 1960s. The effect is a ranking of countries from top to bottom of the larger diamond according to their overall potential for strife. Moreover, we can make general statements about the types and intensities of strife to be found in the countries of each quadrant.

I. These are the turbulent and unstable democracies. Strife is likely to be chronic in them even when social discontent is relatively low. When it is intense, rebellion is highly likely. Ten of the 14 highest "rebellion" scores in the democracies, 1961–65, were registered by these 15 countries. Their chances of democratic survival are not particularly high, either.

Between 1960 and 1970 there were successful antidemocratic coups in 5 of the 38 democracies, of which 4 were in this group: Turkey, Bolivia, Brazil, and Greece. Only Costa Rica of the 15 countries seems exempt from these generalizations.

IV. These are the peaceful and stable democracies. Strife is likely to be low in them even when social discontent is high. Peaceful protest is more common than rioting, and rioting, though rare, is more common than serious attempts at rebellion. The only serious rebellion in any of these countries during the 1960s occurred in the United Kingdom, in Northern Ireland. Even Puerto Rico, which as a self-governing colony seems anomalous in this company, experienced little of the turbulence of the United States in the 1960s, despite the presence of organized advocates of independence.

II and III. The five countries in (II) have the cultural and political dispositions that elsewhere support peaceful and stable democracy, but not the institutional or coercive structures. The seven countries in (III) have the opposite combination: traditions of violent conflict are combined with a social balance that supports stability. Other things being equal, we would expect the countries in (III) to be both more turbulent and more stable than those in (II). An intensification of social discontent in a country in either group is likely to cause an increase in strife, more so than in the peaceful, stable democracies of (IV). But in the (IV) countries any consequent rebellion would likely be more limited, quickly suppressed, and of less political effect than in the countries of (II). The evident exception to these characterizations is Libya, whose constitutional monarchy succumbed to a national socialist coup d'état in 1969. The categorizations in Figure 8.4 are, in effect, a set of general predictions. The reader may find further support or disconfirmation for them in events that occur between the time of writing (October 1971) and his reading.

8.4 Alliances and War

The question posed in Singer and Small's 1968 study of "Alliances and War" was whether an increase in the extent of alliances in the international system increased the likelihood and extent of war. The answer was sought in a year-by-year analysis of all consequential alliances and wars between 1815 and 1945. The basic results of this study have been mentioned at several points above: the relationship is negative in the nineteenth century and positive in the twentieth. The analysis of these results can be summarized and interpreted quite briefly.

Validating the "War" and "Alliance" Measures

Two kinds of correlational comparisons were made of the time-series data on alliances and war. Five different indications of the extent of war and seven indicators of alliance aggregation were constructed and separately compared to ascertain how well they represented the underlying variables. Then the test correlations among the "war" and "alliance" indicators were made for several time periods..

The five indicators of "onset of war" were listed in Figure 5.2. They represent successive, overlapping three-year periods: 1816–18, 1817–19, 1818–20, and so forth. The "war" indicators are very closely related to one another, with r's ranging from .95 to .99, except for "number of wars begun," which correlates with the other indicators in the .2 to .3 range. Singer and Small concluded from the consistency of these results that the measures are all valid indicators of the incidence of war.

Seven indicators of "alliance aggregation" were used. They included percentage of all nations in *defensive* alliances, and percentage of major powers in defensive alliances; similar indicators for *any* alliances; percentage of major powers allied with minor powers; and two indicators of "bipolarity." The correlations among these indicators were somewhat lower but almost all were statistically significant; their average intercorrelation was .51. Correlations based on the alliance patterns of nations in the central system of nations were generally higher. The researchers conclude that "there exists a very impressive intercorrelation among these several alliance measures. In the central system, every indicator correlates strongly with every other. . . . Again, but to a considerably lesser extent than with war, we are tapping approximately the same structural phenomena" (Singer and Small 1968, p. 277).

Comparing Alliance Aggregation and War

Once the researchers were satisfied that their indicators of war and alliance aggregation were valid, they could evaluate the basic relationship in which they were interested: whether and how alliance formation and onset of war were correlated. The various alliance and war indicators were compared for three different time spans: the entire period, 1815–1945; the nineteenth century only, 1815–99; and the twentieth century, 1900–45. They were also compared for two different groups of nations: the total international system, and the central system only. Since there were seven indicators of alliance aggregation and five of war, this yields a total $7 \times 5 \times 3 \times 2 = 210$ r's with which to test a single hypothesis. A representative set of results for two of the "war" indicators is shown in Table 8.8. These r's very nearly do "speak for themselves," and highlight the major finding of the study: *In the international system of the nineteenth century, the greater the alliance aggregation the less war; in the twentieth century, the greater the alliance aggregation the more war.*

The r's in the center column of Table 8.8 show that over the entire time span, alliances have a weak to moderate positive relationship with extent of war. When the two eras are separately analyzed, weak to moderate

TABLE 8.8   *Correlations between Some Indicators of Onset of War and Alliance Aggregation for Different Eras*

	Era		
Comparison	1815–99 N = 85	1815–45 N = 130	1900–45 N = 45
Battle deaths, all nations, compared with:			
% all nations in any alliance	−.27	.34	.56
% central system nations in any alliance	−.45	.35	.50
% majors allied with minors in the central system	−.33	.34	.46
Central-system bipolarity, initial	−.34	.15*	.19*
Central-system bipolarity, alternative	−.30	.18*	.32*
Nations-months of war, majors, compared with:			
% all nations in any alliance	−.04*	.28	.46
% central system nations in any alliance	−.19*	.34	.49
% majors allied with minors in the central system	−.13*	.34	.47
Central-system bipolarity, initial	−.17*	.15*	.24*
Central-system bipolarity, alternative	−.16*	.13*	.36*

* Significant at less than the .01 level.

negative relations are found for the nineteenth century, somewhat stronger *positive* ones for the twentieth century. The *r*'s for the total period are positive rather than approximately 0 because of the relatively stronger relationship in the recent era. This time-dependent pattern of *r*'s appears consistently in all the correlational comparisons for the whole international system and for the central system only; for all indicators of alliance aggregation and bipolarity, and for all indicators of the severity and magnitude of war. The reversal in the relationship is unambiguous, unexpected, and unaccounted for by any extant theory that speculates on the linkages between alliances and international conflict. "In sum," conclude Singer and Small,

> whether we measure amount by number of wars, the nation-months involved, or battle deaths incurred, alliance aggregation and bipolarity predict strongly away from war in the nineteenth century and even more strongly toward it in the twentieth. One might say that those who generalize about the effects of alliance activity—and most postulate a destabilizing effect, especially in regard to bipolarity—have been so preoccupied with more recent history that they have neglected the patterns which obtained in an earlier, but by no means incomparable, period...(Singer and Small 1968, p. 283).[3]

---

3 The principal criticism that has been made of the Singer and Small study is that the results are not a precise test of "bipolarity" theories of international conflict, because the investigators' indicators of bipolarity do not quite accord with what the concept usually signifies (Zinnes 1967). Singer and Small's reply to the criticism appears in the final section of their 1968 report (pp. 285–86).

8.5   For Further Research

The studies we have just reviewed should demonstrate that politimetrics offers powerful and systematic ways of studying vital questions. The questions of men's values, social change, conflict, and peace are major issues of social theory. They are of great and obvious human relevance as well. You may be concerned that politimetric methods do not seem to provide definitive answers to such social questions. But no one scientific study ever does provide definitive answers. Science is *cumulative*. The first study of a problem clears away some of the confusion, the second one adds a bit more to our understanding, and so on through successive studies.

We must also recognize that social science does not and cannot offer the kinds of simple, dramatic "answers" we expect of poets, priests, philosophers, politicians, reformers, or revolutionaries. What such men usually offer as guides to action are individual insights. They may be valid enough for those who want to believe them, but they are seldom of demonstrable accuracy. In brief, what they propose requires faith, which is a different thing from confirmed knowledge. To create and maintain satisfying social life in a complex and changing world requires some social *science* as well as insight. We need objective assessment of the patterns and principals of the human, social, and political condition at least as much as we need inspiration. Uninformed inspiration, translated into action, has been the cause of much human grief and profound uncertainty about mankind's future.

There is no grand research design by which we can make final, definitive studies of any one, much less all, vital political and social issues. Political science, like all other sciences, develops by accumulating precise but partial answers to a series of small and medium-sized questions. These empirical answers become part of a larger scheme of knowledge. They are evidence, evidence in support of theoretical models or still in search of theoretical explanation. Political scientists thus far have accumulated a good many confirmed findings and many more unconfirmed hypotheses. The slow process of testing models, and of explaining evidence and limited models by more general ones, is well begun, but it has a long and difficult way to go. The techniques and studies described in this book should give you some of the means to understand, and contribute to, the empirical basis and scientific objectives of modern political science.

Bibliography

Abell, Peter. 1971. *Model building in Sociology*. London: Weidenfeld and Nicholson.

Adams, Hebron Elliott. 1970. The origins of insurgency. Ph.D. dissertation, Department of Operational Research, University of Lancaster (England).

Alker, Hayward R., Jr. 1964. The long road to international relations theory: problems of statistical nonadditivity: *World Politics* 18: Spring, 623–55.

———. 1965. *Mathematics and politics*. New York: Macmillan.

Alker, Hayward R. J., and Bruce M. Russett. 1966. Indices for comparing inequality. In Merritt and Rokkan (1966) 349–81.

Angell, Robert C., Vera S. Dunham, and J. David Singer. 1964. Social values and foreign policy attitudes of Soviet and American elites. *Journal of Conflict Resolution* 8:December, 329–491.

Averch, Harvey, and John Koehler. 1970. *The Huk rebellion in the Philippines: quantitative approaches*. Santa Monica, Calif.: RAND Corp., Report RM-6254-ARPA.

Baker, Robert K., and Sandra J. Ball. 1969. *Mass media and violence*. Washington, D.C.: Staff Study Series Vol. 9, National Commission on the Causes and Prevention of Violence.

Banks, Arthur S. 1965. Review essay: *World handbook of political and social indicators*. *American Political Science Review* 59:March, 144–46.

Blalock, Hubert M., Jr. 1960. *Social statistics*. New York: McGraw-Hill.

———. 1963. Correlated independent variables: the problem of multicollinearity. *Social Forces* 42:December, 233–37.

———. 1964a. *Causal inferences in nonexperimental research*. Chapel Hill: University of North Carolina Press.

———. 1964b. Controlling for background factors: spuriousness versus developmental sequences. *Sociological Inquiry* 34:Winter, 28–40.

———. 1967. Causal inferences, closed populations, and measures of association. *American Political Science Review* 61:March, 130–36.

———. 1969. Multiple indicators and the causal approach to measurement error. *American Journal of Sociology* 75:September, 264–72.

————. 1970. Estimating measurement error using multiple indicators and several points in time. *American Sociological Review* 35:February, 101-11.

————. 1971. *Causal models in the social sciences*. Chicago: Aldine, Atherton.

Blalock, Hubert M., Jr., and Anne B. Blalock, eds. 1968. *Methodology in social research*. New York: McGraw-Hill.

Bohrnstedt, George W. 1969. A quick method for determining the reliability and validity of multiple-item scales. *American Sociological Review* 34:August, 542–48.

Bone, H. A. 1965. *American politics and the party system*. New York: McGraw-Hill.

Boudon, R. 1965. A method of linear causal analysis: dependence analysis. *American Sociological Review* 30:365–73.

————. 1968. A new look at correlation analysis. In Blalock and Blalock, eds., 1968, 199–225.

Brunner, Ronald D. 1970. Data analysis, process analysis, and system change. Paper read to the American Political Science Association, Los Angeles, Sept. 1970.

Buchanan, William. 1969. *Understanding political variables*. New York: Scribner's.

Bwy, Douglas. 1968. Political instability in Latin America: the preliminary test of a causal model. *Latin American Research Review* 3:Spring, 17–66.

Campbell, Donald T. 1958. Common fate, similarity, and other indices of the status of aggregates of persons as social entities. *Behavioral Science* 3:January, 14–25.

————. 1963. From description to experimentation: interpreting trends as quasi-experiments. In Harris, ed. 1963, 212–45.

————. 1969. Definitional versus multiple operationism. *Et Al.* 2:Summer, 14–17.

Campbell, Donald T., and Donald W. Fiske. 1959. Convergent and discriminant validation by the multi-trait–multi-method matrix. *Psychological Bulletin* 56:March, 81–105.

Campbell, Donald T., and Julian C. Stanley. 1966. *Experimental and quasi-experimental designs for research*. Chicago: Rand-McNally.

Caporaso, James. 1971. Fisher's test of Deutsch's sociocausal paradigm of political integration: a research note. *International Organization* 25:No. 1, 120–31.

Caporaso, James A., and Alan L. Pelowski. 1971. Economic and political integration in Europe: a time-series quasi-experimental analysis. *American Political Science Review* 65:June, 418–33.

Carroll, John B. 1961. The nature of the data, or how to choose a correlation coefficient. *Psychometrica* 26:December, 347–72.

Christ, Carl F. 1966. *Econometric models and methods*. New York: Wiley.

Coombs, Clyde H. 1964. *A theory of data*. New York: Wiley.

Coplin, William D., ed. 1968. *Simulation in the study of politics*. Chicago: Markham, 1968.

Curtis, R. F., and E. F. Jackson. 1962. Multiple indicators in survey research. *American Journal of Sociology* 68:195–204.

de Hoyos, Reuben. 1969. The Catholic Church and the army in the Argentine revolution of 1955. Ph.D. dissertation, Department of Politics, New York University.

Doran, Charles F., Robert E. Pendley, and George E. Antunes. 1971. Reliability of cross-national measures of civil strife and instability events: a comparison of indigenous and secondary data sources. Unpublished paper. Houston: Department of Political Science, Rice University, mimeo.

Duncan, Otis Dudley. 1966. Path analysis: sociological examples. *American Journal of Sociology* 70:July, 1–16.

———. 1969. Some linear models for two-wave, two-variable panel analysis. *Psychological Bulletin* 72:177–82.

Duncan, Otis Dudley, R. P. Cuzzort, and B. Duncan. 1961. *Statistical geography*. Glencoe: The Free Press.

Eckstein, Harry. 1962. Incidence of IWs 1946–1959. Princeton: Center of International Studies, mimeo.

Edwards, A. 1957. *Techniques of attitude scale construction*. New York: Appleton-Century-Crofts.

Farrar, Donald D., and Robert R. Glauber. 1967. Multicollinearity in regression analysis: the problem revisited. *Review of Economics and Statistics* 49:February, 92–107.

Feierabend, Ivo K., and Rosalind L. Feierabend. 1965. Cross-national data bank of political instability events (code index). San Diego: Public Affairs Research Institute, San Diego State College, mimeo.

———. 1966. Aggressive behaviors within polities, 1948–1962: a cross national study. *Journal of Conflict Resolution* 10:September, 249–71.

Fen, Sing-nan. 1968. The theoretical implications of multivariate analysis in the behavioral sciences. *Behavioral Science* 13:March, 138–42.

Fitzgibbon, Russell H., and Kenneth F. Johnson. 1961. Measurement of Latin American political change. *American Political Science Review* 65:September, 515–26.

Forbes, Hugh Donald, and Edward R. Tufte. 1968. A note of caution in causal modelling. *American Political Science Review* 62:December, 1258–63.

Galtung, Johan. 1967. *Theory and methods of social research*. London: Allen and Unwin.

Gold, David. 1964. Some problems in generalizing aggregate associations. *American Behavioral Scientist* 8:December 16–18.

Goodman, Leo A. 1953 Ecological regressions and the behavior of individuals. *American Sociological Review* 18:December, 663–64.

———. 1959. Some alternatives to ecological correlation. *American Journal of Sociology* 64:May, 610–25.

Goodman, Leo A., and William Kruskal. 1954. Measures of association for cross classifications. *Journal of the American Statistical Association* 49:723–64.

Graham, Fred P. 1969. A contemporary history of American crime. In Graham and Gurr, eds. 1969, chap. 13.

Graham, Hugh Davis, and Ted Robert Gurr. 1969. *Violence in America: Historical and comparative perspectives*. Washington, D.C.: National Commission on the Causes and Prevention of Violence, Staff Studies Vols. I and II.

Guetzkow, Harold, ed. 1962. *Simulation in social science*. Englewood Cliffs, N.J.: Prentice-Hall.

Gurr, Ted Robert. 1966. *New error-compensated measures for comparing nations: some correlates of civil strife*. Princeton: Research Monograph No. 25, Center of International Studies, Princeton University. (Reprinted in Gurr with Ruttenberg, 1969.)

———. 1968. A causal model of civil strife: a comparative analysis using new indices. *American Political Science Review* 62:December, 1104–24.

———. 1969. A comparative survey of civil strife. In Graham and Gurr, eds. 1969, chap. 17.

———. 1970. Sources of rebellion in western societies: some quantitative evidence. *Annals* 391:September, 128–44.

Gurr, Ted Robert, and Muriel McClelland. 1971. *Political performance: a twelve-nation study*. Beverly Hills, Calif: Sage Professional Papers in Comparative Politics, 01–018.

Gurr, Ted Robert, with Charles Ruttenberg. 1967. *The conditions of civil violence: first tests of a causal model.* Princeton: Center of International Studies, Princeton University, Research Monograph No. 28.

———. 1969. *Cross-national studies of civil violence.* Washington, D.C.: Center for Research in Social Systems, The American University. (Distributed by U.S. Clearinghouse for Federal Scientific and Technical Information, Springfield, Va.)

Guttman, Louis. 1944. A basis for scaling qualitative data. *American Sociological Review* 9:April, 139–50.

Haas, Michael. 1966. Aggregate analysis. *World Politics* 19:October, 106–21.

———. 1970. Dimensional analysis in cross-national research. *Comparative Political Studies* 3:April, 3–35.

Hannan, E. J. 1970. *Multiple time series.* New York: Wiley.

Harris, Chester, ed. 1963. *Problems in measuring change.* Madison, Wisc.: University of Wisconsin Press.

Hays, William L. 1963 *Statistics.* New York: Holt, Rinehart & Winston.

Holsti, Ole R. 1967. Cognitive dynamics and images of the enemy: Dulles and Russia. In *Enemies in politics,* 1967, eds. David J. Finlay, Ole R. Holsti, and Richard R. Fagen. Chicago: Rand McNally.

Holsti, Ole R., and Robert C. North. 1966. Comparative data from content analysis: perceptions of hostility and economic variables in the 1914 crisis. In Merritt and Rokkan eds., 1966, 169–90.

Holsti, Ole R., Robert C. North, and Richard A. Brody. 1968. Perception and action in the 1914 crisis. In Singer, ed., 1968, 123–58.

Holt, Robert T., and John E. Turner, eds. 1970. *The methodology of comparative research.* New York: Free Press.

Holt, Robert T., and John M. Richardson, Jr. 1970. Competing paradigms in comparative politics. *In* Holt and Turner, eds., 1970, 21–72.

Hotelling, H. 1936. Relations between two sets of variates. *Biometrika* 28:321–77.

Janda, Kenneth. 1969. *Data processing: Applications to political research.* 2nd ed. Evanston: Northwestern University Press.

———. 1970. *A conceptual framework for the comparative analysis of political parties.* Beverly Hills, Calif.: Sage Professional Papers in Comparative Politics, 01–002.

Kish, Leslie. 1959. Some statistical problems in research design. *American Sociological Review* 24:June, 328–38.

———. 1965. *Survey sampling.* New York: Wiley.

Krishnaiah, Paruchuri R., ed. 1962. *Multivariate analysis-II.* New York: Academic Press.

Kruskal, Joseph B. 1968. Statistical analysis: transformations of data. In *International encyclopedia of the social sciences.* New York: Macmillan and The Free Press, Vol. 15, 182–93.

Kuhn, Thomas S. 1964. *The structure of scientific revolutions.* Chicago: University of Chicago Press, Phoenix ed.

Lasswell, Harold D., and Abraham Kaplan. 1950. *Power and society.* New Haven: Yale University Press.

Lazarsfeld, Paul F., and Herbert Menzel. 1961. On the relation between individual and collective properties. In Amatai Etzioni, ed. 1961. *Complex organizations: a sociological reader,* pp. 422–40. New York: Holt.

Lazarsfeld, Paul F., and Morris Rosenberg, eds. 1955. *The language of social research.* Glencoe, Ill.: The Free Press.

McClelland, David C. 1961. *The achieving society.* Princeton, N.J.: Van Nostrand.

Merritt, Richard L. 1966. *Symbols of American community, 1735–1775* New Haven: Yale University Press.
———. 1970. *Systematic approaches to comparative politics.* Chicago: Rand-McNally.
Merritt, Richard L., and Gloria J. Pyszka. 1969. *The student political scientist's handbook.* Cambridge, Mass.: Schenkman.
Merritt, Richard L., and Stein Rokkan, eds. 1966. *Comparing nations: the use of quantitative data in cross-national research.* New Haven: Yale University Press.
Miller, Rupert G., Jr. 1966. *Simultaneous statistical inference.* New York: McGraw-Hill.
Morrison, Denton E., and Ramon E. Henkel, eds. 1970. *The significance test controversy: A reader.* Chicago: Aldine.
Mosteller, Frederick, and Robert R. Bush. 1954. Selected quantitative techniques. In *Handbook of social psychology,* ed. Gardner Lindzey, chap. 8. Cambridge, Mass.: Addison-Wesley.
Mosteller, Frederick, Robert Rourke, and George Thomas. 1961. *Probability and statistics.* Reading, Mass.: Addison-Wesley.
Mueller, John E. 1969. *Approaches to measurement in international relations: a non-evangelical survey.* New York: Appleton-Century-Crofts.
Namenwirth, J. Zvi. 1968. Some long and short term trends in one American political value: a computer analysis of concern with wealth in sixty-two party platforms. *Computer Studies in the Humanities and Verbal Behavior,* 1:October, 126–33.
Namenwirth, J. Zvi, and Harold D. Lasswell. 1970. *The changing language of American values: a computer study of selected party platforms.* Beverly Hills: Sage Professional Papers in Comparative Politics, Vol. I, No. 01–001.
Naroll, Raoul. 1962. *Data quality control.* New York: The Free Press.
Needler, Martin C., ed. 1964. *Political systems of Latin America.* Princeton: Van Nostrand.
Nesvold, Betty A. 1969. A scalogram analysis of political violence. *Comparative Political Studies* 2:July, 172–94.
Nixon, Raymond B. 1965. Freedom in the world's press: A fresh appraisal with new data. *Journalism Quarterly,* Winter, 3–14.
North, Robert C., et al. 1963. *Content analysis: a handbook with applications for the study of international crisis.* Evanston: Northwestern University Press.
Osgood, Charles E. The representational model and relevant research methods. In Ithiel de Sola Pool, ed., 1959, *Trends in Content Analysis,* pp. 33–88. Urbana: University of Illinois Press.
Palumbo, Dennis J. 1969. *Statistics in political and behavioral science.* New York: Appleton-Century-Crofts.
Pelz, Donald C., and Frank M. Andrews. 1964. Detecting causal priorities in panel study data. *American Sociological Review* 29:836–54.
Pool, Ithiel de Sola, with Harold D. Lasswell, Daniel Lerner, et al. 1952. *Symbols of democracy.* Stanford: Stanford University Press, for Hoover Institution of War, Revolution and Peace.
Prezeworski, Adam, and Henry Teune. 1970. *The logic of comparative social inquiry.* New York: Wiley.
Richardson, Lewis F. 1960. *Statistics of deadly quarrels.* Pittsburgh: Boxwood Press.
Robinson, William S. 1950. Ecological correlations and the behavior of individuals. *American Sociological Review* 15:June, 351–57.

Rozelle, R. M., and Donald T. Campbell. 1969. More plausible rival hypotheses in the cross-lagged panel correlation technique. *Psychological Bulletin*, 71:74–80.

Rummel, Rudolph J. 1963. Dimensions of conflict behavior within and between nations. *General Systems Yearbook* 8:1–50.

———. 1964. Testing some possible predictors of conflict behavior within and between nations. *Peace Research Society Papers* 1:79–111.

———. 1965. A field theory of social action with application to conflict within nations. *General Systems Yearbook* 10:205–11.

———. 1966. The dimensionality of nations project. In Merritt and Rokkan, eds., 1966, pp. 109–30.

———. 1967. Understanding factor analysis. *Journal of Conflict Resolution* 11:December, 444–80.

———. 1970. *Applied factor analysis*. Evanston, Ill.: Northwestern University Press.

Russett, Bruce M. 1964. Inequality and instability: the relation of land tenure to politics. *World Politics* 16:April, 442–54.

———. 1965. Reply (to A. S. Banks' review of *World handbook of political and social indicators*, 1965). *American Political Science Review* 59:June, 444–46.

———. 1972. Techniques for controlling error. In Michael Haas, ed., 1972. *Statistical and quantitative methods*. Evanston: Northwestern University Press.

Russett, Bruce M., et al. 1964. *World handbook of political and social indicators*. New Haven: Yale University Press.

Scheuch, Erwin K. 1966. Cross-national comparisons using aggregate data: some substantive and methodological problems. In Merritt and Rokkan, eds., 1966, 121–67.

Selltiz, Claire, et al. 1963. *Research methods in social relations*. New York: Holt, Rinehart & Winston, revised ed.

Shubs, Peter. 1969. Revolutionary symbology: comparative case studies of the American and Indian independence movements. Paper read at the Annual Meeting of the American Political Science Association, New York.

Siegel, S. 1956. *Nonparametric statistics for the behavioral sciences*. New York: McGraw-Hill.

Sigelman, Lee. 1971. *Modernization and the political system: A critique and preliminary empirical analysis*. Beverly Hills, Calif.: Sage Professional Papers in Comparative Politics, 01–016.

Singer, J. David, ed. 1968. *Quantitative international politics: insights and evidence*. New York: The Free Press.

Singer, J. David, and Melvin Small. 1966a. The composition and status ordering of the international system, 1815–1940. *World Politics* 18:January, 236–82.

———. 1966b. Formal alliances, 1815–1936: a quantitative description. *Journal of Peace Research*, No. 1, 1–32.

———. 1968. Alliance aggregation and the onset of war 1815–1945. In Singer, ed., 1968, pp. 247–86.

———. 1972. *The wages of war, 1816–1965: a statistical handbook*. New York: Wiley.

Small, Melvin, and J. David Singer. 1969. Formal alliances, 1816–1965: an extension of the basic data. *Journal of Peace Research*, No. 3, 257–82.

———. 1970. Patterns in international warfare, 1816–1965. *Annals* 391:September, 145–55.

Sorokin, Pitirim A. 1937. *Social and cultural dynamics, Volume III: fluctuations of social relationships, war and revolutions*. New York: American Book Co.

Stephan, Frederick F., and Philip J. McCarthy. 1958. *Sampling opinions: an analysis of survey procedures.* New York: Wiley.

Stinchcombe, Arthur. 1968. *Constructing social theories.* New York: Harcourt, Brace and World.

Stone, Philip J., et al. 1960. *The general inquirer: a computer approach to content analysis.* Cambridge, Mass.: M.I.T. Press.

Tanter, Raymond. 1966. Dimensions of conflict behavior within and between nations, 1958–1960. *Journal of Conflict Resolution* 10:March, 41–64.

Taylor, Charles Lewis, ed. 1968. *Aggregate data analysis: Political and social indicators in cross-national research.* Paris, The Hague: Mouton, for International Social Science Council.

Tilly, Charles. 1969. Collective violence in European perspective. In Graham and Gurr, eds. 1969, chap. 1.

Torgerson, W. S. 1958. *Theory and methods of scaling.* New York: Wiley.

Tufte, Edward R. 1969. Improving data analysis in political science. *World Politics* 21:July, 641–54.

Tukey, John W. 1961. Statistical and quantitative methodology. In Donald P. Ray, ed., *Trends in Social Science,* pp. 84–136. New York: Philosophical Library.

———. 1962. The future of data analysis. *Annals of Mathematical Statistics* 33:March, 1–67.

Wright, Quincy. 1942. *A study of war.* Chicago: University of Chicago Press.

Zeisel, Hans. 1957. *Say it with figures.* New York: Harpers.

Zinnes, Dina A. 1967. An analytical study of the balance of power theories. *Journal of Peace Research,* No. 3, 270–88.

———. 1968. The expression and perception of hostility in prewar crisis: 1914. In Singer, ed., 1968.

Index